Words for Today 2013

Notes for daily Bible reading

Edited by Nicola Slee

Words for Today aims to build understanding and respect for a range of religious perspectives and approaches to living practised in the world today, and to help readers meet new challenges in their faith. Views expressed by contributors should not, however, be taken to reflect the views or policies of the Editor or the International Bible Reading Association.

The International Bible Reading Association's scheme of readings is listed on the Christian Education website at www.christianeducation.org.uk and the full scheme for 2013 may be downloaded in English, Spanish and French.

Editor: Nicola Slee

Cover image: 'Mary with the bread of life – Element earth' by Lucy D'Souza-Krone, one of the series 'Mary and the four elements': www.lucy-art.de

IBRA gratefully acknowledges the permission of the artist for the use of this image.

Published by:
The International Bible Reading Association
1020 Bristol Road
Selly Oak, Birmingham B29 6LB
United Kingdom

www.christianeducation.org.uk/ibra
Charity number 211542

ISBN 978-1-905893-54-6
ISSN 0140-8275

Typeset by Wordsense Ltd, Edinburgh

Printed and bound in the UK by Mosaic Print Management

Contents

Editorial

This year's striking cover image by the German-Indian artist, Lucy D'Souza-Krone, shows Mary holding in her arms the bread of life. It is one of a series depicting Mary and the four elements (see http:www.lucy-art.de for more of Lucy's work). In the painting, we see Mary squatting on the earth, indeed almost emerging from the earth itself, and the shapes and colours of the painting suggest images of seeds and leaves and fruits. From Mary's arms sprouts a great bundle of wheat and the Christchild seems to be one with this natural element. This is a wonderfully earthy celebration of the Word that gives life and nourishment and is the source of all creativity and fecundity in the world. The Christ who comes to us in scripture and sacrament is not apart from the whole created order but is an integral part of it, coming to us also in creation and in every creature that lives. We are invited to pay the same respect and reverence to each creature that we would pay to God, the source of creation.

What does it mean to pay respect and reverence to God in creation? Whatever else it means, it surely requires us to co-operate with God in caring for the creation, in mothering it as Mary mothered Jesus – protecting and nurturing life, standing against whatever threatens fullness of life, and giving ourselves in costly commitment for the well-being of all. Meditating on this strong and beautiful painting may help us to enter into this work to which we are all called.

After ten years of editing *Words for Today*, changes are afoot at IBRA (see the inside front cover), and it is time for me to hang up my hat and hand over to a new editor. It has been an immense privilege to work with a diverse and gifted team of writers from around the world, as well as the internal team at IBRA, and I have learnt a huge amount from the wisdom and experience of many folks during this time. I would like to extend my thanks to each one who has contributed to the liveliness, richness and challenge of these Bible notes over many years (not only under my editorship), and offer my best wishes to Nathan Eddy, the new editor, as he takes up the baton and works to create something new, yet in continuity with the best of what has gone before. Readers are, of course, also part of the rich exchange of this shared endeavour, and I would like to extend my warm thanks and best wishes to all the thousands of readers who have used the notes down the years. Some of you have written or emailed or phoned to share feedback, and we are always grateful to hear responses to the notes; but beyond such overt response, it has been humbling and encouraging to know that, throughout the world, thousands of you have been using the notes as an aid and support to your own daily discipleship. May you be strengthened and enlivened by the nourishing bread of life, kneaded and baked anew each day.

Nicola Slee – Editor

Prayers and reflections

Come, all you who have discernment,
vocal advocates of the Spirit, prophets
who beheld hidden things in you, true visions.
You farmers who sowed seeds and slept in hope,
rise up and rejoice at the harvest: look in my arms:
I clasp the Wheat-sheaf of life
that provides bread for the hungry
that feeds the needy. Rejoice with me, for I carry
the Sheaf full of joys.

Lucy D'Souza-Krone, according to hymns of Ephrem the Syrian

Thank God for life, for living
Thank God for love, for giving
Thank God for death:
an ending a beginning.

Thank God for lips, for speaking
Thank God for hearts, for seeking
Thank God for weakness:
a stumbling an upsurging.

Thank God for eyes, for seeing
Thank God for soul, for being
Thank God for absence:
a longing an unfolding.

Thank God for life, for loving
Thank God for death, for longing
Thank God with singing.

Mary E Morgan, Caribbean (*Oceans of Prayer*, NCEC, p.57)

Lord, from our imperfect understanding of their suffering, we dare to stand with our brothers and sisters and pray with them.
We pray with children who, still and quiet from hunger, neither laughing nor crying, neither running nor resting, know little of life but hunger and waiting.
We pray with young women, bearing and nurturing the next generation.
We pray for strength throughout pregnancy, safety in childbirth and joy in being the channel of life and love for each precious new being.
We pray with men who, once strong and now weakened by chronic ill-health, struggle to go on working in mines, factories and on the land, made ill by the very conditions which they dare not leave.

Christa Hook, UK (*Oceans of Prayer*, pp.49–50)

How to use a 'quiet time'

Pay attention to your body Take time to slow down, consciously relax each part of your body, and listen to your breathing for a while.

Use silence to relax and empty your mind of all that's going on around you. Know that God's loving presence encircles you, your family, your community and the world. Learn to enjoy God's presence.

Have a visual focus – a cross, a plant, interesting stones, pictures or postcards... create a prayer table on which to display them with other symbols.

Read the **Bible passage** for the day several times, perhaps using different translations, and then the notes. Allow the words to fill your mind. Try to discover their message for you and the world around you.

Listen Remember that the most important part of prayer is to hear what God is saying to us. God speaks to us through the words of scripture, the daily news, and often through people around us.

Include the world Hold the news of the day in your mind. Enter the situation of those you hear or read about and try to pray alongside them and with them.

Pray without ceasing Prayer is not only 'the quiet time' we set aside. It becomes part of the whole of life, a continuous dialogue between God and ourselves, through all that we do and think and say: a growing awareness of the loving presence of God who travels with us and never leaves us.

Abbreviations and acknowledgements

GNB	*Good News Bible* (The Bible Societies/Collins Publishers) – Old Testament © American Bible Society 1976; New Testament © American Bible Society 1966, 1971, 1976.
NIV	Scripture quotations taken from *The Holy Bible, New International Version* © 1973, 1978, 1984 by International Bible Society. Used by permission of Hodder & Stoughton Limited. All rights reserved. 'NIV' is a registered trademark of International Bible Society. UK trademark number 1448790.
NJB	Taken from the *New Jerusalem Bible*, published and copyright 1985 by Darton, Longman and Todd Ltd and Doubleday & Co. Inc, and used by permission of the publishers.
NSRV	*New Revised Standard Version* © 1989, Division of Christian Education of the National Council of Churches of Christ in the United States of America.
REB	*Revised English Bible* © Oxford University and Cambridge University Presses 1989
RSV	*The Holy Bible, Revised Standard Version* © 1973, Division of Christian Education of the National Council of Churches of Christ in the United States of America.

Note

BCE Before the Common Era. BCE and CE are used by some writers instead of BC and AD.

New year manifesto

1 John proclaims Jesus

Luke 3:1-6

Encircling hope

In an empire as big as the world there's a region, and in that region there's a district, and in that district there's a Jewish temple. The emperor rules the governor and the governor rules the puppet king and the puppet king tries to get on with the priests. Amid these encircling powers, John the Baptist is surrounded. He's shouting in that corner of the empire: 'Prepare the way of the Lord.'

The powers that surround John might be puzzled. Why, when there's Herod, Pilate and then Tiberius to look up to, is he talking of another authority? Why, when there's a perfectly respectable synagogue, should John cry in the wilderness about the Lord coming like a king? Luke has prepared us, but not these Romans, for the surprise. We have heard Mary's glorious song about the powerful being humbled. Now, with Isaiah, John speaks of a level plain. Luke is bracing us for an exciting subversion of the world order.

It is daunting to think of that lone figure speaking out, with nothing but expectation to raise. At the beginning of a new year we may wonder who or what is going to govern our life this year. Will anything really change? Afraid of naivety, we may shrink from commitment. But hope draws us on.

Lord, I offer you:
my fear of raising false expectations: heal my bitterness, that I may hope;
my fear of worldly powers that claim control: open my eyes to see what hurts and heals;
my fear of speaking up, especially when surrounded: clear my throat that I may speak of your love.

Notes based on the New Revised Standard Version by

David Warbrick

David Warbrick feels absurdly fortunate as a Birmingham parish priest. Curacy in the Bull Ring shopping centre taught him that no one and no church owns the gospel. Handsworth taught that diversity is a thrill, not a threat. A rural parish then showed why we should love the patience of the Anglican parochial church. He now serves in unpredictable and enriching Kings Heath. He is married to Jenny (see p.27) and father to Anna and Joe.

Provoking honesty

Luke 3:7-14

Perhaps the angry comedians who are rude to hecklers and pick brutally on people in the audience are revealing our secret desire to be shouted at. We are drawn to such comedy with fascination and fear, relishing its scandal and painful scrutiny. John's anger is clearly attracting a very large audience craving some kind of scrutiny, some kind of catharsis. The priest's son shouts 'Vipers!' Wrath, cutting and fire are promised. With violent imagery, he is exposing any selfishness in their curiosity. Can such anger, and our craving for it, be good?

A litmus test for good anger might be: having heard the criticism and taken their anger as a sign of hurt commitment, what is their positive thesis? If there isn't one, it's anger for anger's sake. Someone's insecurities are being projected on to others, like a preacher who enjoys telling people they're sinners a bit too much, keeping people on the cusp of confession without offering any absolution. John, however, does offer a positive thesis and it's disarmingly simple. Whatever your job, however unsavoury, you can turn it into a vocation by doing it honestly, not for status in God's sight, but simply because – just because. The unpopular characters who offer themselves for John's criticism show they are there for good, not indulgent, reasons. 'What shall we do?' We should admire their seeking redemption. Some of us, after all, prefer to be held on that cusp and not have the responsibility of being forgiven.

Reflect on whatever you count as your daily responsibility or job, paid or unpaid. Are there aspects that you would rather not come under scrutiny? Is there anyone whose criticism you find hard to take because it's true?

Pray for humility and honesty.

Watch as your job turns into vocation.

Humbling anger

Luke 3:15-22

'You ain't seen nothin' yet' is a phrase raising both excitement and fear. Something much more impressive is coming, but can you cope when it does? This is the feel of John's preaching now as expectation rises and he challenges rumours. Playing with tenses, back and forth, Luke very densely compacts John's life story, telling of his later imprisonment before describing Jesus' baptism. This makes John's story serve entirely as an introduction to Jesus' story, just as John would wish. Showing us the personal cost of John's ministry, though, Luke's concise workmanship heightens our sense of danger, so when we witness the baptism there is a nervous, eager silence in our hearts. Who is this? How will he cope with danger?

The angry energy of John's preparation means we are surprised by a sudden silence and intimacy at the baptism. Contrast the violent fire of John and the gentle dove. Contrast John's cry to the crowd with God's intimate word of encouragement to his beloved offspring. Contrast the empire clamouring for obedience with the heavenly voice's word of encouragement, 'I am pleased with you.' Death hovers in the story. The encircling powers we named on Tuesday that will imprison both John and Jesus are not banished. Rather, Luke is opening our hearts ready for a surprise: Jesus' gentle strength in the midst of the world's angry powers will show us how to live among them and maybe redeem them.

Lord, when I am angry or hardened against surprise, afraid I haven't enough goodness, help me to remember my baptism and hear your voice saying that you believe in me, even when I don't.

Breeding resentment

Luke 3:23-38

A wealthy government minster held a party at his sumptuous home. Someone was overheard saying, 'The antiques aren't real. He bought them.' It was a jealous dismissal, trying to find a reason not to respect him. That said, there are grains of truth in what they said: you can't buy depth or conjure up heritage; we do like to know where someone is coming from.

John's heritage showed he was worthy of attention: unusual son from the priestly caste. Now Luke shows Jesus' heritage, woven through the roller-coaster story of the Hebrews, including David, Abraham, some villains and many dull characters. Seventy-seven names. That's seventy-seven conceptions. If John 1 conveys Jesus' incarnation in a cosmic poem, Luke does so through the microcosm of human relationships and the narrowness and pressure of the birth canal. His being rises from 'the fury and the mire of human veins' (W B Yeats, 'Byzantium'). The names, moreover, lead back to Adam – everywoman, everyman – whose name comes from the earth itself. Jesus is for everyone and for the real, gritty world.

Whatever they make of him, those who encounter Jesus will not be able to claim he has dropped from heaven and knows nothing of our life; nor can they use poor heritage as an excuse not to listen; nor, by contrast, can anyone claim he is only for them. Them. That's 'us'. With this last bit of throat-clearing done, tomorrow, at last, we will hear from Jesus' own lips. Ready to listen?

Reflect on verse 23. How seriously do you and your church take the words of thirty-year-olds?

Tempting love

Luke 4:1-13

The last *Lord of the Rings* movie has, by my count, seven endings. If it were not so epic, it would be irritating. If Luke's Gospel were a film, this would feel like a fifth beginning. This stuttering start must be for a reason.

The Spirit drives Jesus, oddly, into the vulnerability of silence. There, because he is a strong, devout thirty-something, he is tempted. With all that energy and commitment swirling in the pointless wilderness of solitude, he is dizzy with what he could do. Feed everyone? No. That would take away humanity's opportunity to feed each other. Better to start with the spiritual hunger that would make us address poverty. Take control? No. That would replicate the emperor's encircling powers. Better to trust God's authority; then we might handle our own. Dazzle everyone, proving angels are on his side? No. That would coerce rather than inspire faith, replacing oppressive temple politics with another abuse. Better to live a life so generous that we can feel God, than to try to prove God is there with meaningless tricks.

Luke's multiple beginnings make us almost irritably attentive, rather like the people we meet in the synagogue shortly. With intriguing tension, he raises expectation about Jesus, then asserts Jesus' humility. Luke reveals the beauty and clumsiness of our need. He names the world's danger, while tantalisingly holding Jesus in the centre as some kind of answer. Jesus will not be competitive, nor passive–aggressive but, instead, frustratingly loving.

Reflect on the temptations you live with. Perhaps they are a sign of your strength more than your weakness.

As the first week of a new year ends, **pray** for wisdom to discern where small-seeming decisions may set us in very different directions.

David Warbrick

Sunday 6 January

New year manifesto

Notes based on the New Revised Standard Version by

David Warbrick

See David's biography on p.1.

2 Jesus proclaims himself

Luke 4:14-19

Big news for little places

Jesus has been many times to the capital of faith because his family has annually made an extravagant journey to Jerusalem for Passover. By introducing us to his public preaching back at his nondescript provincial home town, Luke offers us two things to look out for in Jesus' ministry. First, the passage from Isaiah rings with the orthodoxy of Jewish law, protecting the vulnerable and applying the jubilee principle of liberation for slaves and debtors. It is, though, very lavish, promising freedom for the poor and disabled. Jesus seems both conservative and radical, old and new, obvious and daring, moving the staid and anchoring the indulgent pursuer of novelty.

Second, Jesus begins ministry 'in the power of the Spirit': a phrase that rings out in the rather understated northern province of Galilee, with its small village synagogues. Luke shows the Spirit's power is a paradoxical one that may lead to obscurity or sacrifice as much as fame or status. It demands that the respective ministries of his followers should be devoted and imaginative *wherever* they work or worship.

I wonder how you rate your regular place of worship, or your workplace: large or small, famous or hidden, conservative or radical, exciting or dull, Jerusalem or Nazareth? Perhaps, watching Jesus begin in such a place and then make his way to Jerusalem, our grander communities can be humbled and our obscure communities lifted up (the Magnificat again).

Being 'filled with the power of the Spirit' (4:1) clearly means a lot to Luke. This is the sixth time someone has been touched, moved or 'filled', and there'll be many more through the Gospel and Acts. What might it mean to you?

You can't choose your relatives

Luke 4:20-30

It's worrying meeting your children's friends or, for them, meeting yours. 'Will they embarrass me?' each asks inwardly. Jesus' ministry has not begun in a vacuum. He is a man with an upbringing, a culture, habits already shaped by faith and environment. He has learned the scriptures. Luke has shown Mary's and Joseph's meaningful obedience to tradition, making the right offerings at birth, visiting Jerusalem. He has shown their openness to surprise in the annunciation and Joseph's dream-rich courage.

Like any of us who proudly hold our children at baptism, or teach them Bible stories at bedtime, Mary and Joseph may have wondered: 'What will Jesus do with this faithful upbringing?' With rumours circulating about him, they might have felt proud but exposed, as their son appeared in the local synagogue, an adult with his own opinions.

As Jesus' neighbours, playmates and carpentry clients hear the bold claim that Isaiah's promise is fulfilled 'today', it could go either way. Will they be uplifted or threatened by his claim? Will they be glad for their humble town or angry that he got out and now comes back with big ideas?

Startlingly, Jesus seems actively to provoke them, exposing jealousies, stirring disagreement, saying out loud what they're secretly thinking. With old stories he asserts the new truth that strangers will know him better than his own people. As we add 'provocative' to his list of qualities, we remember the cost for those close to Jesus who made room for such character to grow.

When someone I love is criticised, God give me grace to respond well. When someone I love embarrasses me, God give me grace to respond well.

Does chaos reign?

Luke 4:31-37

Having been cast out of his rightful home, Jesus now casts a demon out of the home, or personality, it had occupied. Having not been recognised by his neighbours as the fulfilment of Isaiah's prophecy, he is now recognised by the evil spirits he banishes.

These pairings and contrasts are set within the greater tension of Nazareth/Jerusalem. He is moving from rejection in one towards rejection in the other. They create a dramatic tension in which Jesus' authority gleams dangerously. He startles people because they can see he has not come from the usual seat of learning, nor from those other centres where kings, governors and emperors live, but from the Galilean countryside. Jesus emerged from Nowhereville and heads towards the capital. His authority does not come from Jerusalem. It is going to scrutinise Jerusalem.

Now, if we thought the Emperor was the biggest power to be afraid of, even he is belittled before the disturbance of evil. A man's life has been ruined by some force from another realm that brings chaos to his character. It is only a hundred years since the term 'schizophrenia' was coined. Some say it may name the kind of behaviour we see here. Whether or not you wish to translate the language of evil spirits into controllable modern medical terminology, both descriptions have the same belittling effect, even on heads of state. Jesus' authority, which no emperor claiming divinity can emulate, seems to bear even upon such terrors.

Is there anything that seems chaotic or disorientating to you? How might you assert Jesus' authority over it?

Authority to serve

Luke 4:38-44

Many women readers may have got up to make a meal for their household even when feeling rough, and many male readers may resent sexist caricatures about man flu. Fever in Jesus' day, though, was a rather more serious threat.

The Hebrews received instructions about baking and roasting on Passover night; then, as tent dwellers, they heard how to collect manna. The household has always been a centre point of liturgical memory and religious authority in Jewish faith. While we may criticise aspects of Hebrew law in hindsight, the woman of the house was and is a crucial figure at the heart of table liturgy. Jesus goes from one religious centre, the synagogue, to another, a new friend's home, where the female with household authority is gravely ill.

Jesus' authority changes things here, too. As if to answer our 21st-century questions about illness over demon possession, Luke uses the same word 'rebuked' for exorcism as for illness, as he will when Jesus silences waves and disciples. Jesus asserts authority with tangible power but power that leaves people's world bigger than before: free from possession, illness or pride. Luke shows us the difference between generous, godly use of power and human snatching at authority for self-gratification.

The woman of the house is healed and, perhaps amusingly, immediately returns to her pivotal service. It would be typical for this to be both humour and, at the same time, a powerful illustration that in freely chosen service we are closest to Christ.

Is there anyone whose position of service, of whatever kind, has made you underestimate their authority? Look for anyone, stranger or friend, whom you might now see differently, and pray for them.

'Yes, but no, but yes …'

Luke 5:1-11

If you're quickly embarrassed by principle, unsure how to express feeling or nervous of being cornered into commitment, it's easier to listen if you've got something to do with your hands. Fishermen clean their nets. Simon is indebted to Jesus for healing his mother-in-law, so he already calls him 'Master'. He lends him a boat to preach from. Imagine Peter listening, able to frown at the nets, not letting on that the teaching was trickling into the crevices of his soul. He is already obedient to some extent, pushing out the boat, but letting Jesus know how hard they've been working is a way of asserting distance.

Then, the miraculous catch means Simon can deny his feelings no longer. Saying not just 'Master' but now 'Lord', he plunges towards Jesus, yet tells him to go away. This simultaneous drawing near and pushing away is a tension of faith that most of us live with. We do it with our parents, irritating them in order to attract attention. We do it with our partners, wanting togetherness; wanting to be alone. I need you and I am not worthy to have you. I want you but am afraid of what you might ask of me. I thirst for your affirmation but part of me wants to hold on to my self-loathing.

'Do not be afraid,' Jesus says to us. For in that very tension he sees the honesty, vulnerability and energy that might draw others to God.

Who first showed you that God might care for you? What was it about them that made the idea seem credible? Give thanks and pray for them.

Touching friends

Luke 5:12-26

When Diana, an attractive if troubled princess, touched a child living with HIV, she might not have realised she was, via news footage, shifting public understanding of the condition for good. Fear and prejudice had quickly formed in those early days. Her gesture challenged and reassured.

Jesus could have healed the leper with a command but, with great emphasis, he said 'I choose,' and touched him, crossing medical and prejudicial barriers. Touching showed he offered relationship, not merely cure, dignity as well as health. It was a private encounter that gave the isolated leper so much more than a solution.

In the next scene, we see a sick man who is fortunate to have good friends. Their devotion is impressive and physical. Although cruelly paralysed, at least he knows he belongs. In public now, Jesus heals again, but not before offering forgiveness. Relationship and forgiveness are miraculous gifts, giving meaning to physical wonders.

As news spreads, Jesus must resist all the more the first of his temptations. Quick fixes that gain publicity would fizz and impress like fireworks but end with emptiness. The world doesn't need another celebrity fixer. It needs someone who will bring the best out of it through relationship and reach its embattled heart with forgiveness. That is what Jesus does.

It is ironic that the helpful princess died without properly naming her inward craving for relationship and, maybe, forgiveness. Isolated by celebrity, she missed honest touch. Maybe that was why she reached out to the child.

Reflect on the ways in which you interact physically with strangers and friends. Notice whom you touch and whom not. How might your touch communicate relationship and forgiveness?

Pray for any whom you carry. Give thanks for any who carry you.

Dubious honour

Luke 5:27-39

Soon, a Pharisee will invite Jesus to dinner in order to scrutinise him (7:36-end). The religious leader has a spirituality fuelled by suspicion, making him brittle as an old leather wine-skin. Here, a rich outcast invites Jesus to a meal 'in his honour'. He may be a dubious collaborator with the Emperor's taxation system but he has an instinctive sense that there is something to celebrate lavishly in this preacher's company. To some, his spirituality may seem brash and immature, like over-fruity young wine. 'We prefer the old, mellow ways,' think the establishment snobbishly but, with understanding, Jesus describes their needy insecurity: 'no one after drinking old wine desires new' (verse 39). Luke has established clearly Jesus' continuity and fullness of Jewish faith. Now he must admit there are some who won't be able to hold the old and new together (verses 36-37).

We began the New Year zooming in from emperor to governor, from king to temple. Luke is going to take us to the temple – then, in Acts, zoom out again until Paul takes the gospel to the Emperor. On the way, Luke clearly opens our hearts to the poor and powerless but, if we thought Jesus was here only for the poor, we were mistaken. A man with ill-gotten wealth is throwing a party and inviting others of the same dubious cast of mind. Jesus shatters principled prejudice by eating with them. His transforming presence is even more radical than we thought.

Christ, I bring to you the people whose wealth disturbs, whose taste disgusts, whose ugly past frightens me. I bring them to you because I cannot cope with them. Give them peace. Give me grace to be glad that you help them, and so help me find freedom.

Living differently

1 Changes and challenges

Notes based on the New Revised Standard Version by

Jane Gonzales

Jane Gonzalez is a Roman Catholic laywoman and works as a pastoral assistant in a parish in Hertfordshire. She has just completed a Master of Arts degree in Pastoral Theology.

Genesis 12:1-5a

On the threshold

I love getting a new diary at Christmas. There is something exciting about those blank pages. There are no events pencilled in – yet – and the future seems mine to do with as I will. The New Year begins and, like the diary, offers me space, for change and growth. In the West, there seems to be a great hunger for challenge. People set themselves high targets, take up extreme sports; we are encouraged to push ourselves harder; to feel the burn. Is this symptomatic of spiritual emptiness? Physical challenges won't change the way we feel about ourselves. A song says that 'everywhere you go, you always take the weather with you' (Tim and Neil Finn, 1991).

The call to change is not always about major upheavals. Most of us will never be asked, as Abram was, to leave everything behind and set out into the unknown. Our call and our challenge, perhaps, is to make small but significant changes that will help us become people of integrity. Have we the courage to take the steps that might change us, or our world, in what may be small ways but ways that can have great repercussions – as many as the grains of sand on the shore or the stars in the heavens?

Where, this year, is God inviting me to change and develop?

Thinking outside the box

Joshua 2:1-16

I'm sure that Jesus approved wholeheartedly of this ancestress of his, Rahab, who is astute and focused – though not necessarily of her profession! Like the steward praised in Luke's Gospel (16:1-13), here is someone able to assess a situation and come up with a rapid solution. She comes to a swift decision as to which course of action will best suit her and her family in the face of the crisis that approaches. Apparently, the Chinese character for crisis contains two symbols: that of danger and that of opportunity. Rahab appreciates the danger and seizes the opportunity.

The ability to think on one's feet has helped me many times in my life, apart from the driving test, which unfortunately doesn't lend itself to creative solutions and took me eight attempts to pass! Sometimes results come only through hard work and concerted effort and a lot of practice. But there may be occasions when other elements need to come to the fore: imagination, instinct, wisdom born of experience and discernment. And thinking outside the box. Rahab exemplifies this in her astute reading of the signs of the times and her rapid appraisal of the situation.

There is surely room for both approaches to making choices in our lives. Sometimes we don't leave enough room for imagination in our decision-making; we talk things over incessantly instead of just 'going for it'; we decide that we had better do some further consultation. Do we merely see the dangers and ignore the opportunities?

'The wise woman builds her house, but the foolish tears it down with her own hands' (Proverbs 14:1). Where does true wisdom lie? Can I allow wisdom to guide me?

Jane Gonzales

The path of life

Ruth 1:1-17

Social networking has its critics and its drawbacks but I enjoy keeping in contact with family and friends via Facebook and Friends Reunited. Last year I was able to exchange news with the man who was my boyfriend forty years ago, and it was a joy to hear about his family, his ministry as a pastor of an evangelical church and his plans for the future. We hadn't kept in touch since I ended our relationship all those years before.

Every choice involves a rejection. In our passage, widowhood has brought three women to a moment when life-changing decisions have to be made. They have to choose a path to follow. In the end, Orpah elects for what appears to be the safer route – back to her own people, with the possibility of a marriage there, at home. Ruth decides to stay with Naomi and to venture with her into the uncertainty of the unknown. There must have been a mixture of feelings as they parted: hurt and rejection as well as hope for the future. It is always difficult to go our separate ways, especially if there is little likelihood (in the days before modern communication) of keeping in touch. This does not mean that Orpah's choice is wrong. What matters most is making choices and decisions based on love, and in recognition of God's will and our own needs. And then following that path.

'In the path of your judgements, O Lord, we wait for you; your name and your renown are the soul's desire' (Isaiah 26:8).

Have a look back over the last year. What kinds of choices can you identify? Are they life enhancing or life destroying? How will you choose, this year?

Jane Gonzales

Take off the straightjacket

2 Samuel 6:12-22

Convention, tradition, rules of proper behaviour – these are not necessarily inhibiting or restrictive. Society functions best when there is a consensus as to what is right or wrong, appropriate or inappropriate. However, we can all get so caught up in the rules and regulations that they come to matter more than anything else (a situation not unknown in our churches!).

I feel sorry for poor Michal, hedged in by convention, and unable to think imaginatively and creatively. David's behaviour, which results from his joy and is expressive of his relationship with God, challenges her notions of what kingly behaviour should be. Jesus faced similar prejudices and accusations of impropriety when he ate and drank and spent time with the poor and the marginalised in his society. He didn't behave as he was expected to.

Expectations can be a dreadful burden, especially if we find that we cannot live up to them. Other people often seem to have so much invested in us and we hate to let them down: parents, colleagues, teammates, fellow parishioners... In truth, there is only one expectation that we need to live up to, and that is God's. Joanne Hogg's song, 'Forgive Me' (*Song of Confession*, Thankyou Music, 2008), is one of repentance, and a recognition that sinfulness often stems from living up to everyone else's ideas of behaviour rather than living according to God's law of love: 'I'm sorry. Yours is the only opinion that matters to me.'

Spend some time reflecting on the gifts and talents that God has given you. Are you living up to his expectations in the way you use these?

Jane Gonzales

Get busy living

Jeremiah 1:1-12

One of my favourite films is *The Shawshank Redemption* (1994). It is the story of a man wrongly convicted of a murder, who manages to escape from a harsh penitentiary and rebuild a life in freedom. One of its best remembered lines suggests that we have a choice: to get busy living, or else get busy dying. It suggests that, if we live in fear and without hope, if we avoid challenges and conflict, we don't really live at all. The main character, Andy Dufresne, who speaks these words, knows his Bible from start to finish. He could be describing Jeremiah.

The key words, for me, in this passage are: 'Do not be afraid of them' (verse 8). Jeremiah's call comes when he is young, vulnerable and unsure of his own abilities. He is given the reassurance of God's presence, come what may. This does not ensure a trouble-free existence for any disciple, as the story of Jeremiah bears out. Jeremiah often wants to resist the call, but is compelled by the burning within him to speak out (Jeremiah 20:9). And speak he does, to 'them' (verse 8).

What silences an appropriate Christian response to abuse, oppression, injustice? Is it fear of 'them': the clever, the powerful, those in the know? Is it fear of 'them': our friends or family who may not think or believe as we do, and whom we don't wish to upset, confuse or offend?

'O Lord you have enticed me, and I was enticed; you have overpowered me and you have prevailed' (Jeremiah 20:7). What keeps me from rising to the challenges to live out my baptism fully?

Success in every packet

Jonah 3:1-10

This was the claim of an instant cake mix advert on the television when I was young. You added an egg and some water to the mix, baked it, and *voilà* – a proper 'homemade' cake: success in reward for very little work. Jonah's rather half-hearted oracle of doom produces instant conversion and repentance from every living creature in Nineveh, from the king down to the animals. But Jonah is extremely unhappy with the outcome. His narrow concept of God has been challenged. He was not frightened that the Ninevites would reject his call but that they would heed him. He didn't want the cake to rise.

Terry Pratchett's novel, *The Truth* (Doubleday, 2000), features an aspiring journalist. He is advised by the ruler of the city where his newspaper is based not to offer people news: it upsets them. Most of the people, the ruler says, only want 'olds': the familiar, the comfortable, the stuff that suits their own particular prejudices and thought patterns. In our passage, we have the curious case of the prophet who resists the new and seems to prefer the old, and the pagans who respond to the new with an astonishing alacrity, forsaking their old ways.

Conversion is about news, the Good News, and about forgetting the 'olds', the old way of being, of thinking, of judging. The book of Jonah is a warning to us and a challenge to continual conversion, in our own hearts first of all.

'… first take the log out of your own eye, and then you will see clearly to take the speck out of your neighbour's eye' (Matthew 7:5).

What are the 'olds' in my life? Am I really open to the new insights that the Holy Spirit may want to give me?

Square pegs and round holes

Matthew 18:1-5

I love playing with my goddaughter, Beatrice, aged two. She has a lot of 'educational toys', but they are fun as well as helping her develop motor skills and spatial awareness. She is starting to recognise shapes and colours and to post the right shape in the appropriate hole. She is learning that the star shape doesn't fit in the square-shaped hole.

A distinction is often made, when discussing this text, between 'childish' and 'childlike'. It is a good thing to be trusting and dependent on God, as a child trusts and depends upon a parent; a poor thing to resist maturity and the ways of adulthood. I suppose we all hope that we are on the way to achieving childlikeness and have put childish ways behind us. But have we?

What if we woke up one day and decided that this was the day when we were going to put the round-shaped block into the triangular-shaped hole, and make it fit? When we took a conscious decision to look at things from a completely different point of view? We are programmed to see the world in certain ways, and to behave in particular ways, and a consequence of this can be a narrowing of our perspectives. We can lose the curiosity and creativity of the child who sees no horizon and no limit.

Perhaps adults accept the world as it is too readily, and resist the call to question the way things are. Maybe it's time to try fitting the round peg in the square hole.

'For truly I tell you, if you have faith the size of a mustard seed, you will say to this mountain, "Move from here to there", and it will move; and nothing will be impossible for you' (Matthew 17:20).

Make a resolution this year to listen more often to the child within you.

Jane Gonzales

Living differently

Notes based on the New Revised Standard Version by

Francesca Rhys

Francesca Rhys was raised as the middle one of five children in London, but has lived in China, the USA, Germany, and the Democratic Republic of the Congo as a language learner and teacher. She now lives with her partner in Leeds, learning Yorkshire ways, and resourcing three churches as a Methodist minister.

2 But I say to you ...

Matthew 5: 21-26

Compassion, touchstone for behaviour

Jesus' teaching in the Sermon on the Mount is a guide to living differently, and the foundation of his ministry. Jesus advocates not conforming to social and religious norms but rethinking our lives in terms of love. A transformation needs to take place, where it's our inner state that is given most attention rather than the outward act. Jesus calls for the greater righteousness of compassion and empathy as touchstones for our behaviour. Jesus' demands don't contradict the Jewish Law; they surpass it. Here is a moral vision, ever beyond our grasp, but which beckons us forward.

On my day off I like to swim at the local swimming pool. Most of us there swim at an average pace, dodging round one another. There are one or two more skilled swimmers, and I can appreciate their frustration with us average ones. I am also amazed at their military tank-like behaviour. They forge ahead in a straight line, oblivious of anyone else, hitting out at the odd leg or arm that gets in their way. With all its colourful hyperbole, I believe this passage asks us to cultivate the ability to yield to others for all our sakes.

When true simplicity is gained,
To bow and to bend we will not be ashamed.
To turn, to turn, will be our delight
And by turning, turning, we come 'round right'.

Ann Lee, 1736–1784,
North American Shaker leader

Unspectacular lusts?

Matthew 5:27-32

Most of us experience unspectacular lusts, though some of us may experience more spectacular ones! To be committed in every way to one person all one's life is a tall order, but (unless one has a calling to celibacy) this is our Christian tradition. There is some evidence that the Christian tradition included same-sex unions in its earlier history (See John Boswell, *Christianity, Social Tolerance, and Homosexuality*, The University of Chicago Press, 1980, p.26). These days, wise psychological advice in the Christian tradition about lust would tend to be: 'what is it saying to you about how a primary relationship needs some tender loving care or some rethinking?' Or 'what is it saying to you about the human need for sensual pleasure and appropriately expressing God's gift of sexuality'? There seems to be a differentiation in the Greek language of the passage between acknowledging lust and indulging in it with potentially harmful results.

Jesus was unequivocal about divorce, partly in order to protect the interests of women, who had few means of earning an independent living and scant resources of birth control or family planning. Women should not be left destitute simply because their husband has set his sights on another woman. As disciples of Christ, we are called to ways of being that encompass the realms of thinking and feeling as well as that of acting justly.

We thank you, God, for the gifts of sensuality and sexuality. Help our lives, we pray, to be graced with these gifts in ways that respect one another's vulnerability and boundaries. In your name we pray.

Let your yes be yes; your no be no

Matthew 5:33-42

Zhenggang, a Chinese student who came to the UK to do a PhD in the natural sciences, told of his journey towards becoming a Christian. Invited to a New Year event by a Chinese church in London, he began to explore Christianity and was baptised at Easter 2006. He gave a compelling summary of the impact on his life of becoming a Christian. He said that, prior to becoming a Christian, it felt safe to tell only thirty per cent of his real thoughts, since he was afraid to let people know all his thoughts. Since becoming a Christian he aims to speak the truth in love, so that yes is yes and no is no. Previously, success for him equalled money, power and reputation. Since being born again into Christianity he understands success as fulfilling God's will. Conversely, great failure in life for him is to have been successfully doing things that are not important in God's bigger scheme of things.

As disciples of Christ, we're called to live with integrity and transparency, because we have nothing to hide if we are right with God. But the actions described in this passage also imply having worldly wisdom. To turn the other cheek would require someone to hit you with the back of their hand, assuming they were right-handed. In Jewish tradition this was a greater insult. In a position of powerlessness, non-violent creativity was being employed with the little power that was possessed.

Consider how your attitudes to success and to communication, to security and to relationships, have changed since discipleship of Christ became central to your life. Where does your witness need to be more distinctive?

Francesca Rhys

Demanding hospitality

Matthew 5:43-48

Each of the teachings from the Sermon on the Mount has contrasting phrases that introduce former and new exhortations, enabling people to memorise these. Here it is: 'You have heard that it was said ...' which is transformed to: 'But I say to you ...'. The Leviticus 19:18 command to love your neighbour referred to fellow Israelites. Here, the challenge couldn't be made broader: 'Love your enemies' (verse 44). In my experience, enmity has been bound up with the abuse of power. Someone has felt most like my enemy when I have felt unjustly treated. Does being empowered, not least through the Holy Spirit, and standing up for our rights, help us to love our enemies and pray for those who persecute others?

In the northern hemisphere we are in the middle of the Week of Prayer for Christian Unity. Efforts towards unity on the ground, through the Spirit's working, are sometimes in contrast to official church doctrine and policy. In one part of Leeds, three mainline churches – Catholic, Anglican and Methodist – worship and pray together regularly. I arrived at the Catholic church for our once-a-month shared time of prayer to find that my Catholic priest colleague was on retreat with the Mothers' Union. A lay member of the church ushered me up to the lectern, explaining how I should introduce the various readings, psalms and antiphons. On the ground, they showed me, a lesbian Methodist minister, great hospitality and inclusiveness, even though their official church policy tells a very different story.

In place of hate and vengeance, O God, there is a desperate need for love and peace. In whatever ways are open to us, give us courage to partake in this choice to relate differently to one another.

Returning ten per cent in thanksgiving

Matthew 6:1-4

Do you know about the five pillars of Islam? These refer to the five foundational practices of Muslims. Three of these are also central to the Jewish faith, and are found in Matthew 6 for the benefit of both Jewish and Gentile followers of Christ: charitable giving, prayer and fasting. Jesus, according to Matthew, emphasised right motivation for doing these things; how we should concentrate on acting in God's presence, rather than in the presence of other people. The Greek word for actor is 'hypokrites'. Jesus was warning against a theatrical display of good practices, for example letting everyone know how much one has donated.

For Jews, tithing was the most sacred spiritual practice. The Hebrew 'tzedaw'kaw' means both charitable giving and righteousness. When worshipping with the United Methodist Church in the USA, I was struck by how many people took much more literally and seriously tithing ten per cent of one's income. 'Tithe' in Hebrew means ten per cent. The closer I get to tithing ten per cent of my income, the better the rest of life seems to fall into place. Being fortunate to have a limited amount of disposable income, tithing helps remind me that my leisure time and entertainment can be based on simpler, time-honoured forms such as sharing food, singing and playing music, dancing, sports, storytelling, enjoying God's natural world. These ways of spending leisure time help us remain rooted in community and in real, rather than virtual, interaction. Local churches often excel at this kind of DIY entertainment.

If tithing is considered so central in Jewish, Christian, and Muslim traditions, should you review your charitable giving to reflect this scriptural injunction more closely? How might this have an impact on your life?

'Pray then in this way'

Matthew 6:5-15

A comment of one of my lecturers, Dr Paula Gooder, during my ministerial training at the Queen's Foundation in Birmingham, has stayed with me. The lines of prayer that appear in this passage were not intended as a prayer to be said all at once; they were intended to give examples of the kinds of ways in which we should be praying, and what we should pray for.

There is a mixture of individual integrity and corporate responsibility expressed through these lines, a mixture of spirituality and action. I have chosen to paraphrase these lines with contemporary language, keeping in mind their original meaning. This may help us think freshly about our being and doing as disciples of Christ and to pray the Lord's prayer anew.

We have a relationship of intimacy with God.
The spiritual dimension of experience is important and needs fostering.
Help us to relate as equals in Christ, may we do all we can to further this kind of relating.
Help us in our efforts towards making this earth a better place, more like you intended it to be, O God.
Help us to have enough nourishment for today and not be over-anxious about tomorrow and the future.
Help us feel remorse for ways in which we have hurt others.
Help us set others and ourselves free from past resentments and injury.
Help us live in such a way that we don't reach crisis point, and preserve us as much as possible from harm.

Unto whom all desires be known

Matthew 6:16-18

During Lent, once a week I have chosen to miss breakfast and lunch. In place of the time spent cooking and eating, I've either spent time in prayer, scriptural or other devotional reading, or I've gone out for a walk in the sunshine. I've been surprised how relatively easy this has been for me, and how it has given me a sense of freedom and a different perspective. Has our modern epidemic and awareness of eating disorders frightened us away from fasting? This fasting has helped me have the ability to sit more lightly to the desire to satisfy my hunger. This is a kind of spiritual insight or discipline, which is relevant to other desires.

At the youth club, when I said that fasting is traditionally part of Lent, one of the young people said he thought it was only Muslims who fasted. It seems a shame that a young person could observe that Muslims are more serious, more rigorous, about their spiritual practice than Christians are. I have a minister colleague who felt devastated when a young person who had grown up in his Methodist church converted to Islam. The young person explained he had found in Islam what he felt was lacking in the Christianity he'd grown up with – precisely that sense of rigour and deep commitment to the faith, which covered all aspects of life.

Why not try fasting from one or two meals a week this Lent? Or you could give up meat and contribute the money saved to a development agency.

Give us this day our daily bread, O God, and help us be thankful, generous, and open-handed with the food we enjoy.

Living differently

3 The new way

Notes based on *The Message* by Eugene H Peterson (Colorado Springs, NavPress, 2002) by

Jenny Warbrick

Jenny Warbrick lives in Birmingham, UK. A former teacher, she is now a freelance trainer and writer. She is married to David, an Anglican priest (see p.1), and has two teenage children.

Acts 2:43-47

The power of community

The book of Acts depicts the transformation of a group of timid disciples, mere observers of Jesus' ministry, into confident and courageous spokespeople. Newly empowered by the Holy Spirit, they declare their faith in Jesus Christ publicly and live out their faith joyfully and actively. But their effectiveness lies in their wholehearted embrace of community. Paul's pastoral letters to Christian communities in major imperial cities like Ephesus and Rome, and to Titus on the island of Crete, are a testimony to the powerful missionary effect of this new way of living.

Eighty years after the death and resurrection of Jesus, his story lives on in the lives of his followers. The daily disciplines of praise and prayer, celebration of a symbolic meal, and support for the needy, help create strong relationships with God and with each other. Although no doubt idealised by Luke, this inspiring picture of the early church and the steady growth of the faithful can make dispiriting reading today. However, we should not lose heart. Worshipping together, sharing and supporting each other, are a powerful witness and politically subversive actions. And rather than count 'bums on pews', let's leave room for the work of the Holy Spirit.

What is my daily discipline as a disciple of Jesus? What is my role in the local community? How can my faith encourage others?

Generous living

Acts 4:32-37

We have just celebrated the formal opening of our new village square in Kings Heath, Birmingham. It has been an eventful thirteen-year journey of vision, design, collaboration, fund-raising and crises, to its long-awaited concrete reality. But it was worth it! As I stood on the honey-coloured tessellated path in the autumn sunshine, enjoying the space, admiring elegant seats, bubbling water fountains, poetry etched into the stonework, and the marble labyrinth at its heart, inlaid with mosaics and quotes from the major faiths, I gave thanks for the incredible community effort that had created such a beautiful place. Without the generous amounts of time, money and patience given by so many, this symbol of unity and peace in the centre of a busy high street simply would not exist.

The unity and extraordinary generosity of the apostles and their followers to the less fortunate should come as no surprise. Their selfish impulses have been overwhelmed by the Holy Spirit. Joseph's decision to sell his field and donate all the money was a voluntary and sacrificial gift. We might be impressed by his action, but would hesitate to copy it. However, there are ways of living generously that do not involve giving all your possessions away! Taking time to phone someone who is lonely, inviting a grieving friend round for a meal or welcoming a stranger doesn't cost anything, but are ways of making our lives acts of service to others for God's sake.

For silent prayer: Allow the Holy Spirit to name those neighbours who need your help today.

Jenny Warbrick

Working from the inside out

Acts 15:4-12

I became aware that, with my white face, I was in the minority. I had joined a group of black and white Christian and Asian Muslim women to participate in a 'listening exercise' run by the Christian Muslim Forum. This exists to encourage dialogue between faith communities, to heal relationships and create safe spaces to live in. It was an informal discussion about how our life experiences had shaped our outlook on interfaith matters and what the current issues were, personally, locally and globally. It was fascinating to listen to and share with other women of faith. Speaking as a white person, I think we are often drawn to other secular white people, when in fact we have far more in common with black and Asian people of faith.

Paul's first missionary journey with Barnabas, preaching the gospel of Christ to Jews and non-Jews in the Eastern Mediterranean, won him the title of 'Apostle of the Gentiles' (Romans 11:13, King James Version) but the issue of whether to accept these outsiders into the faith remained divisive. The Pharisees continued to insist on pagans being circumcised as a condition of salvation. Paul is adamant that God treats Jews and Gentiles the same, gave them all the gift of the Holy Spirit and wants free access for all. This is a clear reminder that, regardless of our external packaging, God works from the inside out: cleaning, restoring, loving, calling and leading. We should treat our fellow companions with the same respect.

Find out about interfaith groups in your local area and the opportunities for getting to know people of other faiths.

Jenny Warbrick

Freedom within walls

Ephesians 2:11-22

Paul's letter to the Ephesians was written from within the walls of a prison. But, like Burmese pro-democracy leader Aung San Suu Kyi, house arrest doesn't stop Paul freeing others to live full lives in Christ. The world plays the game of life by certain rules and it is only by rejecting these and turning to Christ that we find out who we are and our true purpose. God's embrace is a healing one. He takes all the strands of pain and joy, anger and contentment, celebration and disappointment, good decisions and bad, broken and life-giving relationships, and weaves them together to make us whole. The peace that follows, as Paul attests, cannot be diminished by any physical confinement.

Moreover, Christ's death on the cross destroyed the metaphorical wall between Jews and Gentiles. It breached the divide of hostility and prejudice and united them into one humanity. Paul wants everyone to feel invited to God's kingdom and know that they belong there. Two millennia later, the irony is striking. We find it all too easy to ignore Christ's message of reconciliation and unity. The Israeli West Bank barrier is a most powerful symbol of this, but we are also guilty of constructing real or metaphorical barriers between us and other people. Let us, with God's help, dismantle these barriers and construct something positive together; a holy building where everyone is welcome and free and within which God's Spirit may dwell.

Pray about a relationship where you feel there is a 'wall' between you and someone else. Imagine taking that wall down, stone by stone, so that you can see and understand each other more clearly. Now build a place together where your relationship can be healed and grow.

Jenny Warbrick

Moving on

Romans 6:6-14

We moved house just over a year ago. But that phrase doesn't really convey the enormity of what that meant for my family. We exchanged a six-bedroomed vicarage with a huge garden in a quiet village for a four-bedroomed terraced house with a very small garden on a busy high street. Our secondary-aged children felt completely dislocated from everything they had known and loved. It has taken a lot of time, tears and prayers, but they are finally adjusting and feeling more positive.

'Dying to sin' is a bit like moving house. Once you have said goodbye, packed up and left, you can't go back. But Paul, in one of the most powerfully persuasive letters of all time, assures us that it is all right to move on. Leaving behind our old, sinful life can be painful, but being 'alive to God' (verse 11) means the promise of a new purpose for our lives. This may take us in unexpected directions but will bring us freedom and fulfilment. We simply have to trust God, as an actor trusts the director for guidance on how to play a scene. Who knows what plans God has for us? It's both an exciting and a scary prospect! But no task is too difficult for us to achieve, with God's help. Even death no longer has any power over us. So kick the bad habits and throw yourself headlong into life on God's terms. You won't be disappointed.

Lord God, help me to overcome my sinful impulses, to trust in your purpose for me and embrace life in all its fullness.

Avoiding burnout

Romans 12:9-21

We had this reading at our wedding and the more anniversaries we celebrate, the more I appreciate the words. It is a brilliant summary of God's priorities and provides us with key guidelines for living. It covers all the ordinary aspects of life: love, friendship, handling tough times, helping the needy, hospitality, how to treat your enemies, sharing others' joys and woes, getting along with everyone. If we were all to follow this advice, what a different place the world would be! By doing good and serving others, God helps to bring out the best in us and so turns the ordinary into the extraordinary.

But there are so many people to serve that it can be overwhelming. Empathising deeply with people and sharing their journey, especially through illness, grief or a family crisis, is emotionally draining. Hospitality is a powerful ministry to friends and strangers, but can feel like an exhausting round of cleaning and cooking. God doesn't want us to burn ourselves out. We won't be able to take care of others if we don't take care of ourselves.

So making space in a busy week to 'be' rather than 'do' is an important discipline too. Keep a blank space in your weekly diary and see what you feel like doing when you wake up. Make a regular date to go out with your partner. Take your child out for some one-to-one attention. By refuelling regularly, we will be even more effective instruments of God's goodness.

Look at your diary or calendar. How does it reflect your priorities? How does it reflect God's priorities? Pray for wisdom to get the balance right between work, service to others and looking after yourself.

Jenny Warbrick

Wise leadership

Titus 3:1-11

Leadership is tough. It requires vision, energy, patience, excellent communication skills, an ability to motivate and inspire others, make difficult decisions and carry ultimate responsibility. Titus has his work cut out for him! Paul is writing to encourage and guide him as he seeks to shape the local Christian community in Crete. Paul imparts three wise principles of spiritual leadership: humility, confidence and unity.

Being cleansed by the Holy Spirit and called to new life in Jesus is a wonderful gift that we are all offered, regardless of our position in society. All that is required is a humble acceptance and a desire to follow. If we are a leader, we need to remain humble about our own abilities and achievements, so that God gets the glory, not us.

God's rescue of us, commitment to us and promise of eternal life are guaranteed. The confidence that comes from this should underpin our lives. Leaders must have confidence in God's love, and God's plan for their lives, keeping close to him so that they feel supported and can respond to any new calling.

Any group of people is likely to disagree, and division in church communities is particularly painful. Leaders need to stop arguments becoming divisive and firmly encourage individuals to seek the common good. God wants the church to be a united and caring community; whether leaders or not, we all have our part to play.

Pray for yourself if you are a leader. If not, pray for others: Lord God, I pray for those in positions of leadership in our community, country and world. Keep them humble in their use of power, confident in doing good and help them strive for unity.

Jenny Warbrick

Sunday 3 February

Living differently

Notes based on the New Revised Standard Version by

Tom Arthur

Tom Arthur is a recently retired URC minister living in Cardiff. Prior to 1988 he served the Presbyterian Church (USA) and has also served as a lecturer at various universities, mostly in English literature. These days, he spends time painting and drawing, writing and teaching New Testament Greek and biblical studies.

4 Hearing a different drummer

2 Corinthians 5:17-21

A new creation?

About ten years ago, a *Wall Street Journal* article claimed that a financial crash in the near future was inevitable. Now, the crash that came in 2008 is still with us and, as I write, European finance ministers are meeting in Brussels to find workable solutions. Their task is similar to that of a mediation lawyer: rather than dwelling on the past or looking for scapegoats, they are seeking solutions for the future. Is that like being ambassadors of reconciliation, not counting their sins against them (verse 19)? There is no condemnation of the rapacious, dog-eat-dog world that brought us into this mess. Instead, the nations are struggling to work together. If they can just start working together in solidarity, we may have hope for a different future. Maybe.

Early Christians looked forward to 'the Day of the Lord' when Christ would return and set things right in a new creation. Such hope for a different world is perhaps universal. Paul says that when you are 'in Christ' (embraced by Christ, and living Christ-shaped lives), you are that new creation (verse 17). Now. Already. And more: you are invited into a partnership with Christ in the work of renewing the world. That means no longer sitting in front of the telly complaining about the state of things, but standing up to make a positive difference.

To be 'in Christ' is to live differently, as if you were a 'new creation'. Can there be social, political, economic consequences to your being 'in Christ'?

I'll see you in court!

1 Corinthians 6:1-8

I've started getting spam texts on my mobile phone. The one I got today promised I could claim £3750 for the accident I had had (I haven't had an accident). In the UK, with the advent of no-win no-fee, designed to compensate for cuts in legal aid, ambulance-chasing ads started appearing on daytime television and hospital walls. In the last decade the number of personal injury claims has risen by 75 per cent, with costs to insurance companies, retailers and the National Health Service skyrocketing. The result is a legal system that is more like a casino than an instrument of justice. And it's not just the no-win no-fee business. London has become known as 'the libel capital of the world'. Today's justice system has more in common with investment banking than a traditional court.

What happens to a society that becomes litigation-crazy? What happens when people are set against one another in this way, as adversaries, grabbing all they can get? In Paul's day it was even worse. Civil courts were notoriously biased towards the social elite. Courts became instruments of social inequality. Paul asks why petty disagreements can't be handled in the community of believers, where rancour is minimised in favour of respect for a fair hearing, and, if possible, reconciliation. Again Paul draws on 'end time' language: on the 'Day of the Lord' the saints will join Christ in judging the world in equity and truth (verse 2). Why wait, Paul asks. Can't the church come together as a healing instrument of mediation now?

What does it take to move beyond adversarial litigation to resolve conflict as a community, as companions of Christ? Can the church be a model for secular conflict resolution?

Tom Arthur

For goodness' sake

James 3:13-18

In *Age of Greed* (Knopf Publishing, 2011), Jeff Madrick describes innumerable investment bankers, corporate executives and academic advisers who were brilliant in many ways but not 'wise' in the sense James calls us to be. Madrick tells the story of the infamous Ivan Boesky, for instance, who once said, 'Greed is all right ... You can be greedy and still feel good about yourself.' Boesky built a fortune of over $200 million betting on corporate takeovers, but was caught and convicted for illegal insider trading. He informed on a number of colleagues to gain a reduced sentence. Most of the capitalists Madrick describes were not actual crooks like Boesky, but they would have agreed with his philosophy of greed.

James speaks of wisdom that comes from above and wisdom from below. Wisdom from below is the common advice to look after number one, to be a winner, ambitious and competitive – advice taught as a virtual creed in our business schools. Where is the wisdom from above taught these days? Too often what we get in our churches is a soft-focus psychological pillow that does little to challenge the wisdom of the world. Henry David Thoreau, the American Transcendentalist, once said, 'Be not simply good – be good for something' (in F B Sanborn (ed.), *Familiar Letters of Henry David Thoreau*, Houghton Mifflin, 1895, p.197). Ivan Boesky and the rest of them were all good at what they did, and good for themselves. James asks us what good we are for others.

A friend says, 'I may be born again, but I wasn't born yesterday.' Is practical wisdom-in-the-world necessarily in conflict with the compassionate wisdom that is foolish in the eyes of the world (1 Corinthians 1:27)?

Marching season

1 Peter 4:3-11

'If a man does not keep pace with his companions,' wrote Henry David Thoreau, 'perhaps it is because he hears a different drummer. Let him step to the music which he hears, however measured or far away' (*Walden*, Houghton Mifflin, 1854, p.348).

What drumbeats are we hearing? African music begs to be accompanied by offbeat clapping, a one-TWO-three-FOUR rhythm. Uninitiated Westerners will invariably insist on clapping to a more familiar ONE-two-THREE-four rhythm, which sabotages the music's spirit. More often than not, when trying to introduce African music to churches I have served, our musicians will pick up an African drum and beat out a rhythm more typical of the drum section of the Apprentice Boys' marching band in Northern Ireland's marching season – no syncopation, no cross-rhythms. We march to beats we've learned by heart, deaf to the rhythms of other cultures.

The different rhythms we hear and march to as Christians, says 1 Peter, come from the imminent (soon-to-dawn) Day of the Lord, when God will be all in all. For those who can hear, the day becomes not just imminent but, through our discipleship, immanent, already here. In step with its alternative beat, we may be out of step with the martial clangour of the world around us, and misfits in its eyes. But our new world, which I imagine as marching to the rhythms of Zimbabwe's Biggie Tembo and the Bhundu Boys, is filled with justice and joy.

Religion's familiar worship styles and hymns and regularly repeated shared truths give a feeling of security in a chaotic world. Does the apocalyptic story of the destruction of that security enable us to open our lives to a love that is 'broad like beach and meadow', as the hymn says (Anders Frostenson, 1968, *United Methodist Hymnal 120*, United Methodist Publishing House, 1989)?

Getting naked

Colossians 3:5-15

The professor who taught our introductory theology course began a lecture saying 'I've been to Esalen. And I was naïve enough to bring my swimming suit.' Esalen, in California, is a centre for alternative education and personal transformation. Its website says it provides 'intellectual freedom to explore systems of thought beyond the constraints of mainstream academia' (http://www.esalen.org). It's the kind of place where you are invited to strip off emotional barriers and protective preconceptions, to become brutally honest with yourself and your world. In my day, Esalen was an inspiration for 1960s' liberation from traditional constraints.

'Getting naked', as a metaphor for stripping off old, dysfunctional, ego-centred habits, is equally part of the liberation we experience in Christian baptism. We used to do this literally, that is, undress children as part of the baptism rite, and some traditions still do (some Orthodox traditions, for instance). Colossians is speaking of baptism when it says 'You have stripped off the old self' (verse 9).

And then comes something new. Coming out of the water, the baptised is traditionally clothed in white, the symbolic clothing of a witness, as is the young man at the tomb in Mark (Mark 16:5). 'You have clothed yourselves with the new self,' Colossians says (verse 10). You have a new body, the body of Christ (verse 15). In your own experience, you are a witness to the resurrection.

Can we understand baptism or conversion as an experience of liberation, rather than just conformity? How has the Christian life been liberating for you?

Tom Arthur

No longer strangers

Ephesians 4:17-24

Browsing the newspapers at a supermarket yesterday, I saw a front page article in *The Times* about a young man quitting the Occupy London encampment outside St Paul's in disgust. He had joined the demonstration as an idealist, to make a statement with like-minded protestors against corporate greed and financial inequality. But he found too many there seemed more interested in booze, drugs and sex. Similar articles have appeared in other papers about Occupy Wall Street, Occupy Vancouver, Occupy Oakland and so on. We faced the similar reporting back in 'the movement' days, when I was young, demonstrating for civil rights and against the war in Vietnam. It's a way of undercutting the message. The protestors camping by the steps of St Paul's were voicing concerns about economic greed held by the vast majority of the British people.

Reading Ephesians' tirade against the Gentiles and all their wicked ways here, we tend to forget that this letter says Paul came preaching 'peace to you who were far away' (2:17), and it says Paul was in prison 'for the sake of you Gentiles' (3:1). A key to this letter is its celebration of being brought together with those from whom we have long been estranged, whether they are fellow protestors or investment bankers. Protest movements and Christian discipleship make strange bedfellows. Is this what it means to be created in the likeness of God, as if in us the world were given a new start (4:24), a new chance?

Converts can easily become 'true believers' who turn against their past. Does a developed, mature Christian faith overcome such an estrangement from ourselves, and others? What is it, for you, to be in 'the likeness of God' (verse 24)?

Life together

Ephesians 4:25-32

One of the most useful books I've read in recent years is called *Dealing with People You Can't Stand* (Rick Brinkman and Rick Kirschner, McGraw Hill, 2002). It says that the people you can't stand probably can't stand you, either. Different personality types have different ways of solving problems, and get in each other's way. Another book, on families, written by a colleague when I was teaching at Loyola University, had the wonderfully comforting observation that 'all families are dysfunctional'. Such words are tremendous aids to reducing tension. Churches can be extraordinary places of conflict. And Ephesians is refreshingly honest about human nature. It's okay to be angry. But do not sin; work for reconciliation (verse 26).

When I served in Birmingham, I met every week with a group of 'church drop-outs' – former members of strict evangelical churches who had not been allowed to doubt or question. They didn't want to have anything to do with 'church' but were still interested in exploring faith. Eventually, some years after I moved away, I heard that some had made their way back into church communities, open communities that allowed them to grow. One rang me up and told me, with unmasked pride, that she had become an 'adherent' at Carrs Lane Church. Now an 'adherent' is not quite an official 'member'. But what she was experiencing was what Ephesians here calls being 'members of one another' (verse 25): people who, made new in the body of Christ, can affirm one another in open honesty and build up (verse 29), not tear down.

Is there a difference between being a member of a church and being 'members of one another'? What is your experience of being members of the body of Christ? How can you make it better?

Living differently

5 Living as children of light

Notes based on the King James Version (1611) by

Sibyl Ruth

Sibyl Ruth is a freelance writer who lives in Birmingham. She has one stepson, one daughter and a stepdaughter. Sibyl (just about) manages to combine being a rather sceptical person with being a Quaker.

Ephesians 5:1-14

The new deal

Many of us like to think religion is a private matter. Rather than believing faith is fixed, we have 'spiritual journeys'. This phrase makes me think of adventure tours. We can be in one place today, somewhere equally good tomorrow. The author of Ephesians wouldn't approve. This book is not a holiday brochure. It's a contract, outlining the job of being a Christian. Reading it in a modern version, my gut reaction was of not wanting to take on the work. Who could cope with what it demands? But I'm interested in early forms of religious organisation: the Quakerism of George Fox, the ferment of seventeenth-century beliefs. This could be why I went back to the King James Bible of 1611. Its simple language, the alliteration and rhythmic phrasing, make the terms seem almost beautiful. I became more positive about the contract. Whoever drafted it is clear about the commitment involved, what your duties are, to whom you report, and for whom you're responsible. There could even be a little job satisfaction...

But I'd like to vary some clauses at the start of this chapter. That opposition between light and dark seems dodgy. Is darkness 'unfruitful'? Surely seeds germinate in the dark? In the clear light of day, our eyes can deceive us. Other senses lead us astray. Our ears are susceptible to 'vain words'. Yet I am struck by the idea of trying to copy a Redeemer's 'sweet smelling savour'. Often it's those faculties that we value less highly – taste, touch and smell – that are the truest guide to what is wholesome, and what must be rejected.

Redeeming the time

Ephesians 5:15-21

As Quakers, we are enjoined to 'remember the importance of the Bible'. A modern translation of verse 16 begins, 'Make the most of every opportunity'. It's the sort of thing my daughter's head teacher would say. However, in 1611, Christians were asked to 'redeem the time'. This seems rather more mysterious. I am clear about what's involved in redeeming an item from the pawnbrokers. But redeeming time. How do you do that?

In the New Testament, two different Greek words are both translated as 'redeem'. Ephesians 5 contains the less common term. In an everyday context, it would be used for buying people who were in someone else's power – slaves – and then setting them free. So the author of Ephesians wants to do something that is not ordinary, which goes way beyond convention, with our time.

Perhaps our daily life should be more informed by our experience of collective worship? I'm not thinking so much here about the moral teachings doled out from the pulpit. More, of the opportunity we have to get an entirely different, more meditative, take on time. As a student I used to attend Evensong. Paradoxically, the tight framework of the service would often set me free. My body might be sitting in a pew but my mind would fly back and forwards like a bird. In a Quaker Meeting, the outward rituals are plain, almost minimal. But on an internal level, what can happen defies rational explanation.

Hold Infinity in the palm of your hand
And Eternity in an hour.

William Blake

Cherish the love

Ephesians 5:22-23

That opening instruction, 'Wives submit yourselves,' is most annoying. If I read something that annoys me, I want to throw the book down. But even in our own church, one we've chosen because its teaching suits us, we may hear views that we find abhorrent. In such cases, Quakers – a polite bunch – will refer to ministry that 'didn't speak to their condition'. This phrase was first used by George Fox when he felt let down by the priests and preachers of his day. He was dispirited until he heard a voice saying, 'There is one, even Christ Jesus, that can speak to thy condition. And when I heard it my heart did leap for joy.' Fox believed that what he calls 'the glory' should be given to a Christ we experience *personally* rather than to written texts. On the other hand, if we can bring ourselves to carry on listening, we might hear something useful.

Persevering with gritted teeth, I became intrigued by how the duties of each sex are so different. Women do not have to love their husbands. How liberating! So it's all right to feel resentful at times. What matters is to hang on in there, trying to stick with the deal you signed up to, which in the twenty-first century does *not* involve submission. It is arguable that, as many men have difficulty expressing their feelings, they have the harder task. It is their job to be loving.

And I find that phrase 'no man ever hated his own flesh, but nourisheth and cherisheth it' gloriously affirming. Somewhere, the church got fixated on suffering, mortification. But here we are told to value our own bodies. To nourish. To cherish. This is what counts.

The author of Ephesians does speak to my condition.

IBRA International Appeal

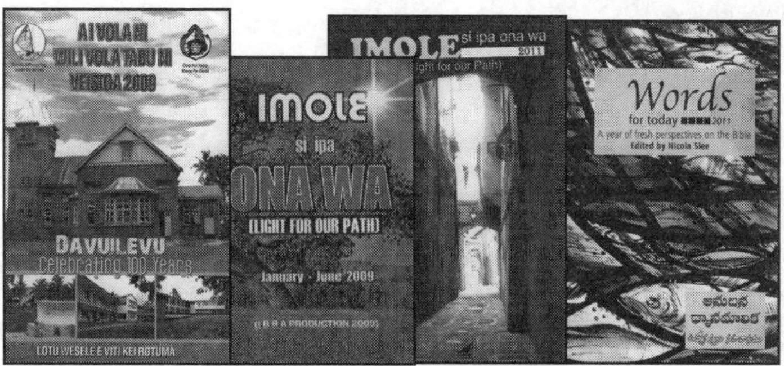

Imagine the only book you have to help you read the Bible is in French (or if you're a French speaker, try Tagalog!). Maybe you can understand bits of it, but imagine your joy when you discover someone has translated it into English for you!

Hundreds of thousands of people around the world experience similar joy when they discover the IBRA books and readings lists have been translated into their language. And this is all through the generosity of IBRA readers.

Each year, the IBRA International Fund provides funds for local groups to translate, print and distribute IBRA Bible notes and reading lists. Last year more than 68 000 people in eleven different countries received copies of the IBRA books which had been translated, printed and distributed by IBRA partners. The reading list was also translated into French, Spanish, Telugu (India), Tokelau (Samaoa) and several Congolese languages, enabling 250 000 people to receive them in a language useful to them.

The funds are given exclusively by IBRA readers like you, who give generously towards the fund, raising over £20 000 each year. With your gift, more people will be able to experience the joy of reading the Bible using notes or a list of readings in a familiar language.

Please consider either giving for the first time, or increasing your donation this year to assist with the development and promotion of our new title. You can donate using the envelope which is part of the leaflet insert that came with this book, or add your donation to your order for next year's books.

Thank you!

International Bible Reading Association
1020 Bristol Road
Selly Oak
Birmingham
B29 6LB
Tel. 0121 472 4242

Wednesday 13 February (Ash Wednesday)

Notes based on the New Revised Standard Version by

Neil Paynter

Neil Paynter has been a street worker for a homeless shelter, a night shelter worker, and a mental health support worker. Presently he is an editor for Wild Goose Publications, and the Iona Community's magazine *Coracle*. His books include *Down to Earth: Stories and Sketches* and *This Is the Day: Readings and Meditations from the Iona Community* (Wild Goose Publications). He is a member of the Iona Community.

Through Lent and Passiontide in poetry

1 Temptations

Matthew 4:1-11

Conversation in the city desert

Near the city centre, I get talking to a young guy, just out of prison. While there, he spent all his free time using the weights and exercise equipment in the yard. Now he wants to do a course at college and get a job in a health club, helping other people to get healthy and fit. 'Brilliant idea,' I say. He can do it, he tells me, with sinew in his voice – and I believe him.

One time he almost died from drugs and drink. He OD'd and passed out: he remembers the blackness. 'Like a pit.' They rushed him to hospital and gave him a shot of adrenaline in his heart. He feels *himself* when he's working out, he tells me. I nod.

He tells me he met an old friend today, down near the market, who told him he had a job to do, and asked him to come in on it with him. 'A job?' 'Robbery job.' 'He said to me: "Why struggle and sweat it? Why wait to get into a crappy little room, crappy little course?" He told me that nothing could go wrong: that he had protection on the inside. I just faced him down. Told him to go to hell. Not even tempting.'

'No?' 'Nope. Easy: I've been dead once.' We talk a little longer. Then he rolls up his sleeves, and shows me his arms – like solid rock. Like armour.

Jesus, this Lent, help us to keep in our hearts those facing great temptation and undergoing real sacrifice.

Money and manna

Deuteronomy 8:1-5

When I was a mental health support worker, I used to visit a young man who lived in a tower block in a rough area of Edinburgh. We'd sit and drink tea and talk. His flat had been broken into three times. He'd been beaten up by a gang who said he was gay. Every day was hard for him. He'd had a job long ago, in a museum, but had a nervous breakdown and ended up homeless; then 'trapped in the system'.

He would go to charity shops and buy cheap reproductions of paintings with a portion of his giro money. His flat was full of masterpieces – Monets, Van Goghs, Botticellis, Chagalls ... Underneath, the walls were peeling; punched and kicked in by previous tenants. The walls out in the corridor were all graffitied, and echoed when you walked in them, as if the building were vacant of soul. There were needles and syringes and empty bottles lying in corners. He'd burn incense in winter to cover up the mouldy smell in his flat. The smell of incense helped 'put him in a better place', he said.

Another thing he'd do was go to the Hermitage, a wood nearby. He explained that some days he just felt 'too surrounded by concrete and greyness'. He'd go and sit under the trees for a few hours. Walk the quiet paths. Look at the wild flowers.

When I asked him why he collected paintings, and took walks in the Hermitage, he thought a moment, and said: 'It's the way I keep hope alive.'

Jesus Christ, as you yourself learned, it is so often the poor who reveal to us the true value of money, manna.

A conversation about angels

Psalm 91

Sitting round the night shelter, we got talking about angels. Sarah, a young volunteer, said she thought that everyone had their own guardian angel who helps you during hard times in life. Nat, who gave the impression that he'd never believe in angels in a million years, said, yes, he believed in angels too; and told us how he was almost killed one time. Some junkies broke into his flat and stole his stereo equipment – stabbed him in the head and ribs. He thought he was falling asleep, but he was really dying. 'I had this feeling. Like someone suddenly reached out and touched me ... My guardian angel, my mum said.'

Ollie, a shelter worker like myself, remarked that in the Bible angels had announced the birth of Jesus; had helped Peter escape from prison. 'Wish I could have one of *them* as *my* guardian angel,' interjected Marco, and we all laughed. Marco was for ever in court; always doing time for something. He pulled a funny face. Ollie said that he believed in angels too, but thought that a lot of times angels were *people*; like the drugs counsellor who picked him up after he'd hit rock bottom. 'Yeah, the nurses and doctors at the hospital were *real* angels,' said Sarah.

And while we talked some more about angels, Sarah reached round and unfastened the necklace she wore, telling Marco to close his eyes and hold out his hand. 'Huh?!' he said.

'No, just do it,' she said. 'Open up your fist.' 'There ... Now you have your own guardian angel,' she said. And there in the scarred palm of Marco's open hand lay a little silver angel on a chain.

Christ, your hands are our hands here in God's world.

The Liberator God

Deuteronomy 6:13-19

The most fitting way to serve the Liberator God is (obviously) to work to help liberate others. Let me tell you about some friends of mine.

Rick, who lives in Canada, is a Buddhist who counsels men who were sexually abused as children and works to liberate them from those who held them captive.

Stuart, who lives in a peace camp outside an arms manufacturer, is a humanist and former businessman who works to help free money and resources that could feed the world.

Jamila, an American, is a Muslim who helps to fund-raise for Amnesty International and works to free prisoners of conscience, to expose torturers, and to speak out for the silenced.

Mika, who sleeps on a platform up a two-hundred-year-old oak tree, is a pagan and eco-warrior; she puts her body on the line to guard the spirits of the trees, the sacred body of Mother earth, and precious water and air for future generations.

Much of the time, I feel I have a lot more in common with people like these than I do with fellow Christians. Many Christians I meet believe that God and religion is 'a private thing', and that 'there is no place for politics in church'. And when I talk to them about my wonderful, passionate, committed, Spirit-filled friends, they inform me that my friends will not be saved and will not go to heaven. To prove it, they then quote the Liberator Jesus, who said: 'No one comes to the Father except through me' (John 14:6). I wonder which Jesus they are following.

May your Spirit be upon us, our Liberator God.

From the song 'Liberator God',
Kathy Galloway, *Iona Abbey Music Book*,
Wild Goose Publications, 2003

Through Lent and Passiontide in poetry

Notes based on the New Revised Standard Version by

Lynne Frith

Lynne Frith is a presbyter in the Methodist Church in New Zealand, Te Haahi Weteriana o Aotearoa, and is currently appointed to a central city parish in Auckland.
Her creative expression includes stitching with threads and fabrics, writing poetry, tutoring in liturgy and homiletics, and being with family and friends.

2 Enemies and opposition

Mark 10:32-34

Facing the consequences

At various times in my life I have been a participant in political protest, sometimes in small groups, but more often in a large crowd. I remember the mixed feelings on such occasions: an air of excitement as a crowd gathers, conviction that this is a just cause, nervousness or even fear at the sight of ranks of police or unsympathetic onlookers, awareness of elements of risk.

It's not always possible to predict what will happen during a protest action. Some protests have better organisation than others, with the organisers or leaders explaining carefully what to expect – from onlookers, from the police – and how to keep safe.

As I reread these few verses in Mark's Gospel, I find myself having some sympathy for the nervous, fearful disciples, lagging behind their intrepid leader. Some were amazed at what they were hearing. Others were afraid. Jesus does what any good leader would do, explaining carefully the possible consequences of his actions. He reminds them that, even though he is likely to be mocked and vilified, even killed, that is not the end of things. In a very short time, everything he stood for will come to the fore once more.

Pray today, this first Sunday in Lent, for all those who are mocked and ridiculed, or who lose their lives, when they stand up and speak out for justice and peace.

Loving the enemy

Psalm 64

I wish I could have the confidence of the psalmist that God will deal unkindly and punitively with those who, in times of conflict or resistance to change in the church, might seem to be my 'enemies'. The trouble is, I cannot escape hearing the words of Jesus: 'love your enemies' (Matthew 5:44), remain in relationship with those who oppose your views, who do not share your passion for justice, who are resistant to change, who are contrary sorts of people. There are plenty of times that I've wished, like the writer of this psalm, for a kind of zapping from the heavens that would just show those difficult people a thing or two!

But I also know, deep down in my heart, that that's not the way to build community, not the way to resolve differences, not the way of Jesus. And then I have to take the difficult steps of seeking peace with my contrary brother or sister, not with the goal of achieving some artificial lovey-dovey state, but with the purpose of restoring community.

Of course there are times when it is impossible to reach across the chasm of injustice and see the humanity of those who foster hatred, commit acts of violence, act unjustly. Restoration of relationship and community may never be possible. Sometimes, for reasons of personal safety, distance must be maintained. Still, I cannot seek divine retribution but must simply and prayerfully acknowledge both my own limitations and those of the perceived 'enemy', trusting that, in time, all will be well.

Pray today for those who perpetuate injustice, those who engage in hate crimes and acts of violence, and their victims.

Unintentional hurt and discord

Psalm 7

I remember well the time when a member of a parish I was in emailed to say that he was withdrawing from active participation in the congregation. When I visited him, he explained that, in a conversation with him and some others, I had made some comments about a particular theological perspective that caused him to think I doubted his sincerity and integrity. I was horrified at the thought and then recalled the conversation to which Fred was referring. We'd been talking about a pastoral situation with which we were both associated. Someone interrupted, I became distracted, and did not finish the conversation with Fred. The unfinished conversation left Fred wondering whether I was doubting his ability to participate in a number of ways in the life of the congregation, and he needed to disengage a little while he considered things.

I was aghast. Fred was someone I trusted, in whom I had confidence, and the last person I would want to hurt, unintentionally or otherwise. I explained my recollection, apologised for the hurt that I had not intended, sought his forgiveness, and expressed the hope that Fred would not disengage completely from the congregation. It was some months before he resumed full participation.

The writer of Psalm 7 recognises the need to repent of the unintentional (or maybe deliberate) harm we have done to our allies or friends, and of excessive animosity and retribution in regard to those who are our foes. It's a hard call, and I need this reminder.

Pray today for those you have harmed or hurt unintentionally, and those upon whom you have exercised harsh and unforgiving judgement.

In desperate need

Psalm 22:12-20

The dramatic picture in verses 14-15 will be all too familiar to anyone who has suffered burnout, depression or persistent fear. If you have been disabled by these or similar circumstances or illnesses, you will know all too well the inability to make your mind and body do what you know they ought, the feeling of being like a floppy rag doll. You may have experienced the helplessness of knowing there are daily tasks that need attention but being completely unable to carry out the simplest of activities; having no emotional or physical energy to cook a meal, pay the bills, do the shopping and, in severe situations, being unable to clothe, feed or wash yourself. Mind and body seem disconnected, thoughts are disordered, and emotions are like an uncontrolled and relentless roller coaster.

Because you may not look unwell, people around you are not forthcoming with offers of help or support, and may even think that the best thing they can do for you is to stay away, to force you to 'pull yourself together'. Whom can you trust? On whom can you rely for loving care and support?

The psalmist pleads with God to draw near, to be prompt in offering help, to provide a safe haven. It's a cry of desperation.

Pray today for those who are in desperate need of protection, care, and love.

The trap of harassment

Psalm 140:1-11

Someone I know was the victim of intermittent harassment from a colleague. He was convinced that she had wronged him in the past, and no amount of mediation or evidence to the contrary changed his mind. Occasionally, at large gatherings of her church organisation, he would stalk her in such a way that only some who were aware of the situation would notice the behaviour.

After one such occasion, my friend sought legal advice and professional support. She was told that there was evidence to indicate that, in at least fifty per cent of cases, such 'low level' behaviour could unexpectedly and unpredictably tip over into extreme violence. The only way she could be sure of her safety while the man lived would be to relocate to another country. This information was duly shared with leaders of her organisation, whose response was to suggest that she have some more therapy so that she could overcome her fears. She felt as if they blamed her for his behaviour, and that they did not take either her concern or the professional advice seriously. The pleas of the psalmist to be delivered from the attentions of evildoers resonated with her.

Churches and related organisations are known for underestimating the possibility of dangerous behaviour by their members or staff. It is often thought that victims are imagining what is happening, or over-reacting, or have somehow caused the unwanted attention. Such attitudes have the effect of condoning evil and violent behaviour, and allow the perpetrator to continue unchecked until someone's life is destroyed.

Pray today for victims of harassment, stalking and abuse, that they may be believed, and find strong support.

Pray also for a transformation of those institutional and personal attitudes that blame the abused person for the behaviour of the perpetrator.

Breaking cycles of violence

Micah 7:1-17

The prophet Micah describes a lonely, isolated adult life, in which friends and family are unable to be trusted. Society has failed. Officials and judges are corrupt, and the powerful have all their desires fulfilled. The faithful have disappeared. Nowhere is safe.

I think of the constant media reports of families in which children are violently assaulted and killed by parents or other family members, of women murdered by former boyfriends or partners, of children being raised in homes that are P (methamphetamine) labs. And I think of the many more children whose physical and mental abuse stays just under the radar and continues undetected and unreported.

I am thankful for the many agencies and individuals who work ceaselessly to break cycles of violence and build families and communities of hope.

I long for the day when Micah's prophecy will be realised, and lives transformed, so that no child need live in fear at home, at school, in the shopping centres or the playgrounds.

Pray today for children whose daily lives are marked by fear.

What kind of God?

Lamentations 2:4-9

When Christchurch was damaged by earthquake in 2011, some claimed that this was the action of a vengeful God: punishment for the sins of the nation. A few weeks after the earthquake, I walked out of a memorial service in my own city when the intercessor suggested that the loss of life was a direct consequence, both of legislation providing for civil unions for same-sex couples, and the wicked ways of Christian churches who welcomed and ordained gay and lesbian clergy. Prior to this, another speaker had claimed that the earthquake and tsunami in Japan was God providing an opportunity for Japanese citizens to be converted to Christianity.

In the ancient world, devoid of the scientific knowledge that we have available to us, there was no other way to interpret natural events and disasters than to attribute them to God. It seems to me that construing God as 'enemy', unpredictable, random, violent and life destroying, is inconsistent with the loving, compassionate, generous and forgiving God described by Jesus. Nor does it take account of what we now know about the nature of this planet earth, of natural forces, and of the consequences of human degradation of the environment.

It is unsurprising that those whose family members, friends and colleagues die in disasters might question why such things happen to them, and search around for somewhere to locate blame, or feel abandoned by God. It is unforgivable, however, to claim that the God revealed in the life of Christ has singled out a particular community to destroy, to make a point, to punish.

Pray for those who are living with the consequences of disaster – earthquake, flood, bushfire, landslide, tsunami – and longing for a restoration of life and livelihood.

Through Lent and Passiontide in poetry

3 Suffering and distress

Notes based on the New Revised Standard Version by

Rachel Mann

Rachel Mann is an Anglican priest, poet and writer based in south Manchester. Her work has appeared in numerous books, magazines and newspapers and she is currently working on her first full-length poetry collection. In 1999 she was diagnosed with Crohn's disease and has subsequently lost far too much of her insides for comfort.

Hebrews 12:1-4

The agony of waiting

Bodies endure it. Minds are strained and sometimes snapped by it. Torturers trade on it. Poets have wielded great art from it. Individuals, communities, societies and whole cultures have been shaped through it. What am I talking about? Suffering. It is one of the unavoidable aspects of human being, as everyday as birth or death. And sometimes it is a place of knowledge, and sometimes, as the cross shows us, along its path lies new life. Without a meditation upon and a reckoning with suffering, our Christian story will be very thin indeed.

As today's reading indicates, the mystery of suffering, as both breaker and maker of our souls, lies at the very centre of Christian faith. Jesus endures the cross and is received in glory. There is encouragement then to 'run the race' of faith in imitation of Christ. What do we do, though, when we are too broken to run? I know that place and it is desperate. Perhaps all we can do is cry out in agony like the crucified Christ. Perhaps we are simply left exhausted. Sometimes it seems as if there is no hope. Endurance can become a kind of agonised waiting. Wait then with God in the darkness. Wait for her to come with everlasting wings.

Living God, wait with us in our struggles and bewilderment.

Eclipse our fears, fill the darkness with hope and good news.

When God dies

Psalm 6

The world can 'end' in a thousand different ways: at the hands of violence, through the loss of livelihood and purpose, in the death of a relationship. In 1999 my world collapsed like a dying star when I became gravely ill with Crohn's disease. I was left unable to work, dependent upon the care of health professionals and then upon my very generous partner. I ended up depressed and having operation after operation. And, I say somewhat shamefacedly, I ended up blaming God. I felt I was being punished by God. 'How', I asked, 'could God do this to me?'

One of the many casualties of suffering is a cosy and safe image of God that says that, if God is good and I am faithful, then nothing bad can befall me. When that image of God dies it can feel like a terrible loss, the loss of our comforter and protector.

What to do when an image of God dies? One faithful response is, like today's psalmist, to cry out, to shout and rail at God and our misfortune. For our God is the living God and, therefore, both present in, and unafraid of, reality – the reality of our distress and of our emotions. God is not in the business of punishment but of bringing us to greater life. When misfortune strikes, she does not wish to hear pious platitudes but wants to meet us in the truth of our loneliness and pain.

Living God,
hear us in our longing and distress,
forgive us when we hide from you,
bring us to greater life,
even when we are afraid
of the things which must die.

The song of the wilderness

Psalm 102:1-11

The wilderness has always been a place of revelation and terror for the children of God. It can be a place of great pain, of crying out like a lonely bird, and yet also of new life. In the wilderness the people of God have often encountered the Spirit waiting to be found. Think of the forty-year wanderings of the Hebrews, their bewilderment and yet their discovery of God's grace. Consider Christ's forty days of temptation and loneliness in the wilderness and, yet, also of the angels comforting him. Remember the great Desert mothers and fathers who sought out the lonely places in order to commune with God. God is a God of the wilderness.

There is such a thing as 'interior wilderness': the experience, within ourselves, of living through a time of desert or wilderness where, as the psalmist puts it, 'I eat ashes like bread' (verse 9). It can take many forms: a sense that one's faith has gone dry, a loss of purpose or direction, a shattering of cherished dreams, and so on. This wilderness strips back and exposes. It brings us down to what we have left. And I want to say it is a place of unsought-for grace, for sometimes God's grace comes like a kick in the gut, knocking us to the floor. This is not the kind of grace we would ordinarily hope to receive, yet sometimes it is unavoidable. For only then can we understand the depth of our dependence upon God.

Living God,
walk with us in the wilderness,
offer us what we need.
Expose us to your grace,
and renew our hoping and dreaming.

Dazzling darkness, dazzling hope

Job 6:1-13

Sometimes suffering genuinely becomes too much. We break and we fall. How do we continue to hope in such situations? In such a place perhaps we add our voice to Job's: 'That God would let loose his hand and cut me off' (verse 9)! It is a place close to despair where comfortable formulas of faith are stretched to, and beyond, breaking point. And yet in this situation, where I, like many, have felt smeared all over the floor, I have encountered God at her most extraordinary and startling. This is the God beyond doctrine or boundaries; this is the God beyond reason and the uses we would make of her. This is the God who is.

It is easy for us to construct for ourselves the God we'd like: the cosy father/mother figure in the sky or gentle Jesus meek and mild. But God will not be made in the image we prefer. S/he is what s/he is and will be what s/he will be. And, curiously, s/he can come to us when we break and fall, for only then are we left with our need.

As for hope? Well, perhaps it is nothing more or less than waiting in the dark, hovering moment by moment above despair. But this dark is no merely negative place. This dark is pregnant with possibility like a womb. New life may yet stir there. The living God is not afraid of such a place and nor should we be. For out of dazzling darkness come fresh beginnings.

Living God,
when our worlds collapse
and we break and fall,
be with us and for us
in the darkness.

The seed waiting to die

Jeremiah 8:18 – 9:6

The experience of pain and suffering is typically intensely personal and throws us back on ourselves. Understandably, suffering can feel a very individual reality, but we know only too well that suffering is experienced by communities and nations. Today's reading, like so many passages of the Bible, draws us back to the pain, not only of Jeremiah, but of the wayward, broken nation he serves. My poem is a response to a modern-day experience of corporate suffering, imagining what one person, caught in the midst of it, might say in response. It is one of the tragedies of our world that it could be set in a thousand places, not merely the Middle East. It is a kind of Magnificat, an echo of Mary's great song of praise, as it seeks to draw hope out of a desperate situation.

Magnificat, Ramallah

My god is a river where goldfinch song soothes
the frightened heart of a son unsure he will
ever find his way home.
My god is a grove, cool with cedar, where sun
warms a man's weary head as he tramples
grapes for wine.
My god is the dream of bread.

In her lingers the scent of thyme, hyssop and
rosemary.
In her incense rises to heal the broken skin of
a child.
In her burning flames renew.

She is the fragments of my heart.
She is the promise which scatters.
She is the seed waiting to die.

The song of the dove

Isaiah 38:9-20

I have had the privilege of being with people as their end is reached. Last time I was in hospital, an elderly lady in the next bed was dying. She was extraordinarily thin, very disorientated and, as her death drew nearer, she began to coo like a bird. I remembered how, as we grow old, our bones can become hollow like birds. I wrote this poem for her, hoping she might know resurrection and ascension in death.

Ascending

To cast off weight, to hollow
out bones, to bend her
voice higher
reaching

she has strength enough for that

for pushing the feathers out
to force the unexpected notes
up through her throat

she is coming down
to what she has left

she is discovering sound –
coos and trills –
body as flute

nothing
will hold her long
she could rise
as easily as dust.

Living God, soar with us,
in both our living and dying raise us up to new life.

Love's exposure

Lamentations 1:12-17

Grief is part of love's harvest. For love, in all its forms, is about exposure, whether that be exposure to the reality of the living God, to one's neighbours or to oneself. And while that may bring great joy and knowledge, there is also a cost: the cost of losing loved ones or precious beliefs or pictures we have about ourselves as we change and move forward. As our vulnerability is exposed, so we may be hurt or weep when people or dreams die. The following poem is an attempt to both acknowledge that truth, in relation to grief, and hint at the possibility of new life.

Time

For now
let tears drop into your palms

let constellations of dust rise and fall

For now
let flowers reveal their fragrance for themselves

there are regions where ice never thaws

soon enough you will raise your hands
receive the first bleak windfall

Living God,
meet us in the midst of our grief.
Wait with us, raise us to new life.

Through Lent and Passiontide in poetry

Notes based on the New Living Translation by

Deseta Davis

Deseta Davis is an Associate Pastor of a Pentecostal church. She works closely with the prison chaplaincy team and has for many years taught in further education. She has in recent years focused on training people for ordained ministry.

4 Being overwhelmed

Matthew 26:36-39

My soul is overwhelmed

It can be difficult dealing with times of anguish in our own lives or those of others. This week's readings explore such times of distress or what John of the Cross calls 'the dark night of the soul', times that can lead to the depth of despair or become a means of transformation. The question is not whether we face times of overwhelming anguish but how we deal with them and how we help others go through their own times of despair.

Jesus became so overwhelmed with what he was about to go through that he admitted he was in despair and his soul was crushed to the point of death. He took his three friends with him, expecting a little support, but ended up utterly alone. His friends having failed him, he could only cry out to God, asking for the situation to be made easier or taken away altogether.

In times of distress we may not be able to depend on others. We may feel very much alone, but in going through the difficult situation we may be given an opportunity for transformation, not only for ourselves but for others also.

Reflect on a time in your life when you were overwhelmed to the point of despair and how you dealt with it. What did you learn from that time?

Sinking like lead

Exodus 15:1-12

Moses and Israel had been freed from slavery. They had experienced the miracle of crossing the Red Sea on dry land. They had seen Pharaoh and his army drowned. This was their time of triumph and jubilation.

The Pentecostal church I am from believes in dancing and rejoicing, especially when seeing the enemy conquered. We would not give thought to the Egyptian army. This is a natural response considering the Egyptians had abused the Hebrews and kept them in slavery for many years. As a Black majority church whose history is from slavery, we would identify with the Hebrew assembly in the text.

The Hebrews had gone through their time of powerlessness. They had been the ones who had been overwhelmed in their situation. They were the voiceless ones with the silent screams that no one else heard. Although many hymns and liturgies today relish high praise and times of celebration, the slaves of old sang songs of lamentation, songs that suited their mood, songs that looked forward to the day they would be free. Suddenly the tables had turned. They had become victorious; they were now in the position of power; but with this power comes responsibility.

The Egyptians, on the other hand, were now drowning in despair. They had no way out, as they sank to the bottom of the sea. The response of the Israelites was to rejoice as the army drowned. Was this the best response for those who were now in power? Did they forget what they had been through? How would you have responded?

Loving God, even though others may have been part of my pain, help me to be like Jesus, who loved, forgave and helped those who played a major role in his difficulties. Help me in my rejoicing not to forget them when they also become overwhelmed.

Into the deep

Jonah 2

You hurled me into the deep,
I am sinking, sinking deeper than ever,
the darkness is gradually taking over.
Little by little I go lower and lower
Till I see no way out.

The waves have hurled me into the deep,
there is no land of rescue I see.
I scream, but no one is there to help.
No one hears, no one listens, no one cares.

The deep has covered and stifled me,
I'm strangled to the point of death,
the waves plunder, pushing me further.
Too much to think about, O what must I do!

O God, I hate these feelings of despair.
I call out and cry to you, but you are not there.
There's no way out, I'm pushing, fighting, seeking,
but I feel so helpless, so powerless to act.

Dear God, help me to feel your comfort, peace and care,
let me know that, through this, you are standing here.
I will grip and hold on as tight as I can,
Till you help me reach the promised land.

Dear God, help me to remember that, even in my darkest hour, you are with me.

'All your waves and breakers'

Psalm 42:5-11

The second book of Psalms starts on a depressive note. This psalmist was exiled in a place far from Jerusalem with only his memories. Thoughts of the celebrations in Jerusalem left the psalmist dejected. He tries somewhat helplessly to praise God in his situation but all to no real avail. After his attempts to praise fail, he becomes more discouraged. God seems distant and his soul is downcast.

Today many are exiled in various lands, in places they don't necessarily want to be, forced out of their homes by war, poverty, fear or trafficking. They long for home and family but are left with only memories. The land they are in may treat them with disdain. They may feel like unwelcome outcasts, with no real means of subsistence. The God they have always worshipped seems absent. Yet they continue to pray and encourage themselves to trust in God. Imagine their despair, their constant anguish, their times of doubt, moving back and forth from trusting God to asking 'why, why have you forgotten me?' Like the psalmist, there may not be an answer at the end; there are times when, going through the deeps, we may not know the outcome.

The implications here are numerous. Among them we may wish to ask questions such as: What does this say about God? How would God want us to respond in these situations? What does it say about us?

Compassionate God, may we remember those who come to this country in desperate need, overwhelmed with the thoughts of home and the hostility of a new land. May we be the hands and hearts you use to show them friendship and grace.

You have overwhelmed me

Psalm 88

I cry out to you in sorrow of heart;
O God, hear my prayer, from me don't depart.
My life's full of troubles, my heart's wracked with pain,
I plead for your help again and again.
Why have you forgotten me? Do you not hear my plea?
I'm cut off as the dead in the depth of the sea.
My friends have all left, I'm abandoned with tears.
Could they not watch with me, help allay my fears?

The land of the dead has taken me over,
The darkness is pouring down like a cover.
But I will plead with you, hear me, you must!
I am helpless, desperate, lacking in trust.
It's on me, like the terrors of a flood –
Let it pass, let it pass, this cannot do me good.
My only company now is tears, the darkness my only friend,
But I'll continue to cry out to God, in the hope that this soon will end.

How do you react when there seems no end to an overwhelming situation?

Out of the depths

Psalm 130

A ray of sun is streaming through,
the scales are beginning to fall;
I sit in the darkness afraid to look,
from the depths of despair I call.

Gradually, slowly there seems a shift;
still through the gloom I crawl.
As if from a dream I slowly awake,
from the depths of despair I call.

The pangs of hell that covered me so
are thick and strong like a wall,
but is that a light at the end I see?
From the depths of despair I call.

Afraid to believe that this is the end
of a long and bitter gall.
I hold on much longer begging for rest,
from the depths of despair I call.

From the depths of despair I call for your help,
desolate, battered and torn.
Through this midnight hour with no seeming end
I am trusting in you alone.

Loving God, even when my faith is lacking and I am filled with doubt, help me to call on you.

Mightier than the breakers of the sea

Psalm 93

What is this that has happened?
The brightness of the day
The shining of the sun
The beauty of the landscape
The calmness of the sea!

I'm now as free as the bird that has found her song
I'm as bright as the star twinkling all night long
I've regained my fervour, my passion, my energy
The cloud has lifted and now I'm totally free.
The overwhelming, engulfing waves are gone – to come no more!

So what is this that has happened?
The hand of the divine has rescued me, from the dark night of the soul.
Though there seemed no escape from the smothering waves
From the violent raging of the seas
God is mightier than the breakers on the shore
God is indeed mightier than these.

Dear God, thank you for your might and power. Help me to tell others of your grace and to help them in their time of need.

Through Lent and Passiontide in poetry

Sunday 10 March

Notes based on the New Revised Standard Version by

Brenda Lealman

Brenda Lealman has been an RE adviser and school inspector, with a special interest in the place of spirituality in education. She is also a published poet and a former chair of the Creative Arts Retreat Movement (CARM). She has travelled widely, including staying in ashrams in India and as guest lecturer at a theological college in the Canadian Arctic. She is retired and lives on the North York Moors.

5 Separation from God

Mark 15:33-39

Cry

The crying of humanity down the ages: cry of the abandoned, of those who are left behind by the world, who cannot keep up.

Through the streets
of half the world
people shove themselves along
on trays and little carts.
They're pulled by the old
whose arms ache and ache,
into jammed columns
on dust roads.
Or are left behind.

Moss is like this:
it scuffs, is legless,
gets no further.
Moss clings to the bark
of willow stumps, to rocks.
We walk over it,
hardly see it, don't hear
its music
a soft solo percussion,
notes here, there,
some with sorrow in them
like the sorrowing in the stares
of those who live
flat to earth.
And are left behind.

Brenda Lealman, 'Moss' in *Is a Religious Poem Possible in the 21st Century?* Flarestack, 2004

Away

Psalm 22:1-11

... And my lament
Is cries countless, cries like dead letters sent
To dearest him that lives alas! away.
G M Hopkins, 'I wake and feel the fell of dark'

'Gone away'. The bleak message on an undeliverable letter: the sort of letter that ends up in one of the Post Office's Dead Letter Centres (Mail Recovery Centres now). A letter sent to someone who is not.

Psalm 22 is a cry to God who has gone away. It expresses intense personal suffering: of abandonment, rejection, abuse. A poet strumming on a lyre, mournfully singing? A psalm used in liturgical worship to express corporate lament? Very likely. The heading 'Deer of the Dawn' is probably an instruction to the temple choir master, the name of the tune to which this psalm was sung, possibly at the early morning offering.

Yet ... God has saved the people of Israel (verses 3-5); has cared for the psalmist in the past (verses 9-11). Is God still there, somewhere, elusive rather than absent? Two contrasting tones now emerge, probably indicating antiphonal singing in worship: interchange between a soloist and congregation. Psalms of lament were accompanied at times by wailing and moaning and weeping. Sobbing, sighing, groaning, labouring, elegiac metre: sounds of grief that can ease our grief.

Broken

Psalm 38:9-22

Heartbreaking poetry expressing torment of mind so intense that it is affecting the psalmist's whole body: bent double with pain, utterly spent and crushed (verse 8), flesh bruised (verse 7), festering (verse 5). He knows he's been foolish and makes no excuses for himself. Bleeding, bruised skin: powerful images of affliction. I felt the pain in my mother just before she died at an old age, not troubled in mind but by increasingly tissue-like, bruising skin. 'You became a flat frock/a sheet of tissue paper/greaseproof paper/scorched in a loaf tin/slit with puce/mackled aubergine/ ... and all the pitifulness/fastened under skin/leaked out.'(Brenda Lealman, 'The Skin', *Time You Left* (Smith/Doorstop, 2000).

The psalmist is so tormented by people that he knows he's likely to make another slip. Please, God, don't let them see me when I fall; don't let them gloat over me when I fail. He has withdrawn in his distress: closed his ears to his tormentors; plays dumb and makes no effort to defend himself.

It is likely that the NRSV translation of verse 18b, 'I am sorry for my sin', does not convey the sense of the original Hebrew. More accurate is the NEB translation: I 'am anxious at the thought of my sin'. 'Sorry' has probably found its way in through its roots in the Old English word 'sar', which has the sense of 'sore' rather than 'sorry'. Raw sorenesses of soul and body, the resonances between the two, expressed through the poetry of this psalm, are almost unbearable.

Plea

Psalm 61

Lamentation is heard across cultures, down the ages: expressions through poetry and music of despair, distress, anger, brokenness, defiance, pleading, alienation from the source of life, God. When the city of Ur was sacked in about 2000 BCE, the sound of laments ran round the city walls, pools of blood were like bronze, the dead melted like fat in the sun. In the West today, blues music echoes the melancholy of African-American work songs and spirituals on the plantations of the southern states of the USA. There is lament in many popular songs, for example, of Bob Dylan, Ella Fitzgerald, Billie Holiday and Annie Lennox. Lament in the plaintive sound of the Kol Nidre sung by the cantor in synagogues on the eve of the Jewish Day of Atonement.

Psalm 61 is a psalm of pleading from the end of the earth, that is, out of dire suffering, just possibly out of exile: the pleading of some individual, or of the king in desperate straits, military, perhaps. The reference to the king in the third person probably signals that those words were sung by a choir. Or those verses could come out of the sense of solidarity of the people with their king: a king fulfilling his obligations contributes to the nation's wellbeing. 'Selah' means 'pause'; it probably indicates a period of silence, of private prayer, or an interlude of instrumental music.

Defiance

Job 19:7-22

Cliffs of fall,
Frightful, sheer

(Gerard Manley Hopkins,
'No Worst, There is None').

The mountaineer Joe Simpson hung in the pitch dark of a crevasse of hideous, unknown depth in the Peruvian Andes. At last he realised the horrific truth: his climbing partner had cut the rope to save himself (he had thought Joe was dead) (Joe Simpson, *Touching the Void*, Vintage, 1998). Job, too, is pitched into the black pit of a dark night of the soul: skin and bone, alive only 'by the skin of his teeth' (verse 20). And the realisation comes: it is God who has cut the rope. It is God who has stripped him of his glory (honour); who has 'taken the crown from my head' (verse 9); who has turned the whole world, even family and servants, against him; who has walled up his way; thrown up siege works against him. Whatever Job has done, he does not deserve this magnitude of suffering; the root of the matter does not lie with Job. His friends continue to maintain that Job is responsible: their accusations are breaking him. 'Have pity on me, have pity on me, O you my friends' (verse 21).

Out of the depths of Job's suffering, out of his dark night, comes his defiant, startling statement: 'God has put me in the wrong' (verse 6). He is preparing to defy God; to take God to task. A worldview of reward and punishment is about to be challenged. Is the idea that God is always in control being questioned, too?

More

Job 26:5-14

Job's friend Bildad has been speaking: Job must remember that human beings are but maggots, worms in the sight of God. With bitter sarcasm Job tells his friends what fine help and wise advice they are giving him in his helplessness; it's as though an evil spirit has got into them (verse 4b). Then follows a passage of great poetic beauty: Job's remarkable description of the cosmos. Even the underworld (Sheol and Abaddon) cannot hide from God. For Zaphon read 'north': Zaphon is a mountain in the north. God stretches the north over an empty place; hangs the earth in infinite space: an astonishingly modern concept. He keeps water in the clouds, sets bounds to the oceans, and overcomes the dragon of chaos that lives in the sea: Sea, Rahab, fleeing serpent (see Isaiah 27:1).

Job opens our eyes to God's power and glory; and his friends have shown that they, too, are aware of God's greatness. But for Job there is more: the signs of God's glory are only 'the outskirts of his ways'; simply glimpses of a tiny part of God's being. 'How small a whisper do we hear of him?'(verse 14) There is more to God; more to suffering; more to the human person than conventional theology has led Job to believe. Most of God is hidden; I am innocent; I am a human being of integrity and dignity. Where is Job's ferociously honest inner searching going to take him?

Remade

Psalm 71:5-21

Psalm for Ludovic, a refugee

Pursue, and seize that person.
Imprisoned. Tortured for doing some printing for people who are seen to be a threat by the current regime in my country.

Lord, you are my hope.
Escape to England. Sent back to my country. Treated brutally by my escorts on the flight. The pain is severe. I can no longer walk properly.

Lord, you are my only hope.
I escape into hiding in fields and forests, into a home where a man risks everything to protect this stranger. Oh, Lord, where are my wife and my small child? Are they alive? In prison? Tortured?

They watch for my life, consult together.
Another police check. Lord, don't desert me now that I have no strength left. Come to my help. Money sent from England buys me medical help. Only one doctor is found who will come to me.

O my God, make haste to help me.
I will hope continually. Wonderful day: the UN has arranged for me to be flown to Sweden.

My God, I will praise you yet more and more.
My wife and child were left to die, locked inside a deserted building. A huntsman heard her cries, shot the lock off the door, and took them to his nearest village to be cared for until our second child was born. Surely my family will be joining me now. O God, from the depths of the earth you will bring me up again. You will remake me.

Through Lent and Passiontide in poetry

Notes based on the Revised Standard Version by

Eleanor Nesbitt

Eleanor Nesbitt is a Quaker, based in Coventry. She has a Hindu family by marriage and her major research focus has been Sikhism. As a poet, Eleanor is especially curious about the Psalms. A Quaker method, 'Friendly Bible Study' (see http://www.read-the-bible.org/FriendlyBibleStudy.htm).has recently introduced her to a new way of interacting with the Bible.

6 Protection and deliverance

Acts 2:22-28

My flesh will dwell in hope

The psalms speak powerfully (and puzzlingly) to us. In each day's reading, let us hope to discern the author's main point, while acknowledging problems that we have with the reading. We can open to 'new light' and ask whether the appointed passage is true to our own experience, and what implications it has for us.

On that extraordinary Pentecost day, when God's amazing actions were being heard about simultaneously in different languages, Peter quoted Psalm 16. For Peter, David's assurance that God will not 'abandon my soul to Hades, nor let thy Holy One see corruption' (verse 27) clearly referred to Jesus, forecasting his transcendence of death. The psalmist's words corroborated Peter's exhilarating sense of a divine plan being fulfilled. Nearly twenty centuries later we can read verses 25 to 28 as uncannily prophetic of Jesus' resurrection, and as conveying David's sense of divine reassurance, and as a universal song of relief and praise. The same words sound differently in different contexts, and carry many meanings and resonances.

When I speak, do I wait to discern that the words have been given to me for that situation? Do I seek to convey hope in confusing times? When I listen, do I expect truth to be multi-layered? Can a treasured poem carry a meaning that eludes prose?

In a deep, deep silence of inward attentiveness, may I be 'full of gladness with thy presence' (Acts 2:28).

Save me in thy steadfast love

Psalm 31:1-5, 14-16, 20

The images of rocks and fortresses evoke an image of God as protective and immovably strong. A very different image is that of God's hand: 'Into thy hand I commit my spirit' (verse 5) and 'My times are in thy hand; deliver me from the hand of my enemies and persecutors!'(verse 15).

Have you noticed how our images of God can be, consciously or otherwise, ones that help shape us as well? We can picture ourselves taking refuge and being plucked out of danger by God's hand and then held in its safety. At the same time, we may find ourselves strengthened to give shelter to others and to stand firm for them when they are in trouble. With God's help, we too can use our hands to help others when they are in distress. Certainly, we do not need to go far to come across 'the plots of men' and 'the strife of tongues' (verse 20).

It was on my first visit to Israel that I realised how welcome a rock can be for the shade that it provides. In the New Testament Jesus speaks of rocks too, as ideal for giving a house strong foundations. And among his closest friends, it was Cephas (Petros in Greek, and thence Peter in English), whose name meant 'rock', whose calling was to be the foundation of the Christian community.

O God, you are my rock. I look to you for stability and protection.
O God, we are in your hands. In our deepest trouble, you come to our rescue.
And may we too be at hand for others.

I love thy testimonies

Psalm 119: 113-120

This psalm is a series of emotive statements: on the one hand the psalmist's love (albeit tempered by fear) for God and his ways and, on the other hand, God's spurning of 'all who go astray' (verse 118).

Today, when the received wisdom is that God hates the sin but not the sinner, many of the verses in Psalm 119, and in other psalms, sound inappropriately harsh.

Fortunately, in today's reading, we can readily identify with the psalmist in his yearning for God, in his love of God's testimonies, and in his commitment to keeping God's commandments. We can ponder whether, why and to what extent other verses do not 'speak to our condition'. When verses present challenges, our mulling over them can yield fresh insight. Let us think laterally and avoid a tunnel vision.

Thus, for Quaker readers especially, the word 'testimony', a word beloved by the translator of the Revised Standard Version, carries an additional resonance. It reminds us of our testimonies to peace, truth, equality and simplicity.

Oh Lord, hold me up, that I may be safe, and not safe just from physical danger. So often (like the writer of this psalm) I feel beset by evil and cunning. But, as a peace-maker, may I commit myself anew to living simply and honestly, even when I feel more like denouncing those who behave cruelly, deceitfully and unjustly. Uphold me according to thy promises.

From whence does my help come?

Psalm 121

Like me, you may first have read, sung or heard a slightly different version of this psalm, one in which I lift up my eyes to the 'hills from whence cometh my help'. There was a hill at the end of the road where I grew up as a child and just looking up to it brought a sense of perspective, stability and assurance.

Later, I worked in the foothills of the Himalayas. I came to understand the reluctance of hill-people to venture higher up after nightfall, when spirits were thought to be about. As dawn lit up the snow-peaks, their breathtaking beauty made it easy to understand that gods might dwell among them and why pilgrims would persevere to reach remote shrines.

The more accurate translation of verse 1 is the question: 'From whence does my help come?' The question moves us away from a God identified with high places, a God more closely associated with one location than another. Here is a God who vigilantly accompanies us everywhere, and provides endless protection.

In the twenty-first century, our awareness of the fragility of our planet's ecosystems, and the vulnerability of the landscape to mining, deforestation and other human encroachment, prompts us to lift up our eyes to the hills with a new consciousness of our responsibilities.

Let us ponder the complex relationships between ourselves, our God and our environment. Will we simply accept the psalmist's assurances of divine protection?

Elsewhere in the Bible, hilltops are sites for receiving God's guidance and witnessing transfiguration.

Pause in wonder. Stop.

We have escaped as a bird

Psalm 124

At about the same time as I read verse 7, 'We have escaped as a bird from the snare of the fowlers; the snare is broken and we have escaped,' I read a verse in the Sikh scriptures, the Guru Granth Sahib. In this verse, Kabir, a poet loved by Muslims, Hindus and Sikhs, describes God as the cage that protects us (the caged parrot) from the marauding cat. At first I was struck by the contrast, and then by the similarity: 'Blessed be the Lord, who has not given us as prey to their teeth!' (verse 6).

Verses 1 and 2 also cause me to reflect: can 'the Lord who was *on* our side' be understood rather as 'the Lord who was *at* our side'? 'On our side' suggests adversarial conflict in a way that 'at our side' does not.

Most of us have not experienced life-threatening floods, but we quail at the images of 'raging waters' that appear on our television screens when such disasters strike. How different from 'the still waters' or 'waters of rest' in Psalm 23:2! In our spiritual journeying we will find water images that convey life's fear and turmoil as well as water images that steady and sustain us.

As we centre down, let us focus on the still waters, while being ready to stand by others when they feel swept away by crises.

Lord, may we sense your presence whenever we feel overwhelmed by forces beyond our control.

Peace be in Israel!

Psalm 125

Here is a difficult psalm. There is the stark classification of people as 'the righteous' and 'those who turn aside upon their crooked ways' and 'evil-doers' (verses 3 and 5). Also, our reading of the psalmist's words is probably affected by the recent history of Israel and by our own sympathies and interests in relation to present-day conflict.

As we read and reread, there may come a realisation that the psalmist is not consigning people to clear-cut, once-for-all categories: 'the righteous' can all too easily 'put forth their hands to do wrong' (verse 3). We are all liable to turn aside. Moreover, and worryingly, preoccupation with being righteous can all too easily result in self-righteousness.

Perhaps visualising the mountain 'which cannot be moved, but abides for ever' (verse 1), like the hills in Psalm 121, strengthens our trust in God. Does the expression 'the sceptre of wickedness' (verse 3) also resonate with our understanding? Importantly, are these images helpful to us or not on our own spiritual path? Through pondering the psalmist's sentiments and his turns of phrase, can we find our own truth? We may wish to formulate our own prayer, in our own images, arising from our own experience.

Let us pray for peace in today's Israel, and wherever there is bitterness and division, aggression and warfare. This may include our country, our local community, our church and our family. May our prayer for peace be one with our commitment to actively bringing about peace and reconciliation in any situations where we can play a part.

I fear no evil

Psalm 23

Appropriately, our week of reflection on themes of deliverance and protection includes a psalm that has comforted millions. Here is the deeply restorative image of green pastures, and how much more meaningful this is if you live in a semi-desert land!

Psalm 23, and Jesus' portrayal in the New Testament as the good shepherd, came to my mind during a day in the hills of west Wales. I was watching sheepdog trials: in turn, each shepherd stood midfield, calling and whistling to his (and occasionally her) dog, in the hope that it would bring three sheep together around the field and into a small enclosure. I identify with the dog, wanting to please, but having to cope with the fickle reactions of the sheep. I identify with the sheep – especially with the one that headed for the undergrowth.

Comforting though this psalm is, it also disquiets me. I do not relate easily to the notion of having a table prepared 'before me in the presence of my enemies' (verse 5). In what way is this true for me?

As I write, a friend is dying, walking through the valley of the shadow of death. Lovingly, let us call to mind those who are sick, and especially any who are close to death. To use a Quaker phrase, let us hold each of them in the light.

Thank you, God, for all the times when I have been followed by your goodness and mercy. May I find the still waters within me. May I fear no evil.

Through Lent and Passiontide in poetry

7 The passion of Christ

Notes based on the New Revised Standard Version by

Geoffrey Herbert

Geoffrey Herbert is a retired Anglican priest, now with a ministry of listening and speaking about our spiritual journey. He is a grandfather. He occasionally writes poetry, and has an interest in studying how poets and other artists represent humanity in the stages of life.

Hebrews 10:5-10

'This is my body'

This week's readings, centred on the cross, have poetry, which can carry a power greater than logic. In today's passage, Psalm 40:6-8 is quoted – originally a poem of kingship sung in the temple. By a leap of imagination it is transposed into the voice of Jesus dedicating himself as a new high-priestly king sacrificing his own body. In contrast, here are some words of Wilfred Owen from the First World War, the voice of millions who gave their lives:

We turn back to our dying.
Since we believe not otherwise can kind fires burn;
Nor ever suns smile true on child, or field, or fruit.
For God's invincible spring our love is made
afraid;
Therefore, not loath, we lie out here; therefore
were born,
For love of God seems dying.

From 'Exposure' in John Stallworthy (ed.)
Wilfred Owen – The War Poems,
Chatto and Windus, 1994, pp.71–2

These men endured terrible suffering, and Owen shared it. The other two men crucified on Good Friday suffered longer than Jesus. In what way was his cross unique? Perhaps he himself saw it as not unique but a way of sharing the indignities and agonies of ordinary people. It was something he felt he had to do, a 'must' (see Mark 8:31), an act of terrified obedience such as soldiers obey. Words on the meaning of the cross were the result of his followers' struggle to make sense of it. The cross is a wordless poem.

Stones that breathe

1 Peter 2:4-8

In Britain our faith is often belittled and rejected by a culture soaked in materialism and atheism. We aren't persecuted, just regarded as silly, deluded or even objectionable because of religious conflicts and moral stances. We are caricatured as an encumbering deadweight on peace and progress, like unusable old building stones. Yet our call is to be shaped and built into chosen and precious living masonry, not encrusted relics. We have a heritage of faith that gives us a strong message for our culture. As part of this, our ancient churches can still put us and even sceptical people in touch with something that makes for wonder and hope. Surely Christ is our cornerstone through the faith and prayer and longing of past eras, and our own. St Giles, Sheldon, Birmingham, was my church for eleven years. For nearly seven hundred years it was the centre of a rural village; today it's on the edge of a main road through a large housing estate.

Remember Lydia, bless her:
she came in here one desperate swirling midnight
to hug a pillar and seek the strength and warmth
breathed into its mediaeval cold by centuries of
prayer.
Whose breath?
God's if, like Lydia, lonely rescuer of refugees,
we seek for ourselves and our false-comforted
age
something absolutely real.

Lord, have you really chosen and honoured me?
May I live this and give freedom and hope.

The cross goes on

1 Peter 2:21-25

Bearing sins goes beyond enduring punishment: sin hurts others, and bearing it involved holding all the results in a great and terrible embrace.

'I will draw all to people to me' *(John 12:32)*

The wounded men of every battle
and all the beggars and lepers of the earth
are festering and dying on my skin.
Every rape is a swordfish in my belly.
There are deserts and volcanoes in my lungs,
and millions of ripped and trapped animals
are howling in my guts.
Victims and torturers, be my wounds.
I want to be your blood brother with my body.
I want to shout Why? and hold you still,
and make a new kind of peace
at the eye of this chaos.
It will mean being racked beyond bearing,
until my bones crack apart
and all the hope and love bleed out of me.
Even then I shall not know that all is well.
We shall be on the dark edge.

Geoffrey Herbert, 'Atonement' in
Geoffrey Duncan (ed.)
Timeless Prayers for Peace,
Norwich: Canterbury Press, 2003, p.286

Pray with a representation of the cross and see Christ as bearing the results of some hurt you have caused and also some wider evil inflicted by humanity on others or the creation. Picture the victims in all this, feel their pain.

Rubbish

Hebrews 4:14-16

The High Priest of the temple was greatly honoured. He alone could enter the holy of holies and make the atoning sacrifices. Jesus is imagined as the last and greatest, yet also humbly one of us. His sacrifice was his body, his holy of holies a public rubbish dump.

Wilfred Owen's Golgotha is the Somme, where the chaplains ('disciples', 'priests') and the jingoistic press ('scribes') have no idea of the cost. The notion of the soldiers' sacrifice as Christ-like was common, but this officer-poet who shared it tells its truth: the propaganda about 'The Hun' was nonsense, and so was the idea of glorious sacrifice. The only men who knew what Golgotha meant were facing each other in the trenches.

At a Calvary near the Ancre

One ever hangs where shelled roads part.
In this war He too has lost a limb.
But His disciples hide apart;
And now the Soldiers bear with Him.
Near Golgotha strolls many a priest,
And in their faces there is pride
That they were flesh-marked by the Beast
By whom the gentle Christ's denied.
The scribes on all the people shove
And bawl allegiance to the state,
But they who love the greater love
Lay down their life; they do not hate.

John Stallworthy (ed.)
Wilfred Owen – The War Poems,
Chatto and Windus, 1994, p.23

Jesus, how much the pain of Golgotha still goes on growing. We imagine you there, wherever it is, the unknown fellow-sufferer.

Living the love

1 John 4:7-16

John sees love as the nature of God, and God's followers as receiving it and living it. But, even in John's community, there was sharp division (1 John 4:1-4). He himself was very sure of what correct belief must be (verse 6), as are some Christians today. They may be right, but it's more important to live the life of Christ: (Matthew 7:16). While the theological and ethical dialogues go on, we're called to reach out in love, to touch the crucified Christ:

Wherever there is a lifting up
from the mud and the gutter

and a holding of lice-infected mortality
close to the heart and the lungs

Wherever one weakened hand
reaches across intolerable pain or loss

to touch another who does not
speak the same language

Wherever the imperative of care
endures despite any difference it can make …

Nicola Slee,
Seeking the Risen Christa,
London: SPCK, 2011, p.131

Drawing on your own experience, write another 'Wherever …' to add to the poem.

When I am weak

Revelation 5:6-14

In verse 5 Christ is given the Old Testament royal titles Lion and Root, metaphors for prowess and heritage. In verse 6, a dramatic leap: the Lion becomes a Lamb. At the beginning of John's Gospel (1:29), the Baptist in a prophetic way also uses this title for Jesus, the Passover lamb to be slaughtered to begin the liberation of the enslaved people of God. The strength of the Saviour is in his weakness, his readiness to suffer and offer himself utterly. In John's vision the seven horns show his power and the seven eyes his ability to see the truth about us and imagine huge possibilities. This kaleidoscope of images is typical of apocalyptic literature such as the book Revelation.

At the heart of today's passage is the weakness and helplessness of Jesus, which are the source of his power to draw, to heal and to inspire worship. When the great Anglo-American poet Denise Levertov (1923 – 1997) was 60 she returned to her childhood faith. She had been writing a fine poem ('Mass for the Day of St Thomas Didymus') that she intended to be from an entirely secular standpoint. When she came to write the song 'Agnus Dei' ('Lamb of God') she was powerfully attracted to the image of lambs as flimsy and helpless, exposed to a coldly fearsome world. She felt strangely drawn to God as a lamb in need of her: 'Must [we] hold to our icy hearts/ a shivering God?' (Paul A Lacey, ed. *Denise Levertov – New Selected Poems*, Highgreen, Northumberland, Bloodaxe Books, 2003, p.136).

Jesus, you are our child, our grandchild, needing us to watch with you, care for you. You are our mother, our father; our needs and our weaknesses are your burden, gladly carried.

The harvest of Paradise

James 5:7-11

In church mosaics, up to the tenth century, the cross is usually shown as a tree of life. In Rome a late example is the apse in San Clemente: on a black cross Christ is upright, unbroken, arms spread as if in blessing; white doves roost on the woodwork; a green vine spreads outwards in spirals with flowers at the centres; more birds have nests there; from the foot of the cross a spring has produced large lush plants; deer come to drink. And all on a gold Paradise background. My wife and I sat for half an hour before it, silenced. In later centuries the mosaics of the cross show bleak agony. This has been written into our theologies and painted in our art – part of the truth; the forgotten part is the tree of life.

In the northern hemisphere the grain harvest can celebrate both the work with its waiting, and a small foretaste of Paradise:

I have ploughed and harrowed,
sown the seed into darkness;
I must wait for the rains
or water the soil's thirst,
wait in hope for the tiny green promises,
for the long rise into golding sun
and the dusty busy fields at cutting time,
for harvest to come home, become milled
richness
mixed and yeasted, loaves for the Kingdom feast.

Lord, we wait in your Holy Saturday silence, sown in the dark soil of hope.

Sunday 31 March
(Easter Day)

Readings in Luke (1)

Notes based on the New Revised Standard Version by

Ian Wallis

Ian Wallis is an Anglican priest, currently based at St Mark's, Broomhill, Sheffield. In addition to parish and chaplaincy work, he has been involved in theological education for over thirty years, including serving as Principal of the Northern Ordination Course. Through his writing, teaching and preaching, Ian seeks to bring the life and ministry of Jesus back into focus in a way that can both inform and inspire contemporary discipleship.

1 Resurrection and ascension

Luke 24:1-9

Remembering the dead

Some of the most fundamental aspects of life can be among the least appreciated. Take the air we breathe, the universe we inhabit or the democratic freedoms many of us enjoy. More often than not, we take these for granted, not out of ingratitude or indifference, but because they are so essential that life without them would be impossible to contemplate. Easter is no less fundamental to Christian faith and yet how often do we consider what resurrection is and how we share in its reality? In the coming days, Luke invites us to reflect on this profound mystery.

Luke starts by taking us to where Jesus isn't. To honour him by observing funeral rites and securing a place of burial is itself a measure of Jesus' enduring impact upon his followers – the bodies of most crucifixion victims remained on the cross, unclaimed, for fear of being found guilty by association. But having offered us this insight, Luke seems keen to stress that Jesus' body was absent, and it becomes increasingly apparent that its relation to his continuing presence is far from obvious.

Another recurring emphasis throughout chapter 24 is the place of memory and correlation within the experience of resurrection. Notice here how remembering Jesus' words throws light on the present (verses 6–9). And remembering for Luke is a communal undertaking without which unbelievable happenings remain at best obscure and at worst irrelevant.

- I wonder if the whereabouts of Jesus' body matters?
- I wonder how community and remembering are able to mediate Jesus' presence?
- I wonder whether I need to express devotion to Jesus?

The womb of resurrection

Luke 24:10-12

Immediately we notice how for Luke the womb of resurrection is not the tomb but the community of faith Jesus called into being. It is among the disciples that his continuing presence is experienced. The gospels reveal that Jesus attracted many followers and supporters, including women. Luke introduces Mary Magdalene and Joanna in chapter 8 where, together with Susanna and many others, they provided for Jesus and his male missionary apprentices 'out of their resources' (Luke 8:1-3). Here, in the company of another Mary, the women act as messengers for their male counterparts, who evidently had remained together in a group that extended beyond the Twelve (verse 9; Acts 1:12-14). One can't but be struck by how infectious this good news proved to be!

But, if it is impossible to keep good news to yourself, then it is equally impossible for it to remain second-hand. The women's testimony was greeted with incredulity. 'Nonsense' seems a more appropriate rendering than the NRSV's 'idle tale' (verse 11), for the apostles were struggling to grasp what was being communicated to them. Rumours of resurrection remain no more than that until validated through personal experience. They are implicit invitations to explore and discover if there is any basis for what is being claimed, just as Peter begins to do (verse 12). For Luke, resurrection is not so much an event in the past as a process of realisation repeated in the lives of those open to the call of the crucified one and possessed of a pioneering faith.

- I wonder if I relate to Jesus' resurrection as second-hand news?
- I wonder how I can seek Jesus' risen presence?
- I wonder where and in whom Christ is to be found?

The witness of scripture

Luke 24:13-27

The Emmaus story is found only in Luke (but see Mark 16:12-13) and, as such, affords our surest insight into the evangelist's appreciation of the resurrection. It helps to recall that Luke was writing two generations removed from the first Easter. His concern is not only to be faithful to the sources at his disposal (Luke 1:1-4), but also to the witness of the Christian community to which he belonged.

Notice how Jesus' presence is communicated. In contrast to the tomb, Jesus' body is apparently seen (verse 15), but it is not the vehicle for encounter, even for those who knew him. The two disciples begin their journey with second-hand news but, as they travel in the company of the stranger, they are encouraged to reflect on recent happenings in the light of the Hebrew scriptures (i.e. the Christian 'Old Testament'). Through this process of corporate remembering, the significance of Jesus begins to emerge as he comes to be seen as the longed-for Messiah who fulfils the hopes of a pilgrim people in search of salvation (verses 25-27). While we may struggle with this explicit Christological interpretation of the Jewish Bible, it was one of the ways in which Jesus came to life for his Jewish followers.

It is also interesting to note how the resurrection is portrayed as Jesus' vindication and exaltation by God, thereby demonstrating that his ministry and death are not simply exemplary in terms of human response to God, but also decisive with respect to the realisation of God's will for humanity.

- I wonder how the Bible shapes my experience of living?
- I wonder in what sense the Hebrew scriptures speak about Jesus?
- I wonder if Jesus is still able to demand attention by the quality of his humanity and his capacity for bringing God to life?

Ian Wallis

Re-membering Jesus

Luke 24:28-35

In these verses, Luke continues to explore Jesus' risen presence among his followers. Now the focus is on hospitality, with strong eucharistic overtones throughout. As the two sojourners approach their place of lodging, they offer shelter and sustenance to their anonymous companion, who accepts. Yet, at table, roles are reversed as guest becomes host and host becomes bread – blessed, broken, given (verse 30; cf. 9:16). The actions are characteristic of the Last Supper, which in Luke's version incorporates Jesus' words, 'Do this in remembrance of me' (22:19) – not so much the institution of a sacramental ritual or injunction to hold memorial meals as a commendation to continue his practice of table-fellowship. In this respect, the meal at Emmaus is the outworking of what Jesus commanded and promised, within the community of faith and the discipleship of its members.

As rumours of resurrection give way to personal encounter, the impetus to share good news finds fresh momentum. Immediately, Cleopas and colleague return to Jerusalem to witness to what they had discovered: Jesus fulfils God's saving purposes revealed in the scriptures and inhabits the faithfulness of his followers as they continue his ministry of hospitality and sharing bread, 'blessed, broken and given', with friend and stranger. Significantly, both today's and yesterday's passages underline how two defining characteristics of Jesus' embodiment of faith continue to mediate his presence and communicate his impetus.

- I wonder in what ways Holy Communion communicates Christ today?
- I wonder how my life expresses the hospitality of Christ?
- I wonder if I am open to the strangeness of Christ's risen presence?

The body of evidence

Luke 24:36-43

This passage stands in stark contrast to the Emmaus encounter, where Jesus' body obfuscates rather than mediates resurrection. Here it is presented as evidence. His wounds and ability to consume food become demonstrations that Jesus is still alive (cf. Acts 10:39-41). The strong physicality of the language seems incongruous in the light of Luke's witness to the resurrection to date and has led some commentators to conclude the evangelist was responding to accusations that Jesus' post-mortem appearances were illusory (cf. John 20:25).

These verses also raise some intriguing questions. For instance, where does the reality of resurrection reside? The word translated 'ghost' in verses 37 and 39 can also be rendered 'spirit', as in the Spirit that descended upon Jesus at baptism (Luke 3:22), was given up at his death (Luke 23:46) and bestowed upon the disciples at Pentecost (Acts 2:4). In the light of this spiritual continuity, in what sense does Jesus' transformed corpse communicate his real presence?

Or, again, what is the relationship between proof and faith? Seeing and touching Jesus' body appears to have engendered a range of responses, but not belief (verse 41). In this case at least, sensory encounter no more precipitates belief in resurrection than it did for the disciples journeying to Emmaus.

How then should we account for this passage? Does it communicate an ancient memory of what took place or is it a creative attempt to convince those of Luke's time unpersuaded by the witness of the Spirit-filled community (cf. Acts 13:43; 18:4, 13; 19:8-9)?

- I wonder about the sources for Luke's resurrection accounts?
- I wonder if proof is necessary for belief?

The authority of experience

Luke 24:44-49

'Witness' is the golden thread running through these verses. They begin with the witness of scripture and the recognition that all three divisions of the Jewish Bible – the Law, Prophets and Writings – attest Jesus as the Messiah.

With respect to the good news of resurrection, however, the testimony of scripture is secondary to personal experience: 'You are witnesses of these things' (verse 48). On a number of occasions throughout chapter 24, Luke refers to 'these things' (verses 14, 18, 21) without specifying what is intended, although he probably has Jesus' entire ministry in mind rather than simply the events of Easter (verses 20-21; Acts 1:20-22; 2:22-32). From this perspective, God's raising Jesus up is the definitive judgement upon that ministry (Acts 2:24) and, as such, the authorisation for its continuance 'in his name' (verse 47; cf. Acts 2:38; 3:16; 4:7-12) and in the power of the same Spirit (verse 49; cf. Acts 2:1-4).

Finally, it is striking how Luke roots Jesus' ministry, exercised largely around Galilee where he resided, in Jerusalem. In contrast to Mark and Matthew, the disciples encounter their risen Lord in the city of David, close to where he was born (Luke 2:4) and crucified (Luke 23:33). In this way, the evangelist locates Jesus theologically within the promise of salvation entrusted to Abraham and the Jewish people (cf. Luke 1:68-79; 2:29-32).

- I wonder if Jesus thought the Jewish Bible spoke about him?
- I wonder how Luke understands the relationship between Jews and Christians?
- I wonder whether that is an understanding I can share?

The heart of worship

Luke 24:50-53

There is a certain irony here easily missed. Having gone to considerable lengths to stress the continuity between Jesus' pre- and post-Easter presence, Luke now wishes to interrupt it or, at least, to re-express it. With the ascension (cf. Luke 9:31; Acts 1:9-11), bodily continuity gives way to spiritual continuity or, more precisely, to the continuance of a ministry and vision of God's kingdom embraced by Jesus' disciples and empowered by the same Spirit at work in and through him.

In this way, Luke distinguishes between two interrelated phases in the outworking of God's promise of salvation for all people. A promise, entrusted to the Jewish people (cf. Luke 1:68-79) is realised in Jesus the Jew (cf. Luke 2:29-32) and fulfilled through the Spirit-filled, ethnically diverse, community, the church (Acts 2).

The ascension, however, is much more than a transition; it speaks of exaltation and enthronement (Luke 22:69; Acts 2:24, 32; 3:15, 26; 4:10; 10:40; 13:30, 37), thereby glorifying Jesus' status ('And they worshipped him', verse 52) while reinforcing one of the key meanings of resurrection for the evangelist, namely that what we encounter of God in Jesus characterises not only a brief chapter in space and time but also the nature and will of God throughout eternity. Jesus' being taken up into the life of God graphically expresses this profound theological insight, while preparing the way for the next manifestation of divine life within human experience – the outpouring of the Spirit at Pentecost (cf. Acts 2:29-36).

- I wonder how I understand Jesus' ascension?
- I wonder where God's Spirit is at work today?
- I wonder if my life bears witness to Jesus?

Readings in Luke (1)

2 Going up to Jerusalem

Notes based on the New Revised Standard Version by

Brother Anselm Smyth SSF

Brother Anselm was born in 1930 and professed in vows in the Anglican Society of Saint Francis in 1956. He worked at St Francis' School, Hooke, from 1966 to 1978; as Minister Provincial from 1979 to 1991; as Vicar of St Bene't's, Cambridge, 1993–2000 – and has since served in Birmingham, and now at Glasshampton Monastery in Worcestershire. He was ordained priest in 1980.

Luke 19:1-10

Lifted up on high

We continue our celebration of Easter with a flashback to the nineteenth chapter of Luke's Gospel, which leads us from the encounter with Zacchaeus in Jericho to the expulsion of the traders from the temple in Jerusalem. Luke prepares the readers of his gospel for the events surrounding the death of Jesus with a series of seemingly unrelated episodes that call to mind the saying of Jesus in the Gospel of John: 'Now is the judgment of this world; now the ruler of this world will be driven out. And I, when I am lifted up from the earth, will draw all people to myself' (John 12:31-32).

The saviour lifted from the earth attracts all of us, the human race, both for judgement (for learning the truth about ourselves, about our wounds – those inflicted on us, those we have inflicted on others), and for the healing of those wounds, for salvation. This involves, for us, the grief of penitence, and joy of redemption.

Luke opens the sequence with the story of Zacchaeus, who lifts himself from the earth to get a better view of Jesus and is consequently accepted, loved and restored by Jesus from a life of greed and theft to his place as a child of Abraham. He faces judgement and is thus redeemed.

God of love, help me to make the story of Zacchaeus the story of me.

A tale of two tales

Luke 19:11-27

Luke firmly links this parable of Jesus at beginning and end so as to make it an integral part of the last journey. It follows the party at Zacchaeus' house (the financier who had walked away from his illicit bonuses), and precedes the entry into Jerusalem. What did it say to his followers (including Zacchaeus)? What does it say to us?

The ruler is Jesus himself. The far country is his death. The kingly power is conferred by his resurrection. ('A little while, and you will no longer see me, and again a little while, and you shall see me': John 16:16.) By rejecting him, his enemies choose to lose their lives. By loyalty to him, all can share his risen life.

The pounds tell of God's generosity and of God's respect for the individuality of his children – but, what are they? Surely, not less than everything? We have nothing that we did not receive. The God of love and longing gave us our being so that we should long for God, give God our love. That same God gave us time in which to do it, bodies with which to do it, and gave us friends to love. God showers us with gifts, pounds if you like, to trade with and return to God.

Loving God, you gave to your son Jesus the gift of resurrection life, which he shares with us your children. Help us always to remember this, and let our cellphones, our wristwatches, the meals we eat, the clothes we wear, our loves and friendships, our sufferings also, constantly remind us that we are debtors, not owners.

The colt

Luke 19:28-40

Having concluded the story that, for those with ears, encrypts the purpose of his journey, Jesus leads the way up the hill towards Jerusalem. He reaches the Mount of Olives, and has planned his entry to the city – he sends for a mount, his triumphal steed. This turns out to be a donkey!

Pilate, too, at Passover time, approaches the city from the direction of Caesarea – and as a demonstration of Roman brute force he rides a cavalry charger at the head of a body of legionaries. This is a demonstration of the nature of the kingdoms of this world – of empires, then and now.

By contrast, the kingdom of God, the father of Jesus, is best revealed by a humble Galilean riding a donkey surrounded by a motley crowd of unarmed peasants. They announce his arrival by shouting 'Hosanna to the son of David!' These words were seditious, a threat to the security of the state, so 'Silence them,' say the Pharisees, 'this is turning into a riot with looting and burning, and forcible repression by the military.' 'If they were silent, the stones would shout,' replies Jesus. The whole of creation witnesses to the kingdom of the creator.

The crusaders, twelve centuries later, ignored the message embodied by Jesus on his donkey and used the imperial might of Christendom in an attempt to regain the holy places from the 'infidel'. A disciple of Jesus, Francis of Assisi, with a companion, passes unarmed and unharmed through the Christian and Muslim lines and converses with Saladin himself. That gesture in itself proclaimed God's kingdom of peace – the greed and rapine of the armies were its denial.

God of peace, today I shall have to choose between Jesus on his donkey and Pilate on his stallion, many times, in many forms. Strengthen me and help me to choose rightly.

Tears for Jerusalem

Luke 19:41-44

The city lies open to his gaze, and Jesus weeps. His were neither the first nor the last tears to be shed over or for Jerusalem – remember Psalm 137; consider the Wailing Wall. Jews, Christians and Muslims all weep for their holy places. The Patriarch, the Christ and the Prophet all made of that small city a crossroads, a focus, alas a battleground for their followers. It is as if the rays so focused fail to provide the light of truth, and instead result in a flame destructive of all that comes to us in the Hebrew Bible, in the New Testament, in the holy and glorious Qur'an.

In the prophecy of Isaiah, and in the revelation to John, God promises that all tears will be wiped away, even those over Jerusalem, even the tears of Jesus shed on the eve of his passion – and resurrection. We make that our hope as part of our celebration of Easter, and rejoice in all signs of reconciliation between Jews, Christians and Muslims. And yes, such signs there are!

God, lover of humankind, bring us together at the last into that unity that is the outcome of the saving events that took place in Jerusalem.

Exit commerce

Luke 19:45-48

Jesus enters the temple in such a way as to challenge publicly those who are plotting his destruction – he violently ejects the traders and moneychangers. They were not selling coffee or improving literature; they were trading on worshippers by selling sacrificial animals for which temple currency was needed. In other words, in order to worship Yahweh, you had to pay through the nose.

Like Zacchaeus at the beginning of our journey, the temple traders face judgement. There is nothing to suggest that they shared his conversion and redemption or that they regarded their position as a loan from God to be repaid with interest – as a 'pound'. They were a living denial of all that the temple stood for as a 'house of prayer for all nations', and thus aroused in the prophet Jesus the strongest possible public demonstration on behalf of God's human children – the 'all nations' for whom that temple is a place of worship.

This leads us to consider our temples, our places of worship – Christian, Jewish, Muslim. Are they places of prayer where all are welcome? Is the stranger welcome? Remember, the stranger is Christ.

God of all people, help me to make of my life, help us to make of our places of worship, channels of welcome to the stranger, truly houses of prayer for all nations.

Authority

Luke 20:1-8

Jesus is challenged by the temple authorities, 'What is your authority for this desecration?' Jesus' teaching about authority is well known to his disciples, but not understood and certainly not practised by them: 'whoever wishes to be great among you must be your servant' (Matthew 20:26). In Luke this is reiterated in the Upper Room at the Last Supper – and still they haven't got the message. The Spirit is not yet given.

His authority? His vocation as servant of all leads him to act in this provocative way so as to open the way to the Father to all. God is his authority. His opponents, even less than the disciples, would not understand this, so he shifts the goalposts. 'Tell me, what was John's authority?' They plead ignorance.

We are disciples of Jesus. To us has the Spirit been given, the supreme gift – the talent of talents, the pound of pounds – so we cannot plead ignorance. Easter living is living a life of service in the knowledge that only so can the life of Jesus be the life of his body, of which we are the members.

Such is authentic authority.

Almighty and servant God, we try to live the life of your servant son in a world of powers that are in denial of his authority. We are sorry for our many failures to do so, and ask that the courage that was his as he drove the traders from the temple may be ours as we witness to his love.

The vineyard

Luke 20:9-19

In the light of Easter, we have been considering the sequence of events recounted by Luke that began in Jericho with the conversion of Zacchaeus, and ended in Jerusalem with the ejection of the traders from the temple. From that point on, initiatives pass from Jesus to his foes – his words and actions are in response to the opposition he encounters from the powers arrayed against him. The climax lies ahead on Maundy Thursday – in the Upper Room he enacts his gospel at the supper table, in Gethsemane he is 'handed over'.

This last passage in our sequence carries a very clear message. It describes the ignominious fate of the beloved son of the vineyard's owner, sent in a last desperate attempt to collect the year's rent. 'With him out of the way, the freehold will be ours,' the tenants reason – falsely. Falsely because in killing the 'beloved son' the tenants have brought about their own destruction. Jesus quotes from a great psalm of victory (118) – the rejected stone is in fact the chief cornerstone. 'This is the Lord's doing' (Psalm 118:23). The murdered son is raised – Christ is risen.

And the vineyard is given to others – to us, in fact. We join, not the ranks of bad tenants, but the succession of emissaries sent to ensure the title of the owner to the property. We can expect the same welcome as that experienced by the envoys in the parable, with the difference that we also share the status of beloved sons and daughters, and the risen life of that beloved son. Francis of Assisi taught that rejection and calumny for the name of Christ represent for the Christian 'perfect joy'.

Readings in Luke (1)

Notes based on the New Revised Standard Version by

Robert Draycott

The Reverend Robert Draycott has had a varied ministry, including working in the local church in Britain and in Brazil. He has worked in theological education and more recently as a school chaplain. A keen sportsman, he has recently been a volunteer and a Games Maker at the London Olympics.

3 The last days

Luke 20:20-26

Indebtedness

When it comes to owing anything to anyone else, most people do not want to be in debt to anybody. This is especially true when it comes to owing money. Yet at the same time we are also aware that we owe a great deal to many others. In human terms it starts with our parents, our wider family, teachers, coaches and so on. As Christians, we believe that life itself is a gift from God. In other words, we are debtors and we usually try to live grateful lives that give something back.

Today's passage contains what is often seen as a fundamental insight into the relationship between faith in God and how one views the state. Those who were attempting to entrap Jesus felt they had left him no room for manoeuvre: he would have to make a choice and he would be wrong either way. Jesus responded with a question, then his answer laid down the challenge, namely: what exactly are the 'things that are the emperor's' (verse 25)? Christians have struggled with that question ever since.

The challenge that faces Christians today, as it has through the ages, is that, while everything is owed to God, not everything is owed to the state. Christians need to be aware of Revelation 13 as well as the rather better-known advice found in Romans 13. Obedience is owed to the state as a Christian duty unless the state is discerned as 'the beast'.

What, if anything, are the 'things of the emperor' in my situation? Do I need to act differently as one whose primary allegiance is to God?

The lens of God's action

Luke 20:27-40

I saw an unusual headstone on a grave recently. First a man's name – he had died suddenly at only 33 years of age. Next came his wife's name, then came her second husband's name. This reminded me of the Sadducees' question that was intended to ridicule the idea of the resurrection of the dead.

As Christians we know that our faith is centred on the resurrection of Christ from the dead. Yet it is very difficult to imagine what that resurrection life will be like. If we take our lead from Jesus, two things can be said, first that it is more a case of what this resurrection life *is* like and, second, that we need to be able to *use our imagination* to picture what is beyond our experience.

It is natural to try to fit the resurrection into our time framework of past, present and future. In one sense we await this event in our future. But if God is the God of the living then we should try to alter our perspective to that of the living God who is eternally present. We read this passage with the benefit of hindsight. We look back at the Sadducees' attempt at ridicule through the lens of God's action in raising his son on what we now call Easter Day. That lens gives our imagination some clues: the risen Lord was the same but different, different but the same. There are also aids to our imaginations through the images we find in the book of Revelation. One example must suffice, that of the 'new Jerusalem, coming down out of heaven from God' (Revelation 21:2)

Teach us, Lord, to see through the lens of your action.

Confrontation

Luke 20:41-47

Most people do not like confrontations. One reason for this is that we remember instances when attempts at confrontation went badly wrong, such as those times when we had listened to only one side of the story and were embarrassed to realise that we had jumped to conclusions that were unfair, or the times when the situation became much worse as a result of our attempts. If only we had kept quiet!

Yet today's passage shows Jesus confronting his opponents. We are reminded that there are times and situations when it is necessary to engage with opponents. Clearly Jesus both had authority and was prepared to use it. In this case he warned his listeners against religious hypocrisy, having first demonstrated his authority with regard to the interpretation of scripture. He seems to be saying that his enemies' understanding of the Messiah was too limited; he challenged them to think more deeply.

One part of our Christian experience today is this question of how to interpret scripture, and the nature of authority. There are several areas of quite fierce debate about 'what the Bible teaches'. Two examples are gender issues, and the relationship between science and religion. How are Christians to work out whom to trust, whom to listen to? There are some general pointers: one is the test of coherence – does the interpretation actually make sense? Does it fit in with what we believe about God, of what we know about the world, about life? Another is the character of the person we are listening to; Jesus used the picture of a bad tree not being able to bear good fruit.

Pray for any situation of confrontation or conflict in which you are involved.

Powerful dependence

Luke 21:1-4

This is a very well-known incident that we can picture in our minds' eye: the rich people making sure everyone saw both them and the size of their contribution, then the poor woman who slips up unobtrusively to offer 'next to nothing'. The amount was, on one level, almost worthless, but on another level invaluable, because it was 'all she had'. The self-forgetful widow provides a striking contrast to the self-important scribes.

Possessing money symbolises both power and independence. The widow looks utterly powerless but in reality perhaps she became a powerful figure through the faith she demonstrated in putting her last two coins in the offering. The scribes took it for granted that they were powerful and independent, not really feeling a need for God. In contrast, the widow knew that she was totally dependent on God.

Jesus challenges us to see beyond appearances to God's reality. We live in a covetous society that at the same time feels itself to be under constant financial threat. It is easy to join in the general assumption that being rich is about what we own. At this point we might recall Jesus' parable about the rich fool. He was actually a *poor* fool wanting to invest in bigger barns, in stark contrast to this widow who was wisely investing in God. This reminds us of the lesson we find so hard to grasp, that we never truly own anything but merely look after things for a time. Our difficulties come because we allow our possessions to possess us.

Does our giving ever delight God? What do we need to change with regard to things we imagine we possess? Pray about this.

Faithful

Luke 21:5-19

In his brilliant allegory *Pilgrim's Progress*, John Bunyan likened the Christian life to a journey on which the pilgrim encounters many difficulties and temptations yet also receives encouragement and support. For a while, the pilgrim has a travelling companion named Faithful. Their task is to follow the 'King's Highway'. At one point, however, they have no choice but to pass through a wicked town called 'Vanity Fair'. Here the two pilgrims are mocked, beaten and imprisoned before being brought to trial. Faithful is condemned and dies a martyr's death.

Bunyan's work reflects his own seventeenth-century context and the way in which Christians were persecuting each other. In his time, people were prepared to, and at times required to, die for their faith. In today's passage, Jesus warns his followers of the cost of discipleship: 'they will put some of you to death' (verse 16). This is a stark reality for some Christians today and should be a matter of concern, prayer and action on their behalf by the majority of Christians who do not face such extreme threats.

We may be part of that majority ourselves, yet we may also find our faith tried and tested in other ways. If we feel uncomfortable at today's challenge, it may help to be reminded of the meaning of the word 'comfort', which is to 'come alongside' and 'to strengthen'. Jesus also said 'I will give you words and a wisdom' (verse 15). He is trustworthy, the one rightly described as 'the faithful witness' in John's vision (Revelation 1:5).

Pray for those suffering persecution and risk of death for their faith.

Robert Draycott

Jerusalem

Luke 21:20-33

The focus of today's reading is Jerusalem. It seems that Jesus foresaw the destruction of both the temple and the city; certainly Luke's readers knew it had happened. The big question for them was, what did it mean? There are various possibilities, some negative, others much more positive.

Negatively, it is possible to emphasise the suffering involved in a siege and its aftermath, to feel that the phrase 'days of vengeance' (verse 22) is significant. Then there is the description of 'signs' leading to 'distress', 'fear and foreboding'. How much weight should we give to those images?

Positively, we could see this imagery as the setting, background or introduction to the heart of the message, which is centred around the phrase 'the Son of Man coming in a cloud' (verse 27). There is something to look forward to – or, rather, someone. The phrase 'for your redemption is drawing near' (verse 28), underlies this point. Jesus is directing his hearers' attention away from the place to the person.

This reminds me of a recent experience when I was invited back to the first church I ministered in. The chapel building was to be demolished and this was to be the final service of worship. There was a certain sadness but a much greater sense of gladness at meeting old friends again. We were being reminded of 'the nearness of the kingdom of God'.

As Christians, the concept of the kingdom now centres around the crucified and risen Lord, the one who brought redemption.

In what ways do we think the kingdom is near? Pray for places and communities where redemption is needed.

Living expectantly

Luke 21:34-38

Christians are meant to live expectantly. One of the great secrets in life is to be able to 'seize the day', as the saying goes. It is easy to live either in the past, looking back and wishing we had done things differently, or to spend so much time planning for the future that we have no time to appreciate the people around us.

Some Christian groups encourage their followers to try to read the 'signs of the times' so as to 'know' when Jesus will return. In such cases the present has no value of itself; it is to be merely observed with an eye to the future. This is to miss the clues Jesus gives of the significance of the present. The parable of the fig tree hints that when the end comes it will be obvious; meanwhile be alert, be prepared.

Martin Luther King was reputedly asked once how he would spend his time if he knew that Jesus was due to return the very next day. He replied that he would carry on as normal. He knew the value of living each day to the full, valuing the opportunities it presented, even if it proved to be his last day.

Living in the present is a vital part of following Jesus. It matters how Christians live their daily lives because the time in between the cross and the return of Christ in glory is the time when the kingdom is near *now*. Every day presents fresh opportunities for service and witness on behalf of that kingdom which is already present. The Lord's Prayer has the two adjoining phrases 'thy kingdom come, thy will be done'. Live expectantly in the here and now because the future is assured!

Pray the Lord's Prayer.

Hosea

1 Covenant and faithlessness

Notes based on the Hebrew Bible by

Rachel Montagu

Rabbi Rachel Montagu teaches Judaism and Biblical Hebrew. She believes teaching people to understand the Bible in Hebrew, without translators' interpretations, empowers them as readers. She has been involved in interfaith dialogue for many years.

Hosea 1:1-3

'You will be like God, knowing good and evil'

Incorporating into his own life both pain and rejection, followed by forgiveness and continuing love, Hosea acts as a living model of the relationship between God and Israel. His writing transmits God's teaching poetically and dramatically to the reader. He wrote before the destruction of the first temple and probably prophesied in the North; this explains why more of his calls to repentance are addressed to Ephraim and Israel. Like Joshua and Isaiah, his name is derived from the Hebrew root for salvation, and salvation is the core of his message. Hosea wants to move the people to repentance and therefore salvation, and to prevent punishment and destruction. Harsh words of condemnation for Israel's betrayal of God by idol worship are constantly tempered by God's promises of mercy and forgiveness. The kings of Judah and Israel mentioned in the introductory verses reigned during the eighth century CE.

God tells Hosea to marry a woman 'inclined to adultery'; this translates 'znunim' better than versions that suggest she was immoral before the marriage. The parallel with the people betraying God by pursuing idol worship after the redemption from Egypt and covenant at Sinai works only if their relationship starts well and then deteriorates.

Grant forgiveness to us, our Creator, because we have sinned; forgive us, our Ruler, because we have transgressed, because you are God who is good and forgiving. Blessed are you, Eternal, who are gracious and abundantly forgiving.

Daily Amidah 6th blessing

Will that name get them teased at school?

Hosea 1:4-11

Usually in the Bible, children are named by one of their parents and the name commemorates something significant about their birth. Hosea and Gomer's children are named by God, as are Isaac and Ishmael (Genesis 16:11, 17:17-19). But Ishmael and Isaac's names say something positive about Isaac's birth and Hagar's relationship to God. Hosea's children's names, Jezreel, Lo-Ruchamah and Lo-Ammi, demonstrate to the people round Hosea the threats God wants them to hear about Jezreel, compassion and peoplehood. 'Lo-Ruchamah' or 'No-Compassion' seems a particularly harsh name for a newborn because the Hebrew word for compassion is connected to the word for womb. Jezreel is harder to understand. It is a place name, and associated with Jehu's massacre of Ahab's sons (2 Kings 10:11). It means 'God will sow' and in Hebrew (Yizrael) sounds more like Israel (Hebrew: Yisrael; both words have been changed when they were transliterated via Greek and Latin into English). So it may be that Hosea is making a positive promise: God will sow and harvest once more. But because of the association with 'No-Compassion' and 'Not-My-People' (the meaning of Lo-Ammi), it seems more likely that Jezreel is a reproach for what was done there. Yet, once the names and the threats were delivered, each name is in turn turned round to a new promise of hope (Hosea 2:23-25).

Ask friends and family why they were given their names and what they mean to them. You may discover some interesting stories.

Eternal our God, have compassion upon us and upon Israel your people. Feed us, nourish us and sustain us, and let us not be put to shame in this world, nor in the world to come.

From Grace After Meals

These compassionate words are Hope's Gate for us

Hosea 2:16-23

These verses declare God's longing for Israel's love. God will 'speak to her heart' (verse 14). 'As in the days of her youth' (verse 15) is similar to Jeremiah 2:2, where God reminisces about Israel's single-minded love and adoration during the years in the wilderness: 'the loving-kindness of your youth and your bridal promises'.

Doreen Wachman, a Jewish author and journalist, has suggested that verse 18 means that Hosea is declaring that, in the future age of perfection, women will call their husband '*ishi*, my man' and not the more domineering '*baali*, my master', a title tainted by its connotations of idol worship. This means that creating more egalitarian relationships between men and women helps ready the world for the era of perfection that Jews call the messianic age; equality between men and women improves the world and is not, as some have suggested, contrary to biblical teaching.

These verses linking human and animal peace and security echo the promises of a future era of perfection from Isaiah 11:6-9, which also end with the knowledge of God as a hoped-for ideal.

Those religious Jews who on weekday mornings put on phylacteries (leather boxes containing verses from Deuteronomy and Exodus wound on arm and forehead – see Deuteronomy 6:8), say verses 21-22 of today's passage while winding the straps round their fingers to remind them of the parallels between the love of God and love for partners and of God's new covenant. They commit themselves to strive towards knowing God and call upon God's promise to respond.

'And I will betroth you to me for ever' – and we will try to follow your teachings for ever.

'And I will betroth you to me in righteousness and justice, with loving-kindness and compassion' – and we will try to act justly and with loving kindness and compassion to those around us.

based on Hosea 2:21-22

'If I must *what*?'
'If I can, you can.'

Hosea 3

Commentators debate whether the woman God commands Hosea to love here is Gomer, whose marriage is described in chapter 1, or another woman. For a passage about adultery and betrayal, this teaches an interesting lesson about the Bible's attitude to love. Like the Song of Songs, this chapter proves the importance of romantic love in the Bible: the woman is described as 'beloved by a friend' (verse 1) as well as an adulteress, showing that marriage means love and friendship as well as a sexual relationship, in fulfilment of the command in Genesis 1:28. Hosea isn't just asked to welcome the woman back to his house but actually to love her again.

It is possible that the woman described was an unwilling captive; the amount Hosea paid may, taking the barley into account, equal the amount paid for the value of a woman or a slave (Leviticus 27:4, Exodus 21:32). But, if she had been abducted and forced, that would provide her with an excuse the children of Israel couldn't claim for their voluntary betrayals.

If the reader empathises with Hosea and how difficult he may have found this, then that may help us to understand how God suffered from the people's flings with pagan gods and other worship-foods – raisin cakes (verse 1) were used in idol worship. Hosea insists on a period of waiting and anticipation before they come to each other and likens this to God waiting for the people again to seek for God and God's manifest goodness.

Make a list of ways in which God's goodness is manifest in your life.

The Eternal, the Eternal God, compassionate and gracious, slow to anger and full of loving kindness and truth, keeping loving-kindness for thousands, forgiving sin, transgression and wrongdoing, and who considers us to be innocent.

Exodus 34:6-7

If with all your hearts you truly seek me

Hosea 4:1-11

Once again, Hosea emphasises knowledge of God as the key to repentance and right living. Human beings may be able to know God to only a very limited extent, but even that limited knowledge ensures that we understand why murder, lying and stealing and the other sins enumerated here are wrong.

The result of the people's adultery and deceit is that the land itself mourns. In Leviticus 18:25-28, too, the land responds to immorality done within its borders. There the land vomits out those who disobey God's commandments. Here when the land is adversely affected by its citizens' immorality, they in turn are affected by the land's grief; the land's distress enfeebles and makes barren its inhabitants, just as anyone ever bereaved knows what it is to feel exhausted while struggling to accept the loss.

In Exodus 19:6, God calls the children of Israel to be a kingdom of priests and a holy nation. Immediately afterwards, God gives them the Ten Commandments. If the Ten Commandments are arranged as two sets of five, as on the two tablets, idol worship and adultery are the second command on each, putting these two betrayals in parallel. Here God says that the people's refusal to know God means they can no longer be priests. Even priests have been involved in worshipping false gods and the people have listened to false prophets like those who made Jeremiah's role so much harder (Jeremiah 23).

You know today and will take it to heart that the Eternal is God in the heavens above and on the earth beneath and there is none other.

Deuteronomy 4:39.
From Aleynu, the prayer said at the
end of all Jewish daily and Sabbath services

If only I could hear your voice!

Hosea 6:1-6

Hosea calls the people to repentance, including himself in the summons. In Hebrew the same word is used for returning and repentance: repentance means a return to our best possible selves. Hosea reminds us that God may punish but always heals us. These passages may be meant to explain to the people that exile and attack from other nations are God's punishment for everything wrong they have done.

If you check 'On the third day' in a biblical concordance, you will find a number of life-enhancing events, including Exodus 19:16-19 and Esther 4:16. Because God 'saw that it was good' twice on the third day of creation (Tuesday in our calendar), some Jews consider Tuesdays to be a lucky day.

The Pentateuch commands worshipping God by regular sacrifices. Hosea, Amos and Isaiah all say that God prefers acts of kindness to offerings, and here Hosea again emphasises the importance of trying to know God. But the way the offerings were made – regularly, every day – can still teach us an important lesson about loving-kindness, which we must try to make a constant in our lives. After the temple in Jerusalem was destroyed by the Romans, the rabbis said that prayer, the worship of the heart, replaced the role of offerings and is now the preferred way to worship God; prayer too should be a constant part of our lives.

May God's great name be exalted and sanctified in the world created according to God's will. May the Eternal who makes peace in the high places, make peace for us and for all Israel and for all the world, and let us say Amen.

From the Kaddish

God still wants to heal bird-brained Israel

Hosea 7:11-16

This chapter begins with God's desire to heal Israel. Ephraim is compared to a foolish dove, birdbrained and flighty, who moves from one dangerous trap to another, not understanding why nothing can be gained by negotiation with Egypt and Assyria, even if this politicking gives them the illusion that they rule their own fate. Unlike Ephraim, we know the whole world is under God's rule.

The sound of cooing doves is one of the many evocative images from nature in the Song of Songs. The word for 'dove' used here is 'yonah'. The dove is also sometimes used as a symbol for the whole people of Israel; because of this, the prophet Jonah is sometimes taken as an everyman, or at least an 'every-Israelite' figure; in this context the importance of his story is not the willingness of the Ninevites to repent but Jonah's anger against God for being, he thinks, far too forgiving. God shows him why all human beings matter to God. The dove in the Noah story and the olive branch she brought back when she found that land had reappeared after the flood are now symbols of peace, because the olive branch was used by the Greeks to indicate a wish for peace and because the dove shows determination and loyalty. Here the dove represents foolish vulnerability compared with the strength of the Assyrian eagle in the next chapter.

Hosea conveys God's exasperation with Israel's continued unwillingness to recognise that they owe whatever strength they have to God.

Our God, help us repent and return to your teaching and to serving you. Bring us back in perfect repentance before you. Blessed are you who delights in repentance.

Daily Amidah, 5th blessing

Hosea

Notes based on the Hebrew Bible by

Rachel Montagu

For Rachel's biography see p.113.

2 God's continued forgiveness

Hosea 8:1-3

The covenant is broken

The role of the biblical prophets is often misunderstood to refer to foretelling the future, while it is really concerned with conveying God's message. If God's message was on the lines of 'repent immediately, or a terrible punishment will come from Assyria', it included a future event that non-prophets wouldn't have authoritative information about. But the key message, the actual prophecy, is 'Repent!' In Hosea, the predicted punishment if the people do not repent does not include the specific, detailed threats of captivity we read in Isaiah and Jeremiah. But hints of disaster at the hands of neighbouring countries do pervade his writings.

Hosea's work echoes in many ways. If the Hebrew is read aloud, complex patterns of assonance can be heard within verses and paragraphs. To understand Hosea, we need to see him in the context of the other books that resound within his writing.

The shofar, or ram's horn trumpet (verse 1), was used both for military signal-calls and to summon the people to repentance. So its use here both warns about possible invasion by the powerful 'eagle' Assyria and calls the people to refrain from sinning and to know God.

Even if our mouths were as full of song as the sea and our tongues with joyful singing as the sound of its waves, and our lips with praise as the expanse of the heavens ... we would be unable to thank you enough, Eternal God.

From *Nishmat*, part of the Sabbath morning service and Passover seder

You shall celebrate the Eternal's feast – not Dagan's

Hosea 9:1-9

Hosea accuses the children of Israel, saying that, rather than celebrating the festivals of God as they are supposed to, they have been practising forbidden pagan rituals. To indicate this, in verse 1, 'the threshing floors of new corn' uses a word for corn identical to the name of Dagan, the pagan fertility God whose temple and followers Samson destroyed (Judges 16:23-30). The reference to Egypt (verse 3) may mean literally exile in Egypt and burial there, despite the warning in Deuteronomy 17:16 that a king who leads you back to Egypt proves himself false. Or it may be a way of saying 'you are regressing to the pagan level you were at before you left Egypt and stood at Mount Sinai'. At Mount Sinai, they learned to turn eating into obeying God (Deuteronomy 12) and to integrate harvests into joyous worship of the Eternal (Leviticus 23).

Hosea is not accusing prophets like himself who truly hear God and pass on God's message, but the false prophets whose cheery reassurances prevent the repentance the people urgently need, thus endangering everyone.

There are several possible reasons why Gibeah (verse 9) holds bad memories. The most likely is the hideous episode in Judges 19–21 where the mob wanted to rape a traveller, who protected himself by handing over his concubine to them; they raped her so brutally she died; this was followed by battle, attempts to isolate the perpetrators, the tribe of Benjamin, who in revenge abducted brides for themselves.

Those who trust in the Eternal will be surrounded by loving-kindness. Rejoice in the Eternal and be happy, all who treat others with justice. Sing out in joy, all who have integrity in their hearts.

Psalm 32:10-11

Let justice roll down like water

Hosea 10:1-8

One of the constant themes of the Bible is the importance of justice. The Holiness Code in Leviticus 19 insists on fair justice and forbids any bias, whether in favour of rich or poor. Abraham challenges God before Sodom and Gomorah: 'Should not the judge of all the world act with justice?' (Genesis 18:25). Isaiah calls upon his readers to learn to do well and seek justice (1:17).

Hosea describes the shift from fruitfulness to poverty caused by God punishing the people's idolatries.

When the people first told Samuel that they wanted a king to lead them in battle like all the other nations (1 Samuel 8), God told Samuel that this meant the people were rejecting God: God should be their only ruler. Now kingship is an established form of rule and it seems that, rather than wanting a king being a sign of rejecting God, divine and royal leadership are now considered a unity; contempt or respect for one implies the same for the other (verse 3).

Jacob erected a stone pillar to God as a sign of gratitude for God's promise to be with him always (Genesis 28:18). He renamed the place where he had seen and heard God Beit-El (House of God). Hosea says that this House of God has become a 'House of Sin' (Beit-Aven, verse 5) because the children of Israel have chosen to erect pillars and idols to pagan gods rather than worshipping the God who promised to be with Jacob and his descendants (Genesis 28:13-15).

Restore our judges, as in earlier times, and our counsellors, as at the beginning. Take away trouble and distress from us. Come to rule over us soon, you alone, Eternal, in compassion, fairness and justice. Blessed are you, who loves fairness and justice.

Daily Amidah 11th blessing

If I am a father, where is my honour?

Hosea 11:1-11

While Hosea makes more dramatic use of the analogy of marriage for the relationship between God and Israel than most biblical books, it also uses the more usual analogy of the parent–child relationship. Both marriage and parenthood as analogies for our relationship with God may trouble the contemporary reader. One difficulty is that, while God is compared to a mother a number of times in the Bible (Isaiah 66:13, Deuteronomy 32:18, etc.), the larger number of references to God as father, and the frequent use of 'Father' in the liturgy, mean that God may be equated with 'father' in our minds. In an anthology exploring women's relationships with their father, two women mentioned that the merging of God and father was problematic (*Fathers: Reflections by Daughters*, Ursula Owen (ed.), London: Virago, 1983, pp.32–35, 70).

Interestingly, the parenting metaphor in this passage seems gender-neutral. Loving, supporting first steps, healing, causing them to eat – these are things either parent can do, although perhaps for many years there was an assumption that a mother provided most of the care of young children.

Admah and Zeboim (verse 8) are places near Sodom and Gomorrah (Genesis 14:2) that were caught up in their destruction.

What is more interesting is the way Hosea describes for us God's thought process, the divine struggle between anger, a desire to condemn the people's idol worship and the protectiveness and compassion that is God's nature (verses 8-9).

God has not dealt with us in proportion to our sins and has not requited according to our iniquities. As far as East is from West, God has removed our misdeeds from us. Just as a father has compassion upon the children, the Eternal has compassion for all who revere God.

Psalm 103:10-13

Repent, keep loving-kindness and justice

Hosea 12:2-6

Ephraim (verse 1) is one of the two grandsons who receive a special blessing from Jacob at the end of his life (Genesis 48:9-20). Here Hosea puns on the meanings of Jacob's two names: Jacob means 'heel' and the verb used here means 'to attack at the heel', which is what Jacob did to Esau in the womb (Genesis 25:22), clutching Esau's heel as they are born. After his wrestle with the angel on his way home from the years living with his father-in-law, Laban, Jacob was told: 'You will be called Israel because you have struggled ['*sr*' in Hebrew] with God and with man and you have prevailed.' Hosea also brings in Jacob's other encounter with angels, this time en route to Laban when he escaped from his twin's fury at being cheated out of his covenant blessing (Genesis 28:10-19). Genesis does not mention during either of these encounters with angels that Jacob wept, but in Genesis 35:3, when Jacob returns to Beth El, he says, 'God who answered me on the day of my distress and who was with me on [my] journey'. Genesis 35 also explains why Hosea links Jacob and Ephraim: Jacob tells his household to put away strange gods, just as Hosea constantly does. God tells Jacob to be fruitful and multiply and Ephraim's name contains the Hebrew word for fruit, '*phri*' (see Hosea 9:16). Also God blesses Jacob; Hosea uses God's love, blessing and covenant promises to Jacob to reinforce the importance of all these for his contemporaries.

Be still and know that I am God. I will be exalted among the nations, I will be exalted on the earth; the Eternal of hosts is with us and the God of Jacob is our refuge.

Psalm 46: 11-12

To err is human, to forgive divine

Hosea 13:1-6

There are many references in Exodus to the craftsmen who skilfully fashioned all the items needed for worship in the shrine, and the wisdom and understanding they possessed in order to do this. Now the expertise of Ephraim is turned from worshipping God to manufacturing idols. This reminds us of the golden calf, which was also described as a 'molten image' (verse 2).

There are many phrases in Hosea that puzzle translators and commentators. It really isn't clear from the language whether verse 2 means 'sacrificers of men' or 'men who offer sacrifices'. The latter seems more probable because such horror is shown for those who worship Moloch (Leviticus 20:2-5) that it seems that, if human sacrifice was among the evils perpetrated by his contemporaries, Hosea would have condemned it more explicitly.

Hosea, whose name means salvation, repeats here that God is the only saviour, and reminds the people that God was mindful of them and miraculously provided for them when they were in the thirsty desert lands (verses 4-5).

The verb 'to know' (verse 4) has a wider range of meanings in Hebrew than English: it can mean 'be mindful of', which would explain verse 5, and 'know by experience', which would be a better way to put verse 4, which echoes the first of the Ten Commandments, 'I am the Eternal Your God who brought you out of the land of Egypt, from the house of bondage (Exodus 20:2)', and this explains why God can ask the people to keep the other commandments.

You favour human beings with knowledge and teach people understanding. Favour us with the knowledge that comes from you, and understanding and discernment. Blessed are you, Eternal, who graciously grants knowledge.

Daily Amidah 4th blessing

I will heal their disloyalty and love them freely

Hosea 14:1-9

Hosea 14:2-10 is read in synagogues as the prophetical reading on the Sabbath of Repentance, the Sabbath between the New Year and the Day of Atonement when we need to know most clearly that we have to work hard at repentance but that, if we do, God welcomes our efforts and delights in forgiving.

Heinrich Heine, the German poet and writer who was born Jewish but later became a Christian because he thought that would make him more acceptable in nineteenth-century Germany, is supposed to have said on his deathbed, 'God will forgive me. It's his profession (*son métier*).' We need a balance between confidence that God does want to forgive and awareness that we need to put effort into repenting with complete sincerity so that our repentance really means something.

The many references to smelling of Lebanon (i.e., like cedar-wood), to lilies and cypress trees, remind us again of the Song of Songs, the ultimate love poem. This ensures that the final message we take from Hosea and his extraordinary book is one of assurance about God's love. In the final verse, Hosea reminds us again of the importance of wisdom, understanding and walking in God's ways, key themes that remind us of the book of Proverbs. So we leave Hosea, realising we must try to know God and to be mindful of God's love and salvation.

Be gracious to me, God, according to your loving-kindness; according to the greatness of your compassion, you will blot out my transgressions. You delight in truth and make me know wisdom. Eternal, open our lips and our mouths will recite your praises.

Psalm 51:1, 6, 15

Fire

1 Fire in the Old Testament (1)

Notes based on the New Revised Standard Version by

Nicholas Alan Worssam SSF

Brother Nicholas Alan is a member of the Anglican religious community The Society of Saint Francis. He has been a friar since 1995 and has lived at Glasshampton Monastery in Worcestershire, England, since 2002.

Genesis 15:17-19

A flaming torch

Over the next two weeks we will be exploring the theme of fire, in the company of two fiery poets, John Donne and Gerard Manley Hopkins. In the Hebrew scriptures the Lord is the ruler of the elements: he strides across the heavens, rides on the clouds as a chariot, and hurls out thunderbolts to strike down his enemies (see Psalm 104:2-4). Both Donne and Hopkins also experience the terror of coming before the throne of Almighty God, and yet also the tenderness of the God who uses his power to heal, cauterising the soul of sin.

Today's passage from Genesis is an ancient, mysterious text. What are the smoking fire pot and flaming torch? Is it a vision, a dream, or a silent ritual of assent? It symbolises the covenant, the agreement between God and Abram involving the gift of land. The fire of sacrifice reaches back far into human memory, perhaps to the first startled use of this primordial gift. Where do the materials burnt go after disappearing? Do they really ascend to the gods in the heavens? It is the experience of transformation, of mutability and impermanence. Fire dries up moisture, turns earth into air.

As we travel these two weeks together, consider:

- Is God to you a guiding beacon of light or an all-consuming fire?
- How have you been burnt by the presence of God?
- How does God kindle the fire of the Spirit within you?

The Lord rained sulphur and fire

Genesis 19:24-29

Pour new seas in my eyes, that so I might
Drown my world with my weeping earnestly,
Or wash it if it must be drown'd no more.
But, O, it must be burnt; alas! the fire
Of lust and envy burnt it heretofore,
And made it fouler; let their flames retire,
And burn me, O Lord, with a fiery zeal
Of Thee and Thy house, which doth in eating heal.

John Donne, *Holy Sonnets*, 5

This week our companion is the English poet John Donne (1571–1631). At first he wrote many sensuous love poems, in a style later described as metaphysical, making reference to the new ideas of science in his day. After ordination in the Church of England he wrote of the stormy love between God and the soul.

Here in Genesis the Lord rains sulphur on Sodom and Gomorrah, whether their sin be seen as lust, or the corruption of the duty of hospitality. Donne, acutely aware of his own sin, calls not for the punishment of others but for the cleansing fire to be poured out on him. He would prefer a softer cleansing – the gift of tears – but fears that they would not be enough. For him the fire of lust and envy could be extinguished only by the greater fire of God's zeal.

How does the fiery zeal of God affect your relationships with others?

In this and subsequent days, let the words of the poet be your prayer to the Lord.

The angel of the Lord in a flame

Exodus 3:1-12

Batter my heart, three-person'd God; for you
As yet but knock, breathe, shine, and seek to mend;
That I may rise, and stand, o'erthrow me, and bend
Your force, to break, blow, burn, and make me new …

John Donne, *Holy Sonnets*, 14

The appearance of God to Moses at the burning bush is one of the pivotal events of the Old Testament. It speaks of the Lord as the God of Moses' ancestors, and climaxes in the revelation of the divine name: YHWH, 'I am who I am' (verse 14). God is in perpetual relationship with Israel, with Abraham, Isaac and Jacob, and all who become their descendants in faith. But God is also 'the One who is', whose name cannot be spoken, who is hidden in a fire that cannot be consumed.

In this famous sonnet, Donne asks for God to consume him. He chides God for being too gentle, for trying to polish him up or glue him back together. He wants to be shattered, melted, altogether remade in the image of God's resplendent son. Sometimes I wonder if my faith is too pedestrian, too reasonable and calm. An incremental reformation is fine for me – rather than a passionate abandonment to God's holy fire. Yet I know that in God's presence only goodness remains; everything else is burnt to dust and ashes. So I hold on to that dual epiphany of God to Moses: the God known to us in a relationship that has sustained our ancestors, leading them step by step, and the God of the fire who cannot even be named.

A pillar of fire by night

Exodus 13:17-22

She's dead; and all which die
To their first elements resolve...
My fire of passion, sighs of air,
Water of tears, and earthly sad despair,
Which my materials be,
(But near worn out by love's security),
She, to my loss, doth by her death repair;
And I might live long wretched so,
But that my fire doth with my fuel grow.

John Donne, 'The Dissolution'

Fire is an ambivalent symbol. It can be seen as a destructive, relentless force; or as a fundamental energy to be harnessed for our good. Just as the pillar of fire leads the Israelites safely through the wilderness, so the fires of our soul can lead us through the deserts of our own despair. God is himself a passionate God, a jealous God, whose love for his bride (Israel, the church, ourselves) is everlasting. Desire, rightly directed, can be a chariot to the divine.

In this poem, Donne mourns the loss of his beloved, whose love he felt had so worn away or refined his corporeal elements that he had become more heavenly than earthly. Now in his bereavement he is brought back painfully to earth; he is consumed by a now frustrated desire, a fire of longing for what he has lost. Yet he hopes that this fire may burn him up with even greater speed, and hasten his reunion with his beloved in death.

God does not want us to be lukewarm in our faith, but to rediscover the fire of our first love (see Revelation 3:15, 2:4). May we know that love which is 'strong as death, passion fierce as the grave. Its flashes are flashes of fire, a raging flame' (Song of Solomon 8:6).

The Lord descended upon Mount Sinai in fire

Exodus 19:16-25

Salute the last and everlasting day,
Joy at th'uprising of this Sun, and Son,
Ye whose true tears, or tribulation
Have purely wash'd, or burnt your drossy clay.
Behold, the Highest, parting hence away,
Lightens the dark clouds, which He treads
upon ...

John Donne, 'Ascension'

Today's passage from the book Exodus is the prelude to the giving of the Ten Commandments to Moses. Mount Sinai, like a volcano, shakes violently and pours out fire and smoke. Only Aaron can accompany Moses; the rest tremble in the valley below. This story prefigures so much in the gospels – the solitary night vigils of Jesus in the mountains (Luke 6:12), the Sermon on the Mount (Matthew 5:1), the Transfiguration (Mark 9:2). Today we think especially of the ascension into heaven (Acts 1:9), the final disappearance of Jesus into the clouds.

Fire and smoke naturally symbolise transmutation and ascent. The psalmist sings: 'Let my prayer be counted as incense before you, and the lifting up of my hands as an evening sacrifice' (Psalm 141:2). Sometimes on a feast day our monastery chapel can be full of incense, prompting a brother once to say from the lectern (as legend has it): 'The Lord be with you ... wherever you are!' Clouds of incense symbolise the prayers of the saints (Revelation 5:8), the cloud of witnesses that surround us as we journey on (Hebrews 12:1).

Each day in the Eucharist we offer 'our sacrifice of thanks and praise'. All of us ascend, in prayer, to where our life 'is hidden with Christ in God' (Colossians 3:3). May we ascend with Jesus as we offer our lives to the Lord.

Out came this calf!

Exodus 32:15-24

… and Thou look'st towards me,
O Saviour, as Thou hang'st upon the tree …
Burn off my rust, and my deformity,
Restore Thine image, so much, by Thy grace,
That Thou mayst know me, and I'll turn my face.

John Donne,
'Good Friday, 1613, Riding Westward'

•

Fire can carry us to heaven, but it can also lead us in the direction of hell. Here in Exodus, Moses descends from the mountain, commandments in hand, to discover the camp turned into a revel. Their treasures have become an idol, as if emerging by itself from the fire.

Jesus said: 'Where your treasure is, there your heart will be also' (Matthew 6:21). Idolatry always misplaces our treasure, makes us grasp hold of something that cannot set us free. St Paul calls it a form of greed (Ephesians 5:5). Fire may create the idol in a physical sense but it also releases us from idols, reducing all material things to ash. For many our idol is in fact our self, our own sense of separateness, our prowess or our need. This setting-up of the ego on our personal altar leads either to self-congratulation as we look down on others, or to self-hatred, as we grow to resent our own incessant demands.

Donne asks rather for the fire of God to burn all that deforms him. He knows his self-worth as a child of God, and asks that his true self be revealed. Who is your true self?

A perpetual fire burning on the altar

Leviticus 6:8-13

O Holy Ghost, whose temple I
Am, but of mud walls, and condensèd dust,
And being sacrilegiously
Half wasted with youth's fires of pride and lust,
Must with new storms be weather-beat,
Double in my heart Thy flame,
Which let devout sad tears intend, and let –
Though this glass lantern, flesh, do suffer maim –
Fire, sacrifice, priest, altar be the same.
John Donne, 'The Holy Ghost'

The Holy Spirit is often associated in the scriptures with fire. John the Baptist spoke of the one to come who would baptise with the Holy Spirit and with fire (Matthew 3:11), and at Pentecost the Spirit descends in 'tongues, as of fire' (Acts 2:3). In this poem Donne describes the Spirit consuming the sacrifice of his whole life, echoing the exhortation of Paul to the Romans: 'by the mercies of God, present your bodies as a living sacrifice, holy and acceptable to God' (Romans 12:1). Thus we, in Christ, become the means, object, giver and place of the oblation of our lives.

Offering oneself to God is a risky business. No one can say beforehand where the act of oblation will lead. With the flame of God's Spirit doubled within us we might become a shining light to others for years to come, or be carried off in a momentary blaze of glory. We will certainly not stay the same. But in the end perhaps this is our only security – to offer ourselves like Isaiah, who, touched by the seraphic coals of fire can only say, 'Here am I; send me' (Isaiah 6:8)!

Fire

Notes based on the New Revised Standard Version by

Nicholas Alan Worssam SSF

For Brother Nicholas Alan's biography see p.127.

2 Fire in the Old Testament (2)

Deuteronomy 4:15-24

The Lord your God is a devouring fire.

Thou mastering me
God! giver of breath and bread;
World's strand, sway of the sea;
Lord of living and dead;
Thou hast bound bones and veins in me, fastened me flesh,
And after it almost unmade, what with dread,
Thy doing: and dost thou touch me afresh?
Over again I feel thy finger and find thee.

Gerard Manley Hopkins.
'The Wreck of the Deutschland', 1

After the stormy passions of John Donne, this week our guide is the rather more elegiac Gerard Manley Hopkins (1844–1889). Hopkins, born in England, spent much of his life in Wales and Ireland. As a young man he converted to the Roman Catholic Church and became a Jesuit priest. None of his poetry was published in his lifetime, and many of his poems express a sense of futility and despair. Yet he was deeply attuned to the beauties of nature and experienced much joy in the world around him, and delighted in the ordinary people he met.

Today's passage from Deuteronomy speaks of God as a devouring fire, a jealous God, and this was often the experience of Hopkins. The stanza above begins an epic poem that marked the rebirth of his creative talent, having renounced all when he joined the Society of Jesus. God was always his master, sometimes stern, always kind, but with a kindness that he struggled to comprehend. He reaches as a child to grasp the finger of God, the one who makes and unmakes him with a touch.

- Where do you find the finger of God in your life?

Then the fire of the Lord fell

1 Kings 18:21-41

Beyond saying sweet, past telling of tongue,
Thou art lightning and love, I found it, a winter and warm …
Hast thy dark descending and most art merciful then.

Gerard Manley Hopkins,
'The Wreck of the Deutschland', 9

Elijah is a powerful figure striding through the Books of Kings. He is the scourge of King Ahab of Israel and his wife Jezebel. He predicts droughts, multiplies loaves, raises the dead and slaughters the priests of Baal. Here he calls down fire from heaven to consume a water-drenched sacrifice in mockery of the worship of other gods. Elijah pronounces the scorn of the God of Israel for all who dare to oppose him. Neither Elijah nor his God is a comfortable figure to soothe a troubled heart.

For Hopkins, God is a mystery to be 'instressed', (Hopkins, *Journals and Papers*, OUP, 1959, *passim*) found in the midst of all things, even in suffering. In 'The Wreck' (1:2) he speaks of 'thy terror, O Christ, O God' at the dawning of his vocation to the religious life. This terror is mirrored in 'the dense and the driven Passion, and frightful sweat' (1:7) of his crucified Lord. How often we sing sweet love songs to Jesus but forget the awful tragedy, and triumph, of his death into life. Yes, God is our Father, our tender-hearted parent; but God is also the one who strikes his enemies with lightning and comes to us in dark clouds of seemingly impenetrable unknowing.

A chariot of fire and horses of fire

2 Kings 2:6-12

The frown of his face
Before me, the hurtle of hell
Behind, where, where was a, where was a place?
I whirled out wings that spell
And fled with a fling of the heart to the heart of the Host.
My heart, but you were dovewinged, I can tell,
Carrier-witted, I am bold to boast,
To flash from the flame to the flame then, tower from the grace to the grace.

Gerard Manley Hopkins,
'The Wreck of the Deutschland', 3

Here Hopkins speaks of the moment of his conversion – not a quiet certitude gazing serenely at a sunset, but a terror-stricken leap from the flames of hell to the flames of God's Spirit. As the saying goes: out of the frying pan, into the fire! But where else could he find complete security? To escape being burned he had to become all flame.

Today we talk little of hell. Perhaps the imagery is too graphic, or too often misused on a credulous audience. But the reality is well known by far too many in this world. What could rival the subterraneous torture chambers that scar our 'civilisations'? Or the daily struggle just to find enough food to postpone starvation? Who can tell what despair Hopkins experienced in the depths of his soul as he was carried on the wings of the Spirit into the embrace of God?

Elijah takes a different leap – into a chariot of fire that ascends the heavens. Elisha stands bewildered on the ground. When we see our spiritual heroes soar above us, do we have the courage to ask for a double share of their spirit?

The voice of the Lord flashes forth

Psalm 29

The world is charged with the grandeur of God.
It will flame out, like shining from shook foil;
It gathers to a greatness, like the ooze of oil
Crushed...

Gerard Manley Hopkins,
'God's Grandeur'

This is one of my favourite sonnets by Hopkins. For one thing it can be read and understood at a single reading! It speaks of the 'dearest freshness deep down things' which is trodden down and hidden by trade and toil. Hopkins always wanted to see into the heart of things, to see what he called their 'inscape' (*Journals*, passim), the inner structures of existence. This inevitably brought him eventually to God, in this case to the Holy Spirit brooding over the world like a bird with 'warm breast and with ah! bright wings' ('God's Grandeur', line 14). For all the sternness of the paternal imagery of his poems, the comforting maternal Spirit speaks to him still.

In today's psalm, God sits as a king 'enthroned over the flood' (verse 10), with a voice that breaks the cedars and shakes the wilderness; but this still re-echoes the moment of creation when the (feminine) breath of God hovered over the face of the deep as God's voice spoke order into chaos (Genesis 1:1). God brings all things into being, and all cry 'Glory' (verse 9)! This indwelling of Wisdom throughout creation is another aspect of God's holy fire. It is the startling recognition of eternity in time, the slow-spreading warmth of the hearth at the heart of God's earthly home.

Fire and hail, snow and frost

Psalm 148:1-14

As kingfishers catch fire, dragonflies draw flame;
As tumbled over rim in roundy wells
Stones ring …
Each mortal thing does one thing and the same:
Deals out that being indoors each one dwells;
Selves – goes itself; myself *it speaks and spells …*

Gerard Manley Hopkins,
'As Kingfishers Catch Fire'

This psalm is one of the most joyful in the whole psalter. Traditionally it was recited every day at the end of the dawn service, together with the two psalms that follow and complete the book. In this way the early monastic night vigil of the recitation of all 150 psalms would draw to a close. Psalm 148 is a wonderful hymn of praise to the God of creation. Saint Francis, our patron, loved psalms like this and, together with his brothers, would have known them by heart, reciting them as they tramped the roads around Assisi.

Hopkins was moved to great joy by the sight of the enormous variety of creation. He could somehow catch the essence of their individuality with a three- or four-word phrase, like a watercolour painter capturing a scene with just a few rapid brush-strokes. Philosophically, Hopkins found this intuitive perception of nature based on the idea of '*haecceitas*' or 'thisness' as taught by the Franciscan theologian Duns Scotus. But the individuality implies no separation from the whole. Ultimately it is Christ who 'plays in ten thousand places,/Lovely in limbs, and lovely in eyes not his …' ('As Kingfishers Catch Fire', lines 12–13). Christ, God's Wisdom, delights in the inhabited world, and makes the heart of the Father immeasurably glad (see Proverbs 8:30f).

The furnace of blazing fire

Daniel 3:13-30

... Brute beauty and valour and act, oh, air, pride, plume, here
Buckle! AND the fire that breaks from thee then, a billion
Times told lovelier, more dangerous, O my chevalier!
No wonder of it: sheer plod makes plough down sillion
Shine, and blue-bleak embers, ah my dear,
Fall, gall themselves, and gash gold-vermilion.

Gerard Manley Hopkins,
'The Windhover: To Christ our Lord'

In this exultant poem Hopkins captures the moment of seeing a falcon or kite in the early morning, hovering on the wind. He is stunned by the skill of the bird 'in his riding of the rolling level underneath him steady air' (lines 2–3), then soaring away in search of its prey. Hopkins, hidden from sight, is moved to wonder at 'the achieve of, the mastery of the thing!' (line 8) And so he asks that the strength and beauty of that bird, so like Christ ('my chevalier!' – line 11), be formed in his own heart; that Christ's fire be set free in him. But he realises that it is not just in the dramatic events of life that Christ shines forth – the sheer plod of the daily round of duties is the soil that he ploughs, lifting behind him a shining furrow of glistening silver earth; and all that seems dull and cold, like embers in a dying fire, in falling reveals a glowing, still burning heart.

In the reading from Daniel, the three young men are thrown, bound, into a furnace. Yet in the middle of the fire the king sees a fourth man – an angel? Christ? – walking with them. Whatever our experience of life, whether exciting or dull, God is there with us. God is the fire within us, ready to flame out when we let loose the control we habitually maintain. Like the falcon soaring on the wind, Christ in us rides the storm-winds of life. Like fire in the coal, he flames through the bleakness of our darkest days.

A refiner's fire

Malachi 3:1-7

... Flesh fade, and mortal trash
Fall to the residuary worm; world's wildfire, leave but ash:
In a flash, at a trumpet crash,
I am all at once what Christ is, since he was what I am, and
This Jack, joke, poor potsherd, patch, matchwood, immortal diamond,
Is immortal diamond.

Gerard Manley Hopkins,
'That Nature is a Heraclitean Fire'

In this poem, Hopkins celebrates the variegated vibrancy of creation – all the endless variation of sight and sound and texture that delights the senses. It is like sparks from a huge conflagration: 'Million-fuelèd, nature's bonfire burns on' (line 9). But the poet mourns the loss of earth's most distinctive spark: the mind of man, quenched in a moment. Or is it? These final lines of the poem assert the comfort of the resurrection that, although all things mortal cease in an instant at death, still, because Christ has taken on our mortality, our adamantine immortality is assured.

The final book of the Hebrew scriptures ends with a warning: 'who can endure the day of the Lord's coming? ... for he is like a refiner's fire' (verse 2). It is a theme picked up by the author of the letter to the Hebrews: 'You have not come to something that can be touched, a blazing fire, and darkness ... for indeed our God is a consuming fire' (12:18,29). We fear the loss of our mortal bodies, and preserve them at all cost. But our true nature cannot be burned: we are created in the image of the divine fire itself. All that is consumed is our greed and our hatred; if we want to we can become all flame.

Fire

3 Fire in the New Testament

Notes based on *The African Bible* (biblical text of the American Bible, Pauline Publications Africa, Nairobi, 1999) by

Godfrey Chigumira

Godfrey Chigumira grew up in Zimbabwe, southern Africa, and served as a priest there before coming to the United Kingdom. He is currently working in the Church in Wales, in north Wales, and has remained constantly in touch with life and events in his home country.

Acts 2:1-12

Pentecost

There is a traditional chorus that announces, 'Fire, fire! There is fire in the gospel … It burns – the Gospel burns … As I forewarned you, it is fiery.' When Evangelical and Pentecostal Christians sing this song, their enthusiasm is evident in countless repetitions, with dancing and clapping. They seem to experience the fiery nature of the gospel in their services, claimed in God's word in the here and now.

Being neither Pentecostal nor Evangelical, I often approach God's word anticipating no burning sensation from it. And I am often neither moved nor touched when I read or listen to it. 'Too familiar a passage and meaning' is sometimes my attitude. Yet I have often been proved wrong. A different context or another person's commentary has brought God's word to life, proving moving and inspiring, even causing a lasting fiery sensation within me.

In what ways could you relive the Pentecostal experience? Are you sometimes too closed within yourself for God's fiery power to move you? How can you ensure your interpretation of God's word depends not solely on your own power?

Dear Lord, may the fire of your Spirit warm my heart, purify, mould, straighten and beautify me. May it penetrate places of darkness within me and enlighten me to strive for wholeness and goodness. May your gospel power continually burn within me and transform me into your image.

Baptism with the Holy Spirit and with fire

Matthew 3:1-12

I did my secondary education soon after Zimbabwe's independence, and it was always going to be difficult for me to grasp intangible scientific concepts in a laboratory that lacked basic science equipment. However, I clearly remember one occasion when, after a simple fire demonstration, I once and for all grasped the concept of a chemical reaction! My science teacher simply burned a paper in the presence of our class and, as we watched, the paper turned into ashes. Then he explained that no one, by whatever means, could turn the ashes back into paper again. And this was the concept of a chemical reaction – the end product could not be reversed, as the original elements had been decisively changed in the reaction.

When John refers to Jesus' baptism involving the Holy Spirit and fire, I sense a similar irreversible character that helps us to see the difference that repentance should make in a believer's life. This is a baptism that changes the person irrevocably. There is no return to any past 'un-Christlike' ways of life!

- Does your baptism mark a definitive turnaround for you?
- To what extent does your society's understanding of baptism influence your own understanding of your baptism?
- What are you willing to do to live a life worthy of one baptised by the Holy Spirit and fire?
- Pray that all people baptised in Christ's name may seek to live a life worthy of their calling.

Calling down fire from heaven

Luke 9:51-56

In Zimbabwe, grass-thatched round huts are still the standard form of accommodation on homesteads in non-urban areas. They have been for centuries. The huts are inexpensive and easy to construct, cool and comfortable during the hot summers. Yet this form of accommodation has always harboured a huge risk – one of the easiest ways to destroy enemies has been simply to light a matchstick and torch their grass-thatched roof. This has often ensured not only the enemies' death, but also the destruction of their bodies, of those close to them, of their property and of most of the evidence. The burning up of an enemy's grass-thatched homestead has been used as a weapon of war.

Yet, by and large, people with differences – even enemies – have coexisted without resorting to such cruelty. Living within such huts for centuries has been possible not only because of the rebuke or punishment that society gives to offenders, but also due to the respect that people have for life.

How much do you owe your existence to others' respect for life rather than to your own self-protection skills? In what ways do you participate in rebuking those who want to call down 'fire' on others in your society?

Pray that the desire to punish others may be restrained in you and in those around you. Pray for the courage to rebuke those who make, sell and keep weapons of mass destruction.

Godfrey Chigumira

Peter warming himself

Mark 14:54, 66-72

The fireplace has been important in Africa for centuries. It is traditionally a place of rest at night-time after a day of hard labour; a place for discussions, when people sit around the fire and share ideas; and where village courts are held and rulings made over difficult issues. It is also a place of reflection, providing comfort not only in the form of warmth, but also a focal point for meditation. African novels often portray their elders staring into the fire as a technique that enhances their mental focus. The burning charcoal, glowing deep within itself, seems to make meditation easier. The flamboyantly flickering colours of flames provide a spotlight of attention as people grapple with issues deep within their hearts and minds. As the eyes penetrate deep into the transparent flames, the mind is seemingly aided to deepen in thought. The light of the fire seems to penetrate the darkness of the mind and heart.

For Peter, too, this was an opportunity to look within himself, to journey mentally and spiritually within the self. Aided by the high priest's maid (verse 66), the bystander (verse 70) and the crowing cock (verse 72), this was for him a moment of revelation, of insight into his identity – and also of change, beginning with the breaking down and weeping (verse 72).

Does the use of light, such as a lighted candle, make any difference to your reflections?

Pray for light that penetrates the darkness of your mind and heart.

The building tested by fire

1 Corinthians 3:10-15

To build themselves modern houses, Zimbabweans very often opt to make their own farm bricks. It is very strenuous work but cheaper than purchasing the finished brick product. They normally choose good-quality soil from an anthill for brickmaking and use planks to mould bricks from the soil. They then make a huge brick oven, by arranging the bricks, about two to four thousand, in such a way as to leave huge pocket gaps between the bricks into which enormous logs of wood are fitted. The oven is plastered by mud to trap the heat. Fire is used as the key element in strengthening the bricks. Huge fires from the logs burn the bricks for two full days.

The greater the intensity of the fire, the stronger the bricks and the better their quality. If the soil is of poor quality, the bricks will crack and break under the intensity of the heat. The heat is so intense it takes another full day for the bricks to cool down, ready for use. The fire acts as the agent that tests the quality of the soil, and that improves the quality of the bricks.

How good are you at dealing with tests, temptations and trials, particularly when they are not of your choosing? Does your best often come out under intense trial?

Lord, we pray that we may grow through our trials and have the courage to see the positives in them; that our faith may see us through difficult moments.

The tongue as like fire

James 3:1-12

Our rainy season is preceded by spring, the time by which most grass in the fields will have dried up. It is an accepted custom within farming communities to burn up the grass during the dry season, creating large fires in the fields, forests and pasturelands. Anyone can start the fires. Very little that comes into contact with the scorching fire is capable of surviving it – dry grass, trees and the rich soil texture perish in the process, not to mention the wild animals, insects, ants and other little creatures that inhabit the land. Some homesteads are also caught up.

I know of one religious minister who has taken up the task of challenging and educating the farming community in which he works about the dangers of these fires, in order to end the custom. So far, there is no sign he has succeeded. There seems little notice of, and concern for, the destruction that the fires cause. Some of the farmers believe the fires help fresh grass to grow earlier than usual for their livestock.

Are there instances when your tongue has been like a destructive fire? Are you aware of the extent of the damage caused? At what moments is your tongue most destructive? What could you do to prevent the damage?

Lord, we pray that your Spirit may have control over our tongues, and that we may take time to think about what we want to say before saying it.

Godfrey Chigumira

The lake of fire

Revelation 20:11-15

One of the problems Zimbabwe's urban areas now face is the shortage of burial grounds. Zimbabwean Shonas are among others in Africa for whom cremation is culturally unacceptable. The Shonas believe that, at death, the spirit separates from the body and becomes restless until, first, its body is properly buried and, second, it is ritually welcomed back into the family. The spirits of the dead are known as 'the living dead', who can experience pain and undertake vengeance or, alternatively, can be made by ritual to feel more comfortable and in turn bless and protect the family members. At cremation, the scorching fire is believed to hurt and infuriate the spirit, which could fight back by causing problems such as sickness and bad luck within the family.

The ideas of a second death and judgement do not seem so far from this set of beliefs. Physical death is only a stage in life, and the 'living dead' still perform good and bad acts, and so could still be liable to God's judgement. The 'living dead' also detest the terrible 'pain' of fire.

How can ideas of end-time judgement of the first century be expressed so as to make sense to the modern world? Is earthly life more likely to end by our own doing (for instance, by the use of nuclear weapons or through environmental damage) than by divine action?

Lord, when our end comes, may we be found ready and willing.

Acts 6 – 12: From Jerusalem to Antioch

Notes based on the New Revised Standard Version by

Elizabeth Fisher

Elizabeth Fisher has spent much of her life teaching the New Testament to adults and university students, most recently lecturing in an Anglican theological college. She has also worked for Christian unity, in the UK and Europe and in the synodical life of the Church of England. She is a lay canon of Birmingham Cathedral and now lives in a Pennine village in the north of England, where she enjoys fell-walking and baking.

1 Disciples increasing in number

Acts 6:1-7

The challenges of growth and the cost of discipleship

We join the Acts of the Apostles as the fledgling church is about to spread its wings and carry the gospel way beyond the Holy Land. But the author ('Luke' as we call him: we can't know his identity for sure but we do know he wrote the Acts as part two to the gospel that bears his name) shows that this successful mission was not without pain. Increasing numbers brought new problems, and the preaching of the good news led to bitter persecution. But death, we will see, is the most powerful witness to Christ.

Today we read of the marginalisation of widows within the church. This is not seen as a failure to follow Jesus, the friend of the marginalised. Rather, the apostles take the initiative in correcting the oversight, suggesting the appointment of seven men for a new form of ministry to the community affected. The twelve are not to give up their primary task: preaching the word.

These seven were set aside for their official ministry, which was both practical and evangelistic, by prayer and the laying on of hands. Two of them will appear later. Nothing more of the widows is heard: presumably a problem solved.

Look again at some of the troubles that afflict your church. Could your prayers help them to become points of new life and witness?

Preaching with boldness

Acts 6:8-15

Appointed as the result of a practical problem, Stephen is seen to excel in oratory and debate. He was 'full of grace and power' (verse 8) and disputed with other Greek-speaking Jews like himself, but who did not follow Jesus. These Jews were of the 'synagogue of the Freedmen (as it was called)' (verse 9), and of others from the Greek-speaking world including Cilicia, the birthplace of Saul. Freedmen were those who had been emancipated by being released from slavery or by buying their freedom. Perhaps they or their parents had been enslaved after Pompey's victory in 63 BC and now they had returned to Jerusalem. Perhaps others were merely visitors in Jerusalem. Simon of Cyrene, who carried the crossbar of Jesus, may have originally attached himself to this synagogue when he arrived in Jerusalem.

Stephen clearly won the arguments, for no one was able to defeat him in debate, but false evidence was fabricated that resulted in his being dragged into court. There he was accused of blasphemy against 'the holy place' (verse 13) – the temple – and the law. This is reminiscent of the false accusations levelled against Jesus, whose actions in the temple clearly brought him into opposition with the authorities, and foreshadowed its fall.

If the seven were appointed to 'serve tables' (Acts 6:2), at least Stephen's ministry went far beyond that, and he is remembered for his fearless commitment to Jesus. Whereas Jesus was silent before his accusers, Stephen had plenty to say. Jesus had said 'everyone who acknowledges me before others, I will also acknowledge' (Matthew 10:32).

O God, if I ever think that preaching is 'not my job', just remind me of Stephen and help me to acknowledge Jesus.

Flinging down a gauntlet

Acts 7:1-8

The eyes of all in the council looked intently on Stephen and saw in his face something of an angel. Of all the speeches in Acts (they make up about a third of the whole), his is the longest. It begins here, and amounts to a retelling of God's dealings with Israel, starting with Abraham, their founding father. Abraham, we recall, was not born a Jew, but in old age heard the voice of God and left behind his homeland in obedience to that call. Abraham was thought of as the father of the Jews, not by his birth but by his fidelity to God and his readiness to be circumcised in his adulthood. Belief and obedience marked him out.

The whole speech is a recounting of Israel's unbelief and rejection of God. It is not a defence of what Stephen had preached in the synagogue; the two charges are hardly mentioned. It was a challenge to his hearers to read their history afresh, but it fell on 'rocky ground' (Luke 8:6). The speech concludes with 'you stiff-necked people, uncircumcised in hearts and ears, you are forever opposing the Holy Spirit, just as your ancestors used to do' (Acts 7:51), and 'you are the ones that received the law as ordained by angels, and yet you have not kept it' (Acts 7:53).

Stephen here is seen as the model disciple under persecution. Jesus had said 'what you hear whispered, proclaim from the housetops' (Matthew 10:27). Stephen witnessed gladly.

O Holy Spirit of God, unstiffen our necks and make sure our religion never becomes an obstacle to your transforming purpose.

Faith tested in death

Acts 7:54 – 8:1a

If Stephen won the argument both in the synagogue and the court, he was not acquitted. Stephen's powerful speech led to his lynching. However, what Luke wants us to note is Stephen's faith and acceptance of his destiny. He modelled himself on Jesus, his lord, whom he saw as he looked into heaven. The similarities between his death and Jesus' are remarkable: both took place outside the city; both offer prayer forgiving their accusers; both pray that their spirit will be received. As important as these parallels are, so is the vision of Jesus, the crucified one, as the Son of Man standing at the right hand of God, the position of honour.

S(P)aul was present at this lynching. The word 'martyr' literally means 'witness' and in early times witnessing was often through the life and death as much as the preaching. Is there any possibility that Saul of Tarsus (in Cilicia) was present in the synagogue when Stephen preached, thus being where Saul first heard the gospel? We later learn (22:3) that he had studied under Gamaliel, who in 5:34-39 advised the Sanhedrin not to do anything that might lead to opposing God: a more accommodating stance to the gospel than that Saul appears to have taken initially.

Jesus' parable of the great banquet (in Luke 14:15-24) described the bringing in of those on the edge. Stephen has done this in his ministry at table, in preaching and in death. Disciples follow their master in all things.

Glory to you, O God, for the courage you give to the martyrs and the glimpses you give of heaven!

Amazing grace

Acts 8:1b-13

With the death of Stephen, a persecution by Saul and others of some of the early Christians followed. Agonising though that was, it led to the spread of the gospel. Here is the story of a colleague of Stephen. This 'Philip' was not one of the twelve, but one of those appointed to the new ministry, the seven. However, he ranks among those who spread the word. The apostles were safe in Jerusalem but Philip took the initiative to travel, and he journeyed to Samaria, not a country most Jews would choose to visit.

Philip is described as being able to do the same things that Peter had done in Jerusalem: healing, as well as preaching. The story about the spread of the gospel shows that in each generation God provides leaders, and gives them the gifts needed.

The gospel knows no human boundaries or limitations. Whether in Jerusalem or Samaria, the Holy Spirit makes unexpected things happen. Simon, a magician used to causing amazement, was himself amazed by the superior power manifested through the name above all names, Jesus, invoked by Philip.

The preaching resulted in baptism, that rite which included men and women on an equal footing, unlike the Jewish rite of circumcision that privileged men. Thus ancient barriers were broken down. Jesus had promised his disciples would be his witnesses in Jerusalem, Judea, Samaria and the ends of the earth (Acts 1:8). It was then, and is still, a shared task.

In an age when special effects and technical wizardry know no bounds, should we be cherishing the 'special effects' that the Holy Spirit works in human lives – ours, too?

What money can't buy

Acts 8:14-25

In 8:1 the persecution in Jerusalem had not affected the apostles, and now we see that Peter and John were free to go to Samaria. The apostles are shown both to share in the Spirit-led work of mission and also to have a special role in overseeing it, and even in channelling the gift of the Spirit. Simon the magician envied this power that they seemed to have at their command, and wanted to obtain it by fair means or foul. His offer to purchase a spiritual gift gives rise to the word 'simony', the buying of benefit or office in the church.

Some see in this encounter between Peter and Simon a contrast between the right and wrong use of power in the church. Both men were named Simon but Simon Peter showed Simon the Magician that the Spirit cannot be bought or owned. As at Pentecost, the Spirit always comes as gift.

The use of money has been an underlying theme in the early chapters of Acts. Some, like Barnabas 4:36 (and the unnamed disciples in 2:45), had been generous; others, like Ananias and Sapphira (5:1-5), had played false with their financial resources. Simon was not punished like them, possibly because he was on the frontier of mission. Mission in new frontiers may demand flexibility on the part of the authorities. Whereas Ananias and his wife did not repent of their lies and guilt, Simon did ask for prayer, and so responded to Peter's demand for repentance.

O God, may my money be put to your use, and my life be freely open to your Spirit.

The Ethiopian eunuch

Acts 8:26-40

The Ethiopian, like Theophilus in Rome (Acts 1:1), was a high-ranking official – chancellor of the exchequer – but, unlike Theophilus, was a eunuch from faraway Ethiopia in the south. He was in his chariot reading from Isaiah 53:7, having visited Jerusalem, where he would have been excluded from entering the temple. Here he is alone, stationary, at midday when activity stops, on a desert road, all symbolic of his barrenness.

Spirit-led, Philip was directed to the right place, the road to Gaza, and to the eunuch. The Ethiopian is ready for conversion; he was familiar with scripture. What he needed was interpretation; this Philip supplied, showing Jesus, the crucified one, was its fulfilment. His conversion leads to his request for baptism, with mention of what might prevent him – a reference to the physical state that excluded him from circumcision, and from entering the temple. In Christ there is no Jew or Gentile, bond or free (Galatians 3:28). The Spirit leaps over yet another barrier and brings into the community of the church those, however powerful, who also know themselves to be outsiders.

Had the eunuch read Isaiah 56:3-5, he would have found the promise that Jesus fulfilled: despite no physical descendants, eunuchs would be given a name for ever. Christians in Ethiopia regard this man as the bringer of the gospel to their country, their first missionary. The journey he undertook was more than miles covered; it involved a change of direction. Philip has done his job; the Spirit takes him elsewhere.

Thank you, God, for inviting me into your home, just as I am; help me to keep my door open too.

Acts 6 – 12: From Jerusalem to Antioch

2 Light dawns for Paul and then Peter

Notes based on the New Revised Standard Version by

Elizabeth Fisher

For Elizabeth's biography, see p.148.

Acts 9:1-9

The way to change

For the first time in Acts, Saul takes centre stage. He is 'fired up' and on the way. It looks like the opposite of the Christian Way, but perhaps Saul had heard the words of Stephen and was already being inwardly moved by them (see Acts 7:58 and 8:1).

What happened on that famous road is vital to our understanding of Paul. As a zealous Jew he may have been a Shammite, one of a Pharisaical group bent on forcing other Jews to adhere to their interpretation of the Torah. So Tom Wright thinks (*What Saint Paul Really Said*, Lion, 1997). For such a hard-liner, to be converted to the gospel required a radical change of direction. The gospel proclaimed the resurrection of a crucified Jesus, yet the law denounced the crucified as cursed. It was the risen crucified one who 'knocked Paul over' on that road, blinded, making him look inside himself, giving him no choice but to listen.

Saul addressed the voice that he heard as 'Lord'. From then he was Christ's man, bound to him, but also bound to the members of Christ's body whom he had persecuted. New name, new direction, new community, new life but along with these, S(P)aul will also encounter new rejection and persecution. Conversion required courage for him, as it still does for those who, in turning to Christ, find themselves alienated from family and mainstream culture. It did for Nurta Mohamed Farah, a young convert fleeing her family in Somalia in 2010, who was shot in an apparent honour-killing.

Pray for those whose calling or conversion brings conflict, and for those of any faith who suffer persecution.

Love your enemy?

Acts 9:10-19

Assuming S(P)aul's reputation went before him, just imagine Ananias' feelings when he hears what God wants of him. He was, after all, among Paul's intended targets. Luke has not explained how the gospel came to Damascus, but there were believers there: Ananias, Judas and others. Both those names were previously associated with bad faith, Judas in the gospels and Ananias in Acts (5:1-6), but now these names are associated with faithfulness and courage. If Paul had intended to go from house to house to root out believers, in this house he finds safety and instruction from an initially reluctant Ananias.

Ananias was let into God's confidence: he was told of Paul's mission to 'Gentiles, kings and Israelites' (verse 15), even before Paul himself knew of it. Paul, like Stephen before him, will witness to his new faith in the crucified and risen Lord. Acts ends with his witnessing in Rome, the centre of the world, that salvation is for all, Jew and Gentile. What is more, Paul is to suffer too. In Judas' house Paul both saw by regaining his sight, and 'saw' who Jesus really is. He was baptised, and what the future holds will unfold. Baptism had bound him not only to Christ, but also to the very community he had wanted to root out.

Is Ananias the great, unsung, hero of the church's early years? This vignette prompts us to reflect that Acts does not tell the whole story of mission and evangelism. Others besides the well known played vital parts in the story.

Have you been, or could you be, Ananias to anyone?

Identifying with the crucified

Acts 9:20-31

Paul now serves a new master. He does not lie low but heads straight to the synagogues of Damascus. Having received advance notice of his coming (9:1), they are prepared to welcome this fire-breathing tormentor of the 'Christians'. They can hardly have been keen to accept what they get: an ardent follower and preacher of Christ.

For this new Paul, faith in Jesus is not simply an add-on to his previous faith. As Wright puts it, 'Saul had imagined YHWH would vindicate *Israel* after her suffering at the hand of pagans. Instead he had vindicated Jesus after his suffering ...' (*What Saint Paul Really Said*, p.36). It was as if God was redefining his people and, for Paul, identity with Jesus is now the key. By revealing himself in a new way in Jesus, the God Paul worshipped had also given him a new identity, and with it a vocation.

Inevitably the persecutor now became persecuted and had to escape Damascus by night. Paul had already created a circle of followers; 'his disciples ... let him down through an opening in the wall, lowering him in a basket' (verse 25). God was creating openings for his ministry! Back in Jerusalem he needed the support and protection of Barnabas (the son of encouragement of 4:36), who plays the same brave part that Ananias had in Damascus. Now Stephen has a worthy successor in his debates with the Hellenist Jews. He too becomes a target, but he is on the move, and there is work ahead for him.

Is there opportunity around for you to be a daughter or son of encouragement?

The one who believes in me will do the works that I do

Acts 9:32-43

Peter is now a roving apostle, and here he is in two scenes in Lydda, an old city known in biblical times. Here among the new community is a paralysed Greek man, bedridden for eight years. Peter says to him the word he had heard Jesus speak in such circumstances: 'rise'. The Greek implies he must make his own bed, in other words, he has to take responsibility for himself. Had Aeneas been bedridden on his conversion and is he now challenged to take steps in his own journey of faith?

Next we hear of Dorcas, perhaps elderly, certainly a widow. She is a corpse prepared for burial; Peter was asked to visit. Clearly, she had been a wealthy benefactor of the community, providing clothes for those without. In Acts she is the first woman to be called a 'female disciple'. Her death was a sadness for the community in which she was a leader. Peter spoke to her in words similar to those Jesus used to the dead little daughter of Jairus, the synagogue leader (Luke 8:54). Here, as there for Jesus, spectators and onlookers were kept outside. However, news of the event spread like wildfire here and as far away as Joppa.

The new community was made up of young and old, rich and poor, male and female; each now a daughter or son of the God who has conquered death. And the boundaries dividing Jew from Gentile, and between male and female, young and old, are being stormed.

Give us who follow you today, O Christ, the desire and the power to raise up the fallen.

Ears ready to hear the gospel

Acts 10:1-8

Paul was sent home to minister in Tarsus but called in at Caesarea en route (9:30). The scene now shifts to Caesarea-by-the-sea (Maritima). Had seeds of the gospel fallen here during his stay?

The conversion of Cornelius will be told three times, marking its importance (chapters 10, 11 and 15). The account in chapter 10 is narrated in a series of scenes. These verses comprise scene one.

An angel appears to Cornelius. He is a pious god-fearer, that is, a Gentile who is drawn to Judaism, and a centurion based in Caesarea Maritima. Note the contrast with the priest, Zechariah, in Luke 1. In the temple at the afternoon hour of incense, Zechariah was sceptical when an angel appeared; here the Gentile centurion was at home ready to obey when the angel spoke to him at three o'clock. Luke's Gospel tells of two centurions: one asked Jesus to heal his servant; the other, at the foot of the cross, professed Jesus' innocence of the charge against him.

'Devout' Cornelius 'gave alms generously', 'prayed constantly to God' (verse 2). He is not described as a proselyte, which would have indicated that he had undergone circumcision. But neither was he a worshipper of Mithras, a god whom many soldiers worshipped. He was like a seedbed prepared for sowing when he sent for Peter, who was lodging with a tanner, someone on the edge of Judaism. The Spirit was moving Cornelius by the sea, and nudging Simon Peter, lodging with Simon the tanner.

Dear God, if you have more good news for me, make me ready to listen, I pray.

Hearing the persistent voice

Acts 10:9-23a

These verses, located in Joppa, comprise the second scene in the drama. Joppa was on the coast and Peter may well have seen the sails of ships in the harbour. Now he is to see another sail-like object, this time descending from the sky.

Peter, hungry, is on the housetop at noon when he sees the vision of unclean animals. An invitation to 'kill and eat' is refused – three times! He is left perplexed. However, we, the readers, know that the middle of the day is when God chooses to reveal himself: in darkness at Jesus' crucifixion (Luke 23:44); in interpretation for the Ethiopian in his chariot (Acts 8:26); and here. Perhaps Peter should have recalled the voice at the Transfiguration (Luke 9:35). The voice then says 'Get up', using the same words as when addressing Aeneas and Tabitha in 9:40.

Cornelius appears to be open to the angel but Peter's response could sound quite arrogant, even challenging: 'by no means, Lord' (verse 14). Was he wanting to maintain the dietary laws he had grown up to respect? Perhaps eating habits and food laws take that kind of hold on us. The heavenly voice overrules him, three times. Peter the impetuous was certainly slow to grasp this point. He was staying with someone whom a law-abiding Jew would have regarded as unclean, yet he seemed reluctant to budge from his horror of unclean foods. The Spirit will move him on once he hears the one who knocks at the door.

Help me, Lord, to change my habits when they become obstacles to your will.

Blown along by the Spirit

Acts 10:23b-33

The third scene is located back in Caesarea, the capital of the Roman province of Judea, where, in expectation of Peter's visit, Cornelius had gathered together a company of people, including his entire household: his kin, adults and children, slaves and close friends, perhaps fellow soldiers too (verse 24). This is the first time we read of an apostle visiting a Gentile house. In this passing comment Luke recorded the breaking down of an age-old barrier that kept Jews and Gentiles apart. Cornelius was also a representative of the occupying force in the region, so Peter had crossed many boundaries in the miles from Joppa to Caesarea.

Peter had been prepared by the vision and its aftermath to be open to the Spirit that blows where it wills (John 3:8). Perhaps that sheet in Joppa had reminded him of a wind-filled sail of a ship. Could he have reflected on Jesus' sending out of seventy missionaries, representatives of a wider mission than that to Jews? However, were the people who accompanied Peter so ready to cross boundaries and move out of their comfort zone?

And Cornelius, too, had made an internal journey, because he fell at Peter's feet – not what many officials of an occupying force would normally do before a native! Imagine the reaction of those who thought of Cornelius as their master.

The encounter moved on, rehearsing the story. God had initiated the process, and Cornelius was prompt in response. Now it was over to Peter.

How do we detect when the Spirit is working ahead of us, and waiting for us to catch up? When have we been compelled by the Spirit to move out of our 'comfort zone'?

Acts 6 – 12: From Jerusalem to Antioch

Notes based on the New Revised Standard Version by

Peter Fisher

Peter Fisher is a priest in the Church of England. Now retired from paid ministry, he has worked in different parts of England, both in parishes and in theological colleges (teaching systematic theology). He is married to Elizabeth and enjoys her baking, as well as playing the piano and digging the garden! He has been involved for many years in the Faith and Order movement, seeking Christian unity in the UK and the wider world.

3 The church spreads

Acts 10:34-48

Once more with feeling

Parchment was costly, scrolls were limited in length, writing and copying were labour-intensive, so why repeat? And it is repetition – of Paul's conversion and of Peter's encounter with Cornelius – that stares us in the face through these chapters of Acts. Luke is a skilled writer and what he writes is well calculated. Like a composer, he realises that the central themes of the symphony must stand out powerfully. His restatements leave the hearer in no doubt: here is the heart of the whole story.

Here we have the ending of the first version of the story of Cornelius. Before Peter's sermon had ended, the hearers received the Spirit's gift of tongues. Clearly, 'hearing the word' did not depend on hearing everything the preacher wanted to say! Peter's Jewish Christian colleagues were amazed at this outpouring on Gentiles. Peter now asked the question similar to the one the eunuch had voiced earlier: 'can anyone withhold water?' (verse 47), and baptism followed for these assembled Gentiles. The Spirit leads the way into all truth: human beings, disciples, can only follow. Peter caught up with the Spirit, as barriers were breached, and he is now truly the catcher of people that Jesus prophesied at his call on Lake Gennesaret (Luke 5:10).

Just keep on repeating your theme of transformation, O God, until I find myself singing it, too.

Watered-down, or powered-up?

Acts 11:1-18

Was Christianity in danger of becoming Judaism-lite? Peter's unconditional acceptance of Cornelius and his household raised the fear among some of his fellow Jewish Christians that their faith was being sold short: Gentiles were being invited to share its benefits without any requirement to knuckle under and change their lifestyle. This fear that the Gentile mission involved the dilution of Jewish-Christian standards of life did not immediately go away: critics of the new mission may have been 'silenced' (verse 18) for the time being, but the issue rumbled on (see Acts 15). Paul tackled the question head on, not least in the strenuous arguments of Romans 6 – 8. But the writer of Acts does not. Instead, at this decisive turning-point, where the whole future of the gospel is at stake, we are given a repeat of the Cornelius story: a repeat that gives us some interesting new details and finally homes in on the punchline, 'who was I to hinder God?' (verse 17).

Peter is doing what most apostles do best: telling the story, witnessing to the work of God. From this point on, the Christian community will be guided as much by fresh examples as new arguments. The Spirit of God is moving about on earth, Luke is telling us, and where you spot the Spirit blossoming and revealing the likeness of Christ in new faces, there you are seeing the future of the church. And there is nothing 'lite' about lives renewed by the Spirit.

Jesus, life-giver, may your unconditional acceptance of me be the springboard for my new life, not the permanent excuse for my old one.

Blessed is the peacemaker

Acts 11:19-25

With all the excitement of Paul's conversion and Peter's new discovery, we might have forgotten about the persecution in chapter 8. But now, as we read of another group of evangelists – Jewish Christians based in Judea prior to the persecution, but originally from Cyprus and North Africa – we realise that the gospel is advancing on many fronts. The Spirit is prompting these unnamed men to start proclaiming Jesus to Gentiles (Hellenists): so you don't have to be a big name, a Paul or a Peter, to spread the good news.

Barnabas is sent to monitor these startling developments in what we now know as Syria. We were told a bit about him in Acts 4:26, now we learn more. He lives up to his nickname as 'son of encouragement' and shows his openness to new expressions of grace, not only by his positive response to the new gentile converts in Antioch but also by setting out for Tarsus to fetch Saul. Barnabas is the only person called 'good' in Acts (verse 24). He is the quiet hero of the narrative (just as Paul is the flamboyant hero): he can be seen doing in person what the book of Acts attempts to do in words – holding together the diverse personalities and developments of the young Christian movement. That diversity, then as now, always teeters on the edge of conflict. So, now as then, there is a special role for the generous, risk-taking reconciler.

Pray today for those who work for reconciliation and unity in a divided church and world.

You are my disciples

Acts 11:26-30

The community of followers of 'the Way' of Jesus has advanced in Antioch. It has grown in size, and it has encompassed many gentiles. This group calls for teaching and guidance, which Barnabas and Saul help to supply. But it also calls for designation. Who are they? What shall we call them? The wider community comes up with the title 'Christians' (verse 26), identifying them by reference to their adherence to Jesus, the Christ. They are 'Christ-supporters' as others are 'Herod-supporters' (Herodians). The fundamental question for members will not be 'where are you from?' or even 'what do you do?', but 'who do you follow?'

The one whom Christians follow famously shared bread with the hungry, so what follows is no surprise: the church in Antioch, hearing of the predicted famine (which would hit Judea particularly heavily), decides to send relief. The first action of the 'Christians' is 'Christian aid'. This collection is almost certainly different from the one Paul writes to Corinth about in 2 Corinthians 9, but surely Paul would have taught, in Antioch, too, that relief-giving was a test of 'obedience to the confession of the gospel of Christ' (2 Corinthians 9:13).

There are no dates in the margin of Acts and Luke, the writer, does not stick to a strict chronology. He is more concerned to show the growth of 'the Way' geographically and thematically. But evidence from other sources points to a major food shortage in the Roman Empire between 44 and 48 AD.

Let us be conditioned, O God, by the character of the one we follow and the needs of those we serve.

Passover from death to life

Acts 12:1-11

Now the scene has changed: we are back in Jerusalem, back with the eventful story of Peter, for one final chapter. Tradition affirms that Peter was martyred in Rome some twenty years after the events of this chapter, but in Acts his story will soon make way for Paul's.

'If they have persecuted me they will persecute you, also,' Jesus foretold (John 20:15) and so it proves. This 'King Herod', grandson of the Herod of Matthew 2 and nephew of Herod Antipas, before whom Jesus had appeared on trial (Luke 23:7), had the reputation of carefully observing Jewish custom. He makes the arrest 'during the festival of Unleavened Bread' (verse 3). It seems that Peter is following his master's passion step by step. But Passover for Peter will be different.

The narrative of Peter's miraculous escape (verses 6-11) is as vivid as a scene from a film: we see and follow it with our mind's eye. In particular, we can imagine it from Peter's own perspective: he is not the heroic captain of his destiny, rather he is the dopey, passive subject of divine intervention. Only after the event, pacing the darkened streets, does the blur give place to recognition: 'the Lord has … rescued me' (verse 11).

'Whether we live or whether we die we are the Lord's', Paul writes (Romans 14:8). Both James (killed by the sword of Herod) and Peter (rescued by the angel) are playing their part in the 'Christian' story.

You may like to reflect on God's presence in the moments of 'escape' and the moments of disaster in your life.

The extended family of Jesus

Acts 12:12-19

The scenario of Peter's deliverance continues in this scene shot in close-up: we see a particular house and a specific maid (a slave), Rhoda. There is an element of comedy, too, as Peter is left knocking frantically on the door. It is tempting to hear Peter's own voice retelling the story to 'Luke', but we cannot know whether the unnamed author of Acts had personal contact with the first apostles. We are, however, given a glimpse of the early church in Jerusalem.

The first place Peter goes for refuge is a woman's house (Mary's) big enough to have a forecourt and to hold a substantial prayer-meeting, which seems to have included the slave Rhoda. Significantly, we also hear that 'James' should be told of Peter's escape. Clearly not the James whom Herod Agrippa executed: presumably James 'the Lord's brother' (Galatians 1:19), who will be shown a little later in Acts (chapter 15) taking the leading role in the Jerusalem church. In passing, we also pick up the name John Mark (Mary's son); he will soon join with Paul and Barnabas in part of their travels and will later be credited by tradition with writing the second gospel and with founding the church in Egypt.

There is an extended family feel to this early community of disciples: it's a family in which women play a key part, in which leadership seems flexible; and it's a family that is able to accept triumph and (apparent) disaster at God's hand.

Where is the home you would head for in emergency? Is yours such a home?

Whose image and likeness is this?

Acts 12:20-25

Most of Acts tells stories that don't appear in other 'history books'. The doings of Peter and Paul, Mary and Rhoda, figure in no known documents outside the New Testament. But here, with the death of Herod Agrippa, we are in the realm of international affairs. The ancient Jewish historian Josephus gives a parallel account of these events in which the king failed to rebuke those who acclaimed him as a god and was consequently struck down (verse 23). In Acts, Herod has been shown as a death-dealing persecutor of the church, but his own violent death is triggered by something else: it is 'because he had not given glory to God' (verse 23). This fits with the whole emphasis of Luke/Acts. From the first chapter of Luke's Gospel we have been shown how God 'has brought down the lofty from their thrones and lifted up the lowly' (Luke 1:52). All the mighty 'acts of the apostles' are accompanied by disclaimers: 'Why do you stare at us?' asks Peter after curing the man lame from birth (Acts 3:12), just as Paul and Barnabas hasten to tell the crowd in Lystra, 'We are mortals, just like you', when the mob acclaims them as gods on earth (Acts 14:8-18).

God is to be seen in human lives and faces, but always as God was seen in Jesus. 'Grasp the truth of God by using the way he himself provides, since he sees the weakness of our footsteps. That way consists first, of humility, second, of humility, and third, of humility' (St Augustine, *Letters,* 118: 22).

'May you be content with yourself just the way you are. Let this knowledge settle into your bones, and allow your soul the freedom to sing, dance, praise and love' (attributed to Mother Teresa).

Questions in Job

Notes based on the New Revised Standard Version (with reflections on the Hebrew text) by

Robert Parkinson

Robert Parkinson is a Baptist minister. Ordained in 1982, he has served congregations in the United States of America and the UK. He and his wife Dawn have three grown-up children. Robert is minister of Didsbury Baptist Church, Manchester.

1 My servant Job

Job 1:1-5

Have you seen my servant Job?

It might be supposed that good things happen to those who do good, and bad things happen only to those who do evil. The book of Job contradicts such a notion. The fact that bad things happen to good people is not the cheeriest of themes. It is nevertheless good news of a sort. Sufferers who, in addition to their suffering, have had to endure the censure of those who blame them for it know this only too well.

In the opening chapters, Job is portrayed as the most righteous of people. He is so perfect and his circumstances so ideal that the reader cannot think of him as a historical person. This is not to say that there could not have been someone called Job who was patient in extreme suffering, but the story told by the book goes beyond the purview of history. No historian can know that a certain man is so morally upright that 'there is no one like him in all the earth' (verse 8), nor can history tell of the workings of a divine council. Job's story functions like a parable. Posing as a conventional wisdom story it turns conventional wisdom on its head. Employing some of the most imaginative and beautiful poetry in the Hebrew Bible, it demonstrates that the very worst things can happen to the very best people. The question is, will the faithful continue in their faithfulness if calamity occurs?

God help us, when we are prosperous, never to assume we have earned our prosperity. Help us, when we suffer, to endure it with patience; and when others suffer, let us never blame them for their suffering. In the name of our suffering Saviour, Jesus Christ.

Does Job fear God for naught?

Job 1:6-12

The Satan of the book of Job is not the devil of later Christian tradition. I wonder why the NRSV (along with most translations) chooses to present this figure with the proper name, Satan. The Tanach, the Jewish Bible, is much to be preferred with its translation, 'the Adversary'. For always, in the book of Job, the word 'satan' appears with the definite article. It is here more a title than a name. One of the divine beings that sit with God in divine council, the Adversary presents himself to God. His divinely sanctioned role seems to be something like that of a prosecuting attorney.

Closer to the Jewish Satan than the Christian devil, the Adversary of the book of Job is not so much a tempter as a tester of human beings. He does not sit on the shoulder of human victims whispering instructions to do evil. His direct interaction is not with those he tests but, rather, with God. Perhaps he does God's dirty work for him – absolving God of the ultimate responsibility for causing harm. Still, he must get permission from God to inflict suffering on Job in order to ascertain whether Job's faithfulness is based only on the benefits he seems to have accrued from serving God.

Here is a challenge for us all. Do we serve God because God is worthy or in order to get something out of God? Is our service of God a kind of self-service after all?

God our Redeemer, save us from the time of trial and help us to know, when innocence brings few benefits, that you are our reward. 'My flesh and my heart may fail, but God is the strength of my heart and my portion forever' (Psalm 73:26).

'Blessed be the name of the Lord'

Job 1:13-22

In the midst of disaster, after all his children have been killed, Job worships God. This is not because Job does not care about his family; on the contrary! He sacrificed on their behalf in order to stave off just such an eventuality. For Job, all things come from God who is to be worshipped in calamity as well as in prosperity. For many today, such a mindset is difficult to comprehend or accept. Yet it is not unique to Job. Isaiah tells us that God is creator of both weal and woe (Isaiah 45:7).

All who try to speak about God faithfully and truthfully have to confront this difficulty. It is possible to ascribe evil to God in such a way as to say something unseemly, to speak as we ought not. Yet we are confronted with a world in which wonder and disaster occur side by side. At the very least, people of faith must say that God allows the terrible things that happen in our world, but we cannot say that God takes pleasure in any of them. With Job, we try to find a way to say that we must receive bad as well as good at the hand of God, while refusing to charge God with wrongdoing.

Even now, good people all over the world in the midst of suffering bow in worship. These are today's heroes of faith who deserve the admiration and support of us all.

God of all comfort, we pray today for all who suffer because of the loss of a loved one. We especially remember parents who grieve the loss of a child. Be close to all who mourn, that they might find in you both comfort and strength.

Do you still persist in your integrity?

Job 2:1-10

Job's troubles grow progressively more personal, yet even in pain Job continues in faith without cursing God or sinning against God with his lips.

I don't know whether we should make anything of the fact that, in this section of the book of Job, the Hebrew word for blessing and for cursing God is the same! Job hopes that his children will not sin even inadvertently and curse (*brk*) God in their hearts (1:5). The Adversary boasts that, if God allows him to inflict trouble on Job, he will curse (*brk*) God to God's face (1:11 and 2:5). Now, Job's wife tempts Job to curse (*brk*) God and die (2:9). What Job has actually done is to bow and say, 'The Lord gave and the Lord has taken away; blessed (*brk* – passive participle form) be the name of the Lord' (1:21).

We are reminded perhaps that the lips that praise God can also curse God. Although blessing and cursing may be opposite responses, they are somehow not so far from each other. Many of the psalms, for example, rail against the Almighty and yet do so in faithfulness. Before the book of Job is through, Job will do the same.

All God-talk is perilous. So people of faith attempt to speak about God but they do so legitimately only with fear, trembling and humility. The language of theological argument gives way to the language of prayer: 'blessed be the name of the Lord'.

God our strength: let it be your will so to empower us that in any and all circumstances we might persist in faith and so with integrity praise you.

And no one spoke

Job 2:11-13

If the book of Job enjoins faithful worship of God even in the midst of suffering, it does not do so easily. It does not underestimate the appalling nature of human suffering, but rather recognises that suffering can be unspeakably severe. Thus the friends of Job arrive to comfort him in his pain. Upon seeing him from a distance they weep out loud and tear their clothes. When they draw near to him they are reduced to silence. So great is Job's suffering that for a whole week all four can only sit and say nothing.

In my pastoral work I have on many occasions been called upon to visit people in great distress. Sometimes a little conversation is appropriate and needed but sometimes silence seems like the only possible response. I have wondered at such times whether my presence made a blind bit of difference, but if later expressions of gratitude are anything to go by, the quiet presence of a friend can speak volumes. Occasionally I have felt the awkwardness of sitting in silence and wondered whether I ought to say something. Eliphaz, Bildad and Zophar eventually had much to say, too much perhaps; Job might have thought they were at their best when silent. Sometimes, to be there and to say nothing is a much greater gift than to fill the air with eloquent speech.

Think of someone you know who is suffering. Is there a way you might helpfully express compassion? Is there something you might do to help alleviate the suffering of another?

In place of words let us in silence remember the suffering poor. If we are able, let us make a gift to Christian Aid and offer it as a silent prayer.

Why did I not die at birth?

Job 3:1-15

With bitter, poetic brilliance, Job breaks the silence and curses the day of his birth. Although he does not curse God, he surely comes close to it. For God, as Job has already asserted, gives life. God brings to birth and Job curses what God has caused to be. Incidentally, we are no longer told that Job 'did not sin with his lips' and we are left until the very end of the book to wonder whether Job is right or wrong to speak as he does. This is the Job unknown by much of Christian tradition. The patience of Job begins to give way to the unrelenting self-justification of an innocent Job trying to come to terms with his own undeserved suffering.

Jesus says of the one who was to betray him that 'it would have been better for that one not to have been born' (Mark 14:21), but Job had done nothing wrong: his is innocent suffering. Like the innocent sufferer of Psalm 22, Job knows it is God who has fenced him in and only God who can give him relief. There is then restraint in Job's outburst. He longs for death but cannot 'curse God and die'. He is close to despair but will not contemplate suicide. Rather, in the manner of the Psalms of Lament, he raises his voice against unjust suffering and cries out for an answer. Better, much better, to complain bitterly against God than meekly to despair.

God who brings light out of darkness, we pray today for all who are close to despair, especially for those who suffer greatly for no good reason. Give them strength to hold on to life, and bless with wisdom those who give them counsel.

The thing that I fear comes upon me

Job 3:16-26

As a young teenager, I once heard a preacher claim that Job suffered because of his fears. Job's suffering, the argument went, was a direct consequence of fear. If he had not feared loss and illness he would not have suffered it and, if we can keep from fearing disaster, we too will escape it. The preacher wanted his hearers to put away their anxious fears but it had the opposite effect on me. 'Fear', said the preacher 'attracts disaster'; 'faith wards it off'. Far from fearing less, such counsel made me fear more. After all, who does not occasionally (and legitimately) fear that things may go awry, that great suffering may befall us? Now I had two problems: in addition to my fear of disaster I began to fear the power of my own fears!

The truth of the matter is that Job's suffering had nothing to do with his fears. True, he feared and he suffered but his suffering was not a consequence of his fear. The two are unrelated in terms of cause and effect. Job suffered for no good reason. He had done no wrong; he was not being punished and he did not attract his own suffering by his behaviour or his fears. Only when we understand this does the message of Job begin to be comprehensible.

Faith does not guarantee immunity from suffering or disaster, but it can sustain the believer in the midst of it.

Lord God, when all is dark and all seems lost, help us to hold on to hope and put our trust in you. Lead us, we pray, out of darkness and into your light.

Questions in Job

Notes based on the Revised Standard Version by

Ruth Shelton

Ruth Shelton was born in 1951 in Nottingham, where she still lives, works and writes. After a long period of freelance roles in the voluntary sector she now works for a local homelessness charity.

2 Job's friends venture a few words

Job 4:1-11

Letting the voices speak

The voices in the Book of Job surround and cut across one another in sometimes deceptive harmony and equally deceptive dissonance. Satan appears to be an amiable rogue and God at times a tyrannical megalomaniac. Patient Job is defiant. The baddies are not all bad and the goodies aren't good at all. I have arranged the following meditations like a play that is intermittently interrupted by another play or even real life.

PREACHERS 1, 2 AND 3 SPEAK: Thank you for attending this series of sermons called 'Reasons to Believe' The preachers come from a variety of traditions and will draw on their learning and expertise to explain why you believe what you do.

PREACHER 1 SPEAKS: Don't mistake me – I feel for all of you. You are church goers: all will be well. You have prayed: your prayers have built the church. Outside music thumps from the club doorways, muggers resist arrest. You are not like them! When you suffer (and I know how you have suffered) remember your faith. As you gasp for breath, trust God. As you toss and turn in pain, know your place. If you speak, say your prayers, God hears psalms, not cries and struggles.

Write a short prayer in your own words in the way you would normally speak. No one is going to see this so be as honest as you possibly can be. Reflect on the difference between this prayer and some formal prayers you know.

Preacher 2 speaks

Job 5:1-16

Let me display my understanding before you,
capacious as my sleeves.
Standing, in front of you, I can see the view beyond and behind you, views you are crouched too low to see.
From here I can see across the fields, where workers toil, squabble, sleep, straight into the eyes of God.
He saves, protects, punishes, believe me!
Between him and me the great themes bounce back and forth just as the workers plough, sow, reap.
God weaves his plans in the air, the ripe ground he leaves to itself.

Try to have a conversation with someone whose role you are aware of but whom you don't normally talk to, a taxi driver for instance, or a street cleaner.

Let us give thanks for a God who walked and still walks among us. He walks through the night, works with us during the day.

Let me find the new world in the world, always ready, always waiting for me to share with him.

The parish visitor speaks

Job 8:1-10

Don't try to speak – you are delirious.
Try and rest, I am here now.
Here, have some water.
I have a copy here of the Desert Fathers*,*
it might be some help.
No – it's all right, I understand what you're saying,
I did a course in Pastoral Visiting.
I am so glad to be able to give something back.
I'll be back next week!
Just remember – God looks after his own.

Pick up a charity leaflet or newsletter that you haven't yet read. Meditate on the stories and try to imagine them as they are happening. Try to place yourself in the place of the 'helped' or 'victim'.

Let us give thanks for a God who heals and gives us strength to heal, not because we are skilled but because we too are suffering.

Heal us with your humility so that we look eye to eye with those we heal, because only together will we break into your new world.

The tabloid article speaks

Job 11:1-12

Jay B's release may delight his supporters but we are tired of his continual outpourings.
The Parole Board believe his story, but we have heard enough.
The five-year sentence speaks for itself even with unreliable witnesses.
An apology would not go amiss, after all, the CCTV camera showed he was almost certainly there at the time.

Draw a pie chart with sections that represent where your beliefs, morality and views come from. How much comes from your family? How much from the church's traditional teaching? How much from what your friends think and believe? How much from the media?

Let us give thanks for a God who liberates not only people but the ideas and judgements that keep us captive.

Let me truly listen to the stories of others so that their stories shape a world new to me, always ready, always waiting for me to share with you.

The housing department speaks

Job 22:1-11

Please fill in this form.
It is only forty pages.
Without your statement we cannot proceed.
We do have a flat for you, but you have no local connection.
We do have a house for you, but you have not proved 'intention to stay'.
There's a property on our books, but you had an ASBO five years ago.
There's another one available soon but you are in arrears.
It must be hard sleeping rough; here is a list of Soup Runs; but really, you have brought this on yourself.

Let us give thanks for a God who forgives, who meets each need with compassion because he has chosen to suffer too.

Free us to suffer alongside others, without comment or viewpoint, seeing always the possibility of a new world always ready, always waiting for us to share with you.

Preacher 3 speaks

Job 37:14-24

Praise the Lord!
Don't listen to the others, there's nothing worth listening to but the Lord (through me).
If I sound angry it's because I care for your soul, if I am shouting it's because I know that I'm right.
An ambulance siren blares on the street outside – don't listen.
A child plays in the bench in front of you – don't look.
Thunder and lightning beat at the door;
Let them beat your hearts into repentance – that goes especially for you women and children, for you are nothing without him, and the guidance of your minister.

Let us give thanks for a God who raises us all up with a mysterious dignity, who does not ask the oppressed to bow down or the hungry to fast.

May women and children form the contours of a new world, always ready, always waiting for us to share with you.

Ubuntu speaks

Job 6:24-30

I am nine and I help look after my family since my mother died of AIDS.
I have four sisters and three brothers.
I like schooldays best, but I go only once a week.
Some people have helped me, but sometimes their words are confusing.
My name is Ubuntu.
I am HIV positive.
My name means 'I am what I am because of who we all are'.

Do some research today into HIV/AIDS in Africa. Who is most affected and why? What are the barriers that prevent survivors getting the help they need?

Let us give thanks for a God who hears all voices, however quiet; who discerns in the cacophony the song of truth.

Help me to see that I belong to the world, that my voice raised up raises up others, shaping the new world together.

Questions in Job

3 Job calls God to answer

Notes based on the New Jerusalem Bible by

David Ford

The Reverend David Ford is an Anglican priest working in parish ministry and school chaplaincy in the ex-mining town of Hucknall in the East Midlands of England. Central to David's theological outlook and approach to ministry is humility: humility before the God who goes before us and humility towards the context in which we are called to minister. David is married to Liz and they have two grown-up children.

Job 9:1-12

Humility before God

Near where I live is an unassuming English country lane bordered by hedges and open farmland, picturesque and quite beautiful. On a clear day, the vista ahead is magnificent: miles and miles of open, glorious countryside. Conscious of the limitations and failures of humanity, is there anyone who would dare question the Creator before such a view?

Creation at its greatest might silence us for a few moments, yet most of us will swiftly return to picking fights with God, who must bear the brunt of our anxiety, anger, and fear. Just occasionally, however, we have the privilege of meeting someone who chooses not to walk in Job's shoes. Godfrey is one young man who has every reason to argue with God. Living in Southern Uganda, Godfrey lost all his family to HIV when he was still quite young. Despite such trauma his faith is among the strongest I have ever witnessed. His acceptance of his family's story is sustained by that faith which echoes around his village with a vibrancy that would embarrass many a Western church. Walking along that lane in rural England I feel humbled in the presence of the Creator. Yet that is nothing compared with standing before Godfrey as he asserts his faith that we will meet again in heaven.

In the face of the faithful beauty of creation and in the faithful face of humanity, who is going to dare ask God: 'What are you doing?' Some questions are for living through, not answering.

Lord God, may my life be worthy of your creation.

Friendship under pressure

Job 13:1-12

I feel some sympathy for Job's friends Eliphaz, Bildad and Zophar. Their contributions may not be helpful or welcome to Job but their friendship is certainly being put to the test. In his attempts to silence them, Job's friends have every reason to shrug their shoulders and walk away.

The notion of friendship is arguably under threat. Social networking sites are redefining people's understanding of what it means to 'have friends'. Conversation is now reduced to 'tweet'-length exchanges. Chat has replaced dialogue; pronouncements have replaced understanding. In many cultures, the exchanges between Job and his friends would be exceptional today for their length and detail, but especially perhaps for the resilience of those involved. Few would sustain such a friendship for so long.

Job is not yet ready to acknowledge his frailty to his friends. Yet his friends, in their patience and persistence, are expressing humility towards Job that is deeply moving. They can see his pain and are trying to reach him. Job argues back, and his frustration is tangible.

It is always those who love us most who carry the burden of our pain. Every parent and partner knows that to be true, and God knows it most of all. It is, of course, the story of the cross. Sticking with others as they wrestle with their questions and their pain is at the heart of what it means to be a friend.

When has a friend remained by your side despite everything?

Lord and friend of all, give me the patience and the strength to absorb the pain of others.

Listening to the suffering

Job 19:21-29

For Job, injustice meant ill health. Today's passage is preceded by a colourful description of his ailments. His family and household have deserted him in the face of his condition and now he fears his closest friends will leave him also. In response, Job cries out, desperate to be heard and taken seriously. 'Will no one let my words be recorded … for ever' (verses 23-24)?

Listening is a skill. To listen well requires a degree of attentiveness that takes practice to refine. It also involves discipline, for it is easy to be the kind of listener who wishes to interrupt with one's own stories, to jump to conclusions and offer solutions, or to pretend to listen while constructing a speech of one's own. Sadly for Job, Eliphaz, Bildad and Zophar are poor listeners. Listening to the suffering is part of our calling as Christians. There may be little we can do of any practical help but, through listening, we can affirm the humanity and dignity of those who suffer and ensure their stories are 'inscribed on some monument with iron chisel and engraving tool' (verse 24).

That does not address the question of why God allows suffering. But it does give voice to the Christian belief that God detests injustice, takes the side of the poor and, through us, offers healing and wholeness.

What does it feel like when someone truly listens to your story?

God of justice, help us to listen to one another's stories
and lighten the burden of our suffering.

Searching for God

Job 23:1-17

Challenging assumptions about the nature of God is an intrinsic part of my work as a chaplain in a large urban school for 11–18-year-olds. Hence youngsters ask me 'who created God?' to which the reply 'God is' requires a huge shift in their rationalist-led thinking. When I declare that 'I don't believe in the God you don't believe in', eyes open with incredulity, only to be replaced with broad smiles when they realise what I've said.

This seems to me to be the territory that Job occupies. He wants to debate with God as in a court of law, using all his powers of advocacy and persuasion. Yet this depends upon God being a certain kind of God and, despite Job's diligence, his searches for this God naturally prove fruitless. The more he allows himself to be obsessed by his search, the greater his dread of God grows. Sadly, Job is consumed by dread of a God that does not exist.

Whilst atheists and agnostics rightly assert that they cannot believe in a God that is unbelievable, Western Christians are not always effective in presenting a God that is irresistibly believable. The challenge is to invite people on an inward spiritual journey in which God can be discovered and experienced. For it is within the heart that God is known. Other questions about God may have to wait for the world to come.

When and where did you feel closest to God?

Lord of all, help us to search for you where you may be found: in the beat of our heart and the movement of our breath.

It's unfair!

Job 31:16-23, 35-37

I have just returned from leading a retreat on Iona, the small island off the west coast of Scotland that has been a place of pilgrimage for Christians for hundreds of years. It is a wonderful place where God's presence is tangible. Yet, on this retreat, almost everything that could go wrong did. The ferries were cancelled, reducing our already short stay of four nights on the island to two. The heating in the retreat centre failed on one of the coldest nights of the year. Our car broke down and had to be left behind, leaving us to find our way home by train. It rained, and rained and rained. Why me? I cried. What did I do to deserve this?

However understandable, such cries of righteous anguish betray a Job-like perspective on our relationship with God. There is no correlation between right behaviour and divine protection; we cannot bargain with God to ensure he delivers outcomes that meet our desire for self-justification. That is neither how God works, nor how God is to be experienced. Rather, we should seek God in the situation and bring to it God's grace and transforming love.

And that is what happened. Changed plans unveiled new opportunities to grow in friendship with strangers. Hot-water bottles materialised, generosity flowed, and conversations blossomed. Such is the transformative power of the Holy human Spirit. Such is the God of surprises.

Can you recall a situation that was transformed by your openness to God's transforming Spirit?

God of the unforeseen, help us to embrace the unexpected as a gift from you, to discover afresh the opportunity to love and serve in your name.

Humbled by God

Job 38:1-21

I was not the most pleasant of children. On one occasion at the breakfast table, I was talking an endless stream of egotistical rubbish. My father, usually the most mild-mannered of parents, lost his temper. I was left in no doubt that I was not the centre of the universe and that, whatever complaints I might have, they were infinitesimally small and irrelevant compared with those of others. In a moment, I realised my error and wished I could retract my words, start the day again or even be swallowed up in a hole in the ground. My father let up only when he went to work. I went to school with his anger ringing in my ears.

I imagine this is what Job must have felt like in the face of Yahweh's unceasing invective. The tables were suddenly turned: 'Who is this, obscuring my intentions with his ignorant words? Brace yourself like a fighter; I am going to ask the questions, and you are to inform me' (verses 2-3)!

Arrogance is the scourge of our generation. And it is our obsession with self that obscures our view of God's intentions for us. We cannot see when our eyes are focused only on our need to make virtues out of our own shortcomings. This is largely, but not exclusively, a Western phenomenon. Arrogance fed by growing consumerism is creeping globally, damaging community and exploiting people and planet. Be ready to be humbled.

What will it take for humanity to stop, think, reflect and change?

Lord of all, help us to remember that there is only one Creator.

Questions, more questions

Job 38:22-41

'Have you visited the place where the snow is stored' (verse 22)? The childlike innocence of this and other questions in Yahweh's relentless speech is endearing. Imagine oneself back in a pre-scientific age and the question conjures up images of huge warehouses of snow and other wonderfully pragmatic solutions to otherwise insoluble problems. At the same time, it is possible to think of questions to which we do not know the answers today; questions that, in a future age, might sound similarly childlike.

Science and theology are frequently perceived as in competition with one another; that with every advance in science, the need for God and religion diminishes a little further. In practice, every advance in science generates a whole new world of unanswered questions where only awe and wonder make any sense at all. Every time science answers a 'how?' question, the question 'why?' grows in magnitude and urgency.

Frequently confused with weakness, humility is an unpopular virtue and yet it is the source of the greatest of all strengths. To recognise one's need of God, to trust that which cannot be rationally explained or sensually experienced, is to draw closer to the source of all meaning and life. In so doing, we become more human and more divine. 'Blessed are the poor in spirit, for they know their need of God' (Matthew 5:3).

What or whom were you blessed by today?

Loving God, lead me in the path of humility so I may wonder at your greatness and dwell in your presence.

Questions in Job

Notes based on the Revised Standard Version by

Ruth Shelton

For Ruth's biography see p.176.

4 A happy ending?

The subversive nuances and subtleties of the Book of Job have provided inspiration for many writers, artists and poets. Oskar Kokoschkska portrays Job as a betrayed lover trapped in a farcical cabaret. The dialogical energy of Estragon and Vladimir in Samuel Beckett's *Waiting for Godot* mimics the allusions and affinities of the conversations in Job. Perhaps most tellingly for our age, Kafka anticipates in *The Trial* the Jobian fate of countless victims in concentration camps, for whom there was no exit except death. Whose are the voices who carry on these conversations in our time and context? The questions in Job remain questions for us, touching with ironic, playful but painful insights on some of the most difficult areas of human experience.

Sunday 7 July: Job 39:1-12

The voice from the whirlwind

Who am I? Who are you? Where were you?
Are you able to hear me, listen to me?
Look around you, look around you, that's the only answer I can give.
The stall-holders are spreading out their fruit; their bread.
A child waves a drawing of his mother as he runs into school.
Sun shines on the sides of the tower blocks; my voice clatters in the street noises, my answers dodge the traffic.

Take time to reflect on your image of God. Where does this come from? From art? From scripture? From a feeling? Now conjure an image that is the opposite of yours, for instance God as a woman, God as a violent storm. Stay with this image and let it speak to you.

The voice from the whirlwind

Job 39:13-30

Look around you.
8.30 a.m. outside a Day Centre – homeless people are going in.
Some stay outside to finish their cigarettes, one shares his last fag with another.
One leaves his bag on the pavement, ID and papers spilling out, he's singing a Polish song.
Some help the staff to serve breakfast, move tables, already calls are being made to the Job Centre, the Benefits Office.
The day ahead needs courage and tenacity.
There are battles to be fought and no one can do it alone without dying a little.

Buy a copy of *The Big Issue* today or as soon as you can. Talk to the vendor and ask about his or her life.

Homeless or home-full, help me to understand my own fragility, the things I depend on.

Let the God who came as a homeless baby give me a home in him.

Help me find a home by seeking out the lost.

The voice

Job 40:1-14

Why do you speak to me as if you were speaking to yourself?
As if I were made of mirror-glass only showing you your own face?
Are you afraid of an answer you don't already know?
Don't say you have no voice – I gave it to you.
Don't say you have no clothes to wear – you are beautiful as you are.
Do you think that I made you without power, like a lifeless doll?
Look around you; your brother is wounded.
Look around you, your sister is dying.
Believe that your hand can heal him.
Believe that your words are life.

Look at your face in the mirror for a full minute, noting changes, tics, characteristic expressions. Remember ambitions, dreams, visions that may have got lost or have been diluted. See the strength and determination in your face that reflect those dreams.

Help me to understand my own power, with all its tensions and temptations. I pray for freedom, for independence from my own identity, the addictions that tell me who I am.

Help me to be as strong as you made me by being as weak as you became.

The voice

Job 40:15-24

Dust or royalty?
Royalty or dust?
What hours you spend, you and your friends, talking about these things!
You are both and neither.
You are full of a wonder that you have not recognised.
You are part of a universe that is unknown.
Your silence is your voice, your weakness is your power.
You are able: able to drink with me; able to follow me; able to work with me.

God of Gods, of multitudes and millennia, of a world of infinite beauty: help me to beat the vanity that says 'I am helpless.' Help to accept that you made me strong enough to work for your creation.

The voice

Job 41:1-11

Sometimes I know you can't find me, you become tired looking for me in the wrong place.
Just as the sermon explains me, or the text reveals me, a child cries, a storm breaks, the street signs have been altered, the map torn up.
When you look up from wiping the child's eyes, or bending low over a sickbed, things have shifted a little.
No doctrine can define me, no grave can seal me in.
Your eyes must be open to the world in all its dereliction and hopelessness.
Then I can renew, then I can replace.
If your prayer works, it is because you have travelled and suffered with me.

List your outside work and home activities. Strike off one and resolve to engage in an entirely new one within the month.

Speak to me today with an unheard voice. Let me catch a glimpse of you in the familiar routine where I don't expect you to be. Remind me in a way I haven't thought of how you went to the depths to find me.

Answering voice

Job 42:1-6

My fears and hopes were something different –
now they are the same.
I thought the dust I sat on was different from me
– now I am one with the ground.
Most of all, I looked to the sky for an answer and
heard a cacophony of sounds.
I looked at books for healing and missed the hand
on my shoulder.
I cried to heaven for God, as he sat at my
kitchen table.

Thank you for speaking to me face to face. Thank you for seeing me eye to eye. Thank you for seeing me as I really am – as I will fail to be but also truly am: beautiful, strong, complete, capable of joy.

Ubuntu

Job 42:7-17

Now I am going to school and so are my eldest brother and sister.
A nurse comes each week and there is clean water in the village.
We are working to build more houses and we had a feast for all who worked alongside us.
I miss my mother every day but I believe I have a future and she would be proud.
I listened to the world and the world has listened to me.
'If you have come to help me you are wasting your time, but if you have come because your destiny is bound up with mine come, let us walk together.'

from South Africa AIDS activists

Teach me to rejoice in the beauty of every face in the world: in our need for one another – my need for others and their need for me. Help me to see others as beautiful, strong, complete, capable of joy.

Mountains and valleys

1 Mountains

Isaiah 2:2-4

Vision from the summit

Mountains attract our gaze and compel us to look upwards, and this week we shall be looking at biblical mountains as places to encounter God or to get a wide perspective. Yet climbing can be hard work, physically, psychologically and, as we shall see, spiritually, as we find a path to the summit.

The iconic image of Everest points us to the heavens, to a place so high human beings normally need artificially supplied oxygen in order to breathe and survive. Mountains are creation's natural spires pointing us to God. When people think about Isaiah's vision, they recall the dramatic events of chapter 6 and Isaiah's profound encounter with God in the temple. Yet chapter 2 offers a grander vision, one that runs throughout the rest of the book: the temple as a symbol of our most profound worship. This vision is seen at the summit of the mountain of God, which claims all nations and all peoples in all times, past and present. This vision is of the almighty God who desires our worship as we respond to God's love and mercy, justice and judgement, peace and truth.

Reflect on the vision you have of God and how this shapes the way you live your life.

Notes based on the New Revised Standard Version by

Alistair Ross

Alistair Ross is a Baptist minister, practical theologian, academic psychoanalyst and ethical philosopher. He writes and researches on spirituality, psychoanalysis, theology and ethics. Alistair is currently writing a book on sacred psychoanalysis. He works at Oxford University as Director of Psychodynamic Studies and is Dean of Kellogg College. In his spare time Alistair scrambles up mountains, and has a particular love of the Northern Highlands in Scotland, the land of his birth.

Wild and free

Isaiah 2:12-19

In a few parts of the Scottish Highlands, there exists a rarely seen creature called a wildcat. This feral and ferocious creature may look like a large domestic tabby but all resemblance fails at this point. It can never be tamed. It exists wild and free. One of the tragedies of contemporary church life is that we have tried to domesticate God. Isaiah reminds us of the terror and majestic brilliance of God (verse 19). Even the highest mountains will be levelled in the day of God's encounter with creation and all people. The mountains here represent the height of human pride and arrogance that one day will be seen for what they are: empty words and achievements.

Isaiah's call to the people of Israel, and by inference to the church today, is to be the place where God is encountered, wild and free. May that drive us to go out into the wider community with confidence and hope that God is and will always be.

Stop. Be still. Wait for God to reveal a word or image from this passage that is for you today. Let it settle. Do not rush on. Allow space and time to be in the presence of God.

- We confess our human arrogance and pride, our desire always to be in control.
- We lament the mess we have made of our own lives and the lives of others.
- Creator God, allow us to see enough of your glory to inspire us, not terrify us.

The mountain of God

1 Kings 19:1-10

There are places we go back to again and again, and one such place for me is Tryfan (literally 'pointed peak') in Snowdonia. Within two hours' drive from my home I can be scrambling up this 3000-foot peak, never using the same route twice. There is always something new to encounter, a new person to meet on the journey, or in winter some new weather system to endure. Despite once slipping and cracking a rib, I come back.

Horeb, literally the mountain of God, is where Elijah is taken to encounter God. Stretching back in time, Horeb (the same as Mount Sinai) was where Moses met God as recorded in the book of Exodus (Exodus 19:3). Elijah needed a fresh start. Despite his exhaustion, despair and depression, God still has plans for his life.

For Elijah, and for ourselves, life does not always follow the path we wanted, fit with our plans or fulfil our dreams. A time comes when we have run out of emotional and spiritual resources. What better time could there be to rediscover God's claim on our life? Our part is to be in the location God wants us to be, and that may mean figuratively moving from where we are. In this place we can only listen to all that God needs to say to us at this time.

God, grant me the wisdom to listen and to hear what you say. Help me shut out the clamour that deafens me to your words for today.

Still small voice

1 Kings 19:11-16

Elijah's encounter with the 'still small voice' of God (verse 12, King James Version) is justifiably famous and speaks to us again and again. It demonstrates that God's perspective is so very different from our own. We can only be amazed at the splendour, power and majesty of a God who can shake the foundations of the planet, spew lava into the heavens from the molten core of the earth, or send a hurricane that devastates all in its path. Yet these natural phenomena are not as powerful as being in the presence of almighty God, waiting, listening and, most importantly, obeying all that God requires of us.

What God requires of Elijah is that he stops being the prophet of God and passes this role on to the next generation. We live in a world where so many people – politicians, leaders, dictators, media moguls and financiers – become addicted to power, and it is rarely a pleasant sight. In it all they rarely appear to stop to think 'What is happening to my soul?' The world looks at the external but God sees inside who we are, into the very depths of our soul. Elijah had his life stripped bare and the courage to see himself as seen by God. He had the grace, humility and desire to listen to that 'still small voice' of God and act in obedience. Elijah ultimately fades from the scene but is remembered in biblical history, particularly for this incident.

God of earthquake, wind and fire, speak into my very soul, enable me to listen and to obey.

Last will and testament

Deuteronomy 34:1-6

We know intellectually that death is a fact of life, but so often it comes unexpectedly, with no time to prepare or to say goodbye. For several years I mentored a young minister, becoming involved in his story, his pains, and his struggles with sexuality, his desire for God and passion for the church. The day before our regular meeting a phone call told me he had died. I had so many things I wanted to say that were never spoken.

God meets Moses at the top of a mountain, Mount Nebo (now in the kingdom of Jordan), rising over the Dead Sea, and that gives a panoramic view of much of what is now Israel. Unlike Sinai, it is not a revealing of a future but, in his old age, a revelation of his end. Moses has the chance to hear God's words on his life and all he had achieved. Moses' life was hardly perfect, with many failures, false starts and decades of frustration. Yet in it all God was at work, and God grants Moses a final vision of his dream of a promised land that becomes a portent of his death.

As you make a space to think about your life, imagine what legacy you will leave to others. Recall those lives that have touched you, and those that you in turn have touched. Give thanks to God for the pathways of love woven through those around us. Tell those people what they mean to you while such words can be spoken.

Too good to be true?

Matthew 4:8-11

One of the joys of mountains is, weather permitting, the view you get at the top,whether you got there by climbing or cable car. The view evokes sensations of awe and grandeur. One summer, at the summit of the Jungfrau in Switzerland, we had the bizarre experience of looking down on two military jets flying below us.

What would it be like to be offered everything we have ever dreamed of? Land stretching as far as our eye could see? Jesus is mysteriously and metaphorically whisked to the top of a mountain. Here he is offered all the kingdoms of the world. From the pinnacle of a mountain Jesus gets caught up in a dilemma: a kingdom at no cost. The catch? The temptation? All he had to do was avoid the cost of incarnation, the messiness and pain of being human, circumventing a barbaric and tortured death by crucifixion. Our temptation is to seek forms of spirituality through short cuts, which bypass our very humanity. Spirituality can focus so much on the self that those vital others we are connected to in community, spiritual or social, get neglected.

Each of us knows the temptation for the quick fix or the easy route, and this is very much a reflection of the culture we are in. The example of Jesus is to see through this illusion and encourage us to commit ourselves to a lifelong living out of our personhood in the love and presence of God.

Pray for courage for a lifelong commitment.

A heart 'strangely warmed'

Matthew 5:1-12

Before concert halls or conference venues, large groups could be addressed only in the open air. In the 1700s, John Wesley (following the example of his colleague George Whitfield) used this approach to offer a radically new form of Christianity that became known as Methodism. Wesley's open-air preaching was following in a long line of biblical figures who did the same: Moses, Joshua, Samuel, Elijah, Jonah and Jesus. Jesus used natural amplification by speaking from the side of a mountain. No thunder or lightning, just Jesus speaking to his followers and the crowds they attracted. Yet, when we read the Sermon on the Mount and let its meaning sink in, it sends a lightning bolt across the sky of our spiritual life, illuminating it in dramatic ways. Jesus calls us to live in humility, wholeness, peace, purity and obedience, pursuing justice and mercy no matter what complexities life inevitably brings.

Jesus models a reflective and mindful approach to Christian living that does not take us out of the world into some separate spiritual existence. Rather, Jesus offers a radical approach that puts us at the very centre of the pain and brokenness of the world so we can share the words of Jesus with any who will listen. We don't need a mountain as a pulpit but we do need to speak.

Find some space to listen to God today. Allow the Spirit of God to burn within you – like Wesley's heart, which was 'strangely warmed'. Let that guide what we can speak out to others.

Sunday 21 July

Notes based on the New Revised Standard Version by

Alistair Ross

For Alistair's biography, see p.197.

Mountains and valleys

2 Valleys

Psalm 139:7-12

God is there

This week we will explore valleys as places of spiritual encounter and revelation, where our faith experiences waiting, questioning, testing, desolation and renewing.

What does the word 'valley' mean to you? What memories does it evoke? What feelings does it generate? Where does it take you? Wherever that is, there too is the presence of God. This psalm begins with the simple and profound declaration: 'O Lord you have searched me and known me' (verse 1). I find this fact immensely reassuring, that the one who searches for me has found me, knows my most profound and profane thoughts and actions, yet remains ever present. I do not get consigned to utter darkness but invited to live in the light, illuminated by the presence of God (verses 11-12).

For the psalmist, heaven and hell are places in which God is present (verse 8). We expect God to be in heaven but this psalm challenges conventional ideas of hell as God's absence. Hell is seen as a valley of death and despair; yet, however we understand hell, nothing and no one is beyond God. Our God is not an impotent God, unable to create or enter into the worst predicaments of our flawed personhood. God calls us into valleys of life, wellbeing and hope. Yet all begins with the searching examination of God.

God, enter into the dark valleys of my life. Transform them into places of healing and growth.

Racing to God

Isaiah 40:3-11

The Mille Miglia Rally is an historic road race in Italy that begins in Brescia (near Lake Garda), goes via Rome and finishes back in Brescia. Only pre-1957 cars are allowed to compete and it is a glorious spectacle of vintage Ferraris, Alfa Romeos, Maseratis and the like. The route plunges down valleys and snakes up winding mountain roads, testing the engine, suspension, brakes and drivers' stamina to breaking point. Yet competitors, even those that inevitably break down given the vintage status of the cars, return again and again.

Isaiah tells us that there will come a time when God enters the world in such a dramatic way that all creation will be affected. The landscape will be changed for ever. What were once mountains, peaks, valleys and gorges will become a level path along which God proceeds. This momentous event will lead to an overwhelming experience of God's glory, and our responses can be only of awe and worship. Yet even in this tremendous experience of God, another dimension emerges: the creator and ruler of the universe is also caring, tender and protective. Here lies one of the most powerful appeals of Christianity: the very eternal God who births universes into existence is also the one who mends a broken spirit and who touches our fleeting and transient lives.

God of infinite space and distant stars, God of finite grace and unseen scars, speak to me today.

Through the fire

Exodus 24:12-18

Travelling across Italy one very hot summer to the Gran Sasso mountains, we drove through what seemed to be a bank of fog. It was only then we noticed flames shooting upwards along both sides of the road. The smoke receded as our journey continued through the plateau towards the mountains, and we escaped the fire hugely relieved.

While Moses is meeting God in the fire and smoke of the mountain, Joshua, Aaron and Hur stay in the valley handling the everyday life of the people of God. Part of a leader's role is both to be in the presence of God, yet also grounded in everyday reality, working with the pettiness, disputes and fallings-out of ordinary people. We know from chapter 32 that it was a lesson Aaron failed to learn as he lost confidence in Moses and returned to the old patterns of worship. God and Moses seemed remote, as the people of Israel wanted something immediate and tangible. Yet it was also a lesson that Joshua learnt well, as he later led the people of God into a promised but disputed land, relying on God's presence each step of the way.

From time to time it is easy to feel that God is remote, and we become stuck in a 'valley' or plateau of depression, anxiety, loss, fear or absence. At times like this we often make poor decisions. Leaders exist to point us back to the mountain top where we can experience God once more, seeing more of ourselves and God.

Pray for someone you know stuck in the valley.

Anger is good for you

Exodus 32:7-8, 15-24

No one likes people being angry with them, yet the biblical message is that God and God's people can and do get angry. Anger is seen as a natural emotion that is neither condemned nor approved. What is important is the context of the anger. Anger is like a large neon sign that points directly to something very important in us or others that is under threat.

Moses, coming out of the holy presence of God, exhibits anger at the foolishness of God's people and the failure of Aaron's leadership, when he hears of their creation of a gold idol. His anger is fuelled by his utter sense of God's glory and the spiritual blindness and short-term vision of God's people. Such anger is best channelled into action. So many of the great pioneers in church history have been stirred either by God's presence or in response to terrible injustice, enabling them to take extraordinary steps in following God, despite opposition.

I met Archbishop Desmond Tutu when he was invited to Oxford to launch a new Centre for the Study of Governance and Transparency. The cost of corruption constitutes a major obstacle to reducing poverty, inequality and disease in the developing world. Following the example of Desmond Tutu, these are things that the church should be angry about and involved in. There may be other issues close to your heart, but God calls us to pursue love, justice, truth and mercy and to become angry when these are denied to so many.

What makes you angry? How do you use your anger constructively for the wellbeing of others?

Now you see me, now you don't

Mark 9:2-8

When we are frightened we blurt out the first thing that comes to mind. Peter, as always, was the first to verbalise, to speak before he thought through what he was really saying. In doing so he missed the enormity of what had just happened. What had happened? At the top of a mountain, in a private place, away from the crowds and the other disciples, there was the most complete visual and verbal revelation of the being of God in Jesus Christ they would ever experience. Not just some great Old Testament prophet like Moses or Elijah but rather 'this is my Son, the Beloved; listen to him' (verse 7). Then it is all gone, as if it were some hallucination, waking dream or out-of-body experience.

How does God reveal her/himself to you? What do you do with that? How does it leave you? Where do you go with that? What gets stirred in you? Whether we find ourselves figuratively at some mountain-top experience or in some deep and dark valley where all presses in around, God calls us to listen. The love of God experienced through God the Father or Mother to God the Son is what we are invited into, just like Peter, James and John.

God invites us to belong, and with that belonging come love and affection. No matter how good or bad the pattern set by our own parent/s, it is an opportunity to discover the depths of God's transfiguring love.

Down to earth with a bump

Mark 9:14-29

N T Wright sees this passage as crucial for understanding the mission of Jesus and the kingdom of God (*Mark for Everyone*, SPCK, 2001). Working within a first-century world view that understood spiritual life as a cosmic battle between good and evil, in this story the good is represented by Jesus, the son of God, in opposition to the evil represented by illness and the demonic. To demonstrate visibly to people around him that Jesus brings good news of hope for the future, he shows authority over death, illness, nature and demons. Just as the Transfiguration revealed Jesus in a unique way, these encounters with demons show that Jesus brings a new power and authority to life now and life beyond. The disciples get so caught up in arguments with other religious leaders they miss out on helping those in need. They tried but failed, thus earning a rebuke from Jesus. Jesus, however, looks to the heart and finds an honest depth of encounter in the troubled son's father: 'I believe, help my unbelief' (verse 24).

At times all of us doubt and find it difficult to believe. Some may even struggle with the mention of demons in this passage. The message is clear: cry out to the God revealed in Jesus, who hears, responds and reaches into us to affirm belief in the midst of our doubt and despair. We can discover the truth that Jesus releases us from the knots we tie ourselves in, intellectual, emotional and spiritual.

I believe, help my unbelief!

Highs and lows

Psalm 84:5-7

Over these last two weeks we have scaled the heights and been dragged to the depths, and the theme running through each section has been how God enters into our experience and stays with us, through good or bad. In the psalm for today, commentators cannot decide how best to understand 'valley of Baca' in verse 6. It is literally 'a place of tears', indicating a barren, desert place. When people think of valleys in the Bible they often recall Psalm 23 and its reference to the 'valley of the shadow of death' (Psalm 23:4 King James Version). The barren place or the shadow place is one that we all know well. When there, our prayers seem filled with empty, lifeless words. Our worship is mechanical or begrudged, if we worship at all. Yet still God is there and we are invited to journey on and not stay in this place.

'Valley of Baca' can also mean a place of balsam trees, indicating fertility and growth. Valleys are also symbols of fertile places, of abundant growth, or rich habitat in which life blossoms. In the context of the earlier verses about the joy and desire of worship, God calls us into a life-giving and life-affirming relationship that can endure deserts, literal and metaphorical.

Read the rest of the psalm. Let the sheer excitement and enthusiasm of the psalmist bathe or soothe your soul with wellbeing, peace and joy. God longs to be with us and we with God, which makes faith, worship, witness and service a thrilling journey of discovery.

Fresh from the Word

It may seem early, but copies of the new Bible reading book are now available to order.

Order now:

- with your local IBRA Rep*
- in all good bookshops
- direct from IBRA

online: http://bit.ly/IBRAbooks

email: sales@christianeducation.org.uk

phone: 0121 472 4242

post: using the order form at the back of this book

Price £8.75. If ordering direct, postage is free of charge.

Ebook versions priced at £8.00 inc.VAT are available from our website.

Become an IBRA rep

*If you purchase 6 or more print copies, and you live in the UK, you can sign up as an IBRA Rep and claim the 10% IBRA Rep discount on all IBRA products. You will also receive a free poster and samples to help you share IBRA more easily with family, friends and others in your church. Contact staff at IBRA to sign up now!

Paul for today

1 A re-formed life: in Christ

Notes based on the New Revised Standard Version by

Lori Rizzo

Lori Sbordone Rizzo is an itinerant teacher of at-risk youth in New York City. She is recently married and the two are waiting for word from Lori's bishop on her application to be an Episcopal priest.

Galatians 1:11-17

More to the story

Saul of Tarsus loved God. He loved law as a way to honour God. These followers of the Nazarene made him nervous. They seemed to flout the law, claiming some sort of new freedom. Then Stephen is dragged before the Sanhedrin. He responds by invoking Israel's heroes, men made brave because of their relationships with a God who spoke, made promises, and remained faithful, even when they were not. Their testimony is so much bigger than obedience to 613 laws. Then Stephen's story comes around to the building of the temple, and here he speaks a very dangerous line, 'the Most High does not dwell in houses made with human hands' (Acts 7:48). That verse, like a two-edged sword, must have pierced Saul's heart. After all, we have this account of Stephen's trial because it lived in Saul's memory like a thorn. Was he guilty of trying to put God in a box? Was he so in love with his own intellect that he cut himself off from seeing that God can act in any way God chooses? It's new wine, the kind Jesus warns will burst old wineskins. It almost burst Saul, until God gave him the opportunity to be made new.

God revealed himself through the law, but there was more to the story. The truth about God is beyond any human's capacity to grasp. We get pieces, hints, but we are still looking through the glass darkly, longing for the face to face.

Help me, God, to be open to you, even if you need to astound me.

Eternity

Colossians 3:1-4

Evelyn Underhill defined mysticism as 'the art of union with reality' (*Practical Mysticism*). Reality is everything that's eternal. Everything else is transient. Some of the transient stuff is fun: a new car, a leather jacket, toys. Transient things can also be needful, such as food, shelter and our mortal bodies. We treasure them, thank God for them, but inevitably their time's up. Beauty gets no pass from time; neither goodness nor fairness. Time is an indiscriminate serpent devouring the just and the unjust. But there is another kind of time that cannot be measured from head to tail. A professor I knew once explained the differences between the two Greek words for time by asking me to imagine a one-inch line on a sheet of paper: 'The line represents all of human time running from past to present, and the paper is God's time.' God's time surrounds us. It is infinitely dimensional. Past, present and future coexist. Jesus is the lamb who was slain before the foundation of the world. He is the Alpha and Omega, even while he was on the cross.

'Set your mind on things that are above, not below,' Paul says to us today (verse 2). Don't just live on the line, where yesterday and today think they can speak for tomorrow. Seek the one who is eternally true. As Ms Underhill observed, 'Eternity is with us, inviting our contemplation perpetually, but we are too frightened, lazy, and suspicious to respond; too arrogant to still our thought, and let divine sensation have its way' (*Practical Mysticism: A Little Book for Normal People*, Aziloth, 2011).

In fear and trembling I ask you to have your way in my day, that I may dare to glimpse my life through your eternal eyes.

By any means necessary

1 Corinthians 9:16-23

Paul is not afraid to be inflexible in theological debates but he admits to the Corinthians that he is willing to adjust his relationship to the law if that will create an opening to introduce someone to Christ. The rule is: there must never be a barrier to the gospel. Jesus ate with adulterous women and tax collectors; Philip climbed into a chariot to explain Isaiah's prophecy to an Ethiopian eunuch. Paul will certainly keep kosher, if this will bring to the table someone who is open to hear the good news.

There is a song Paul sings in jail. It is 'recorded' in his letter to the Philippians. Here is the first verse: 'Let the same mind be in you that was in Christ Jesus, who, though he was in the form of God, did not regard equality with God as something to be exploited, but emptied himself, taking the form of a slave, being born in human likeness. And being found in human form, he humbled himself and became obedient to the point of death – even death on a cross' (Philippians 2:5-8).

Paul knows that dietary laws have nothing to do with one's righteousness; he is convinced that he has no righteousness whatsoever except for that which has been given freely from God. Does this mean he will walk into a kosher home carrying a ham and cheese sandwich? Of course not. Rather than exploiting his freedom, he empties himself so that the grace of God can be revealed.

Lord Jesus, give me grace to put on your mind, so that your glory can be revealed in the great and small movements of my day.

Rejoice

Philippians 1:3-21

The word 'joy' or its verb form 'rejoice' appears 16 times in this short letter of Paul to the Philippians. What makes this remarkable is that this letter was written in jail. There are different options about which jail this was written in (Paul was in a few). I believe this letter was written in Rome, after Nero burned it down and blamed the Christians for his crime. If I am right, then Paul knows he is not likely to escape death, although anything is possible. He is writing to say goodbye to a church family he dearly loves. He wishes he could return to them, watch them grow more in love with God and each other, but he is confident that the God who began a good work in them 'will bring it to completion' (verse 6). He has one final word for them: Rejoice. Rejoice in persecution; God is near. Rejoice in want; God is faithful. Rejoice in all things, whether you feel like it or not, and God's own peace will be with you.

Somewhere in the palace, a monster recites forgotten verses. He is remembered solely for his madness. Somewhere amongst the prisoners, saints are rejoicing, singing songs that continue to be sung by Christians across the world: Rejoice in the Lord always. Again I will say, Rejoice! (Philippians 4:4).

When people of faith rejoice, oppressors fall, darkness scatters and freedom is a foregone conclusion.

No matter where we are, we are always in your hand.
O joy!

Living with contradictions

Romans 8:1-7

Our lives are hidden in Christ. The creator of all is our Abba. The king of glory is our brother. By virtue of God's Spirit alive inside us, we are free from sin and death. So says Paul, but it's a stretch to believe. Everything, from my personal experience to my observation of the world, contradicts it.

Paul seems to know we are going to have trouble with this, so he offers as proof the fact that our souls cry out to God with bold familiarity. We know that there is little holy within us yet we dare to approach God by his most intimate name. When Isaiah came before God, he cried, 'Woe is me! I am lost; for I am a man of unclean lips, and I live among a people of unclean lips' (Isaiah 6:5). We're just running up and calling him 'Papa.' We are either very foolish, or we know something. Somehow we seem to know that God has seen our worst and loves us anyway. Before Isaiah could come into God's presence, a coal had to be taken from the altar and touched to his lips. Paul is saying that this same coal has been applied to our hearts by the Spirit burning inside us. If we have figured out that God is not going to destroy us, it is no credit to us. The Holy Spirit has revealed God's heart to us, sharing with us secrets that are known only amongst family.

So how do we live with contradictions? Tolstoy's advice sits over my desk, 'The business of a Christian is everywhere and always one: to increase one's fire and let it give light to everyone.'

Holy God and Abba, Here am I, send me.

Be the kingdom

1 Corinthians 12:12-26

Anarchists are often asked, 'Come the revolution, who will collect the garbage?' Everyone. Come the revolution, we will understand that we must each take responsibility for our own messes. If some individuals feel compelled to make sure that our garbage is disposed of in an environmentally friendly way, then we bless them in their work and love them for it. I lived through a garbage strike in New York. When the garbage man finally came up the street, we were ready to elect him mayor.

Pastor Paul is worried that this Corinthian community is threatened by divisions. Some of the members feel they have more say than others because they have 'more important' positions in the body. Paul will allow none of this. The head of the body is Christ, who washed his disciples' feet. Christian community, therefore, is characterised by service, where all members are honoured and celebrated for the unique gifts they bring to the body. The preacher and the gardener are both proclaimers of the gospel. The priest and the food pantry workers are all simply banquet workers. All equally hear God, all are indispensible to the life of the community.

I am not claiming Paul was an anarchist but passages such as these reveal that his vision of community was much less hierarchical than most modern-day churches. I believe Paul would say that our churches should be patterned less on the kingdom of this world and more on the kingdom of God. Imagine if visitors could come upon our gatherings and feel as if they had stepped into heaven. What better way is there to proclaim the gospel than to be the kingdom?

Eternal God, grant me to see the marvellous orchestra of gifts that will come together to create your in-breaking kingdom in my life today.

Shine

2 Timothy 4:1-8

If Philippians was written within weeks of Paul's death, this letter was probably composed within hours of the executioner. Timothy, the recipient of the apostle's last words, is a beloved apprentice and companion in the gospel, the one Paul has entrusted to continue his life's work. He urges Timothy to stay out of trouble, be kind, study scripture, and depend on God's unfailing grace.

Many have commented on Paul's confidence in verses 7-8. Apparently, the tone of his self-eulogy is scandalously boastful. But who knows more than Paul how conflicted the human heart is? He confesses in Romans, 'I know that nothing good dwells within me ... I can will what is right, but I cannot do it' (Romans 7:18). His confidence is completely in God so, despite the fact that he is about to lose his life at the whim of a madman, he can proclaim, 'I know the one in whom I have put my trust, and I am sure that he is able to guard until that day what I have entrusted to him (2 Timothy 1:12). Paul is certain that God will meet him with 'a crown of righteousness', not because he has been good, but because he has loved the Lord and 'longed for his appearing' (verse 8).

To 'fight the good fight' we must simply offer God our conflicted hearts and set out each day to represent God in the world. The best we have may not be all that good but, if we offer it to God like the child who gave Jesus his two fish, God can feed a multitude and make the kingdom shine right through it.

Send me out into this day, dear God, confident in your power within me.

Paul for today

Notes based on the New Revised Standard Version by

Janet Corlett

Janet Corlett is a Methodist minister now working in Bermondsey, London. Before training for ministry, Janet was an agricultural scientist and worked in the Philippines, India, Zimbabwe and Italy. She has since worked as a mission partner in the Bay Islands, Honduras.

2 Sharing good news

Acts 22:1-21

Speaking the same language

While studying agriculture in the Philippines, I took a jeepney ride to visit the famous Pagsanjan Falls. The best way to see the waterfall is by boat and I could hear the driver discussing with the boatman just how much they could charge this tourist. When I asked them a question in Tagalog their attitude towards me suddenly changed. Not only did I get a bargain price, but my beginner's Tagalog was stretched to the limit as they wanted a real conversation and wanted to know how I knew their language.

Paul was on the point of being killed by an angry mob in the temple (21:36) when first of all he surprised the Roman soldiers by speaking fluent Greek (21:37), then silenced the crowd by speaking Hebrew (22:2). Once he had their attention, he was able to tell them his dramatic story of conversion and calling. He 'spoke their language' and so communicated successfully on many levels, speaking to their context, their world view, their history and their aspirations.

Read through the passage again and pick out all the words or phrases that define Paul's multifaceted identity.

How do I define my identity? Can I speak the language of those with whom I desire to share the good news?

Who am I?

Romans 3:1-20

The postmodern identity prevalent in countries like the UK leads people to pride in being non-judgemental and strongly resists the identity of 'sinner'. In the 2009 song 'The Fear', Lily Allen describes, somewhat tongue-in-cheek, the individualistic, image-conscious identity of someone seeking fame, fortune and the perfect body. 'Now I'm not a saint but I'm not a sinner', she proclaims in one breath, and then admits to confusion in the next breath; to not knowing what is right, or real, or how to feel. All the freedom she thought she had in being and buying her way into a secure identity has only left her insecure and anxious.

In his letter to the Romans, Paul is clear that both Jews and Gentiles share a common identity before God; we are all sinners, but loved sinners, reconciled to God in Christ. In today's reading Paul concentrates full-square on our identity as sinners. He seems particularly concerned with how we talk, and mentions throats, tongues, lips and mouths. Perhaps Paul concentrates on our speech to remind us that much of what we say to God and to others easily becomes pure self-justification. We're not saints but then we are really not sinners either. Perhaps only when our tongue is still and we stop making excuses for ourselves can we really listen to God. When we listen to God and become aware of God's loving gaze upon us, we become more aware of both our disease and our cure.

Can I be silent and still for long enough to hear what God wants to say to me?

The necessity of humility of branches

Romans 11:11-24

When Saul met Jesus on the road to Damascus, he was challenged to turn from being a Christ-persecutor to become a Christ-follower, but this did not mean he stopped being a Jew. At the point Paul is writing to the Romans, there was no separate Christian religion, rather the followers of 'the Way' (Acts) formed a small sectarian group or faction within Judaism. This group had grown quite rapidly in Rome through welcoming people whether they were ethnically Jewish or not. It is possible that Jewish followers of Jesus, returning to Rome after a time of expulsion, had found a predominantly Gentile group meeting in the name of Christ. Perhaps there were tensions between Jewish and Gentile Christ-followers as they sought to understand their common life and faith. Paul speaks to them using the metaphor of grafted olive branches.

I don't know much about olive grafting but as a scientist I spent several years studying drought-tolerance in the fruit tree *Ziziphus mauritiana* (or Indian jujube). Cuttings of heavy-cropping (cultivated) trees were grafted on to wild rootstocks that had vigorous and deep taproots. The deep and spreading roots meant that the trees could produce fruit in the semi-desert and even in years of drought when other crops failed. Paul's metaphor of the olive tree is 'contrary to nature' as he envisages wild branches (Gentiles) grafted into the cultivated root (Israel or Yahweh?). None of the branches should feel superior to any others though, since we all depend equally on the living water that comes to us from God, our deep and spreading root.

Are there people in my church that I look down on for being too liberal or too conservative?

Lord, give me the humility of a branch that knows its reliance on the richness of the holy root.

Essential marks of Christian identity

Romans 14:13-23

When Christians of different ethnicities, cultures, traditions and denominations meet together, there can be many stumbling blocks to unity in worship and witness. When I lived in South India I learnt to take off my sandals and cover my head when entering a church. 'Walking in love', I also wore modest clothes and sat on the women's side of the church. Much energy can be wasted in arguments around what should be seen as essential or non-essential marks of Christian identity. Even more damaging can be the reflex of condemnation towards the visiting Christian who innocently and unwittingly breaks some cultural or denominational taboo in the host church. As a mission partner in Utila, Honduras, I unintentionally caused offence by wearing sandals in church instead of 'proper' shoes, and when I allowed children to come behind the communion rail and into the pulpit. Sometimes, however, I had to choose between pursuing peace and pursuing righteousness when some taboos needed challenging, such as the white supremacy that resisted inter-ethnic marriages.

Attitudes to food and drink can still cause deep divisions between Christians, especially when the food and drink in question is the bread and wine of that shared sacramental meal meant to celebrate our unity in Christ. Paul exhorts the multi-cultural church in Rome to expend their energy in removing stumbling blocks and in 'mutual upbuilding' (verse 19) rather than passing judgement and creating divisions. Christian identity then is found not in food and drink but in righteousness, peace and joy in the Holy Spirit.

God, please give me the grace to walk in love with my fellow Christians and to pursue what makes for righteousness, peace and joy.

Is your inside like your outside?

Galatians 2:1-10

Appearances can be deceiving. I have an all-time favourite visual-aid to illustrate this point. I open a can of dog-food using a can-opener or ring-pull, and then ask the children in the congregation if they want to eat a spoonful. They express disgust because it looks like dog-food and they imagine it smells and tastes like dog-food too. No one has ever taken up the challenge because only I know that the contents have been surreptitiously replaced with chopped-up chocolate bars and chocolate mousse.

The theme of outward appearance and inner reality runs through the whole of today's reading, just as Paul's attack on the 'circumcision fanatics' runs through the whole epistle. The central question is whether or not to require new followers of Christ to prove their new identity by taking on the external marks of God's chosen people. In Paul's context these external marks were circumcision and the food laws. Paul firmly rejects them as 'non-essential' and as threatening to the gospel of justification through faith in Christ (2:16). What matters is what is on the inside, not the outside, of the can.

Paul also takes a dig at those who were acknowledged as leaders and pillars (verses 2, 6, 9) because he received nothing from them that he had not already received from God. Paul was a mystic as well as a pastoral theologian, and from his conversion onwards was open to God's leading through dreams, visions and ecstatic experience in prayer. These were not seen by Paul as spiritual experience for its own sake, but as an impetus towards growth and action.

What marks of 'belonging' do I expect of new Christians besides their faith in Jesus Christ? Have I ever felt, during my prayers, the surprising/close/mysterious presence of God? How has this prompted me to action?

Janet Corlett

Our identity 'in Christ'

Galatians 3:15-29

Paul continues his passionate defence of 'justification by faith' over and against the 'circumcision fanatics'. Now he draws his argument from salvation history, going back to the promises declared to Abraham as the father of all those who believe (3:8). Paul is reminding his readers that, even before the covenant command to circumcise (Genesis 17:10), God's promises were made to Abram and his offspring, and Abram was reckoned as righteous because of his belief (Genesis 15:6).

Paul then lays out his vision of what it means to be part of the new covenant 'in Christ'. Sometimes we skim over the words 'in Christ'; missing the power they held for Paul as a description of the new personal and communal identity of the Christian. This is a radical shift in identity for those who have died to sin 'in Christ' and, through the power of the resurrection, have become signs and participants in the 'new creation'. Here and elsewhere, we can discern that Paul expects more than unity 'in Christ'. He also expects a radical equality that challenges and subverts the patterns of society now as then.

When I was training for ministry in Birmingham, I had the privilege of placements at several Sikh gurdwaras. The birth of the Sikh religion in India challenged the inequalities and conflicts between castes and between faiths (Hindu and Muslim). For Sikhs, eating together is central and is a sign of breaking down caste barriers and promoting equality. The first guru insisted that all should eat together first in order to create a community fit to worship together.

What does it mean for me to be 'in Christ', and 'in Christ' with others? Are there any ways of increasing the sharing, communal and hospitable character of the Christian group to which I belong?

Janet Corlett

New heart, new lips and new feet

Romans 10:5-15

Today's reading is full of quotes from and allusions to the Hebrew scriptures. If the Jews in Rome wanted a message of hope and restoration after exile and oppression, they might have focused on Deuteronomy 30. This text points to the time when the redeemed will be marked out, not by circumcision of the flesh, but by the circumcision of the heart (Deuteronomy 30:6). Paul asserts that these longed-for promises have come to fulfilment in Jesus Christ. In addition, the gospel is now global – and from the people of Israel good news has gone out to all nations – for there is no distinction. Note the astonishing conversion from mouths that were full of cursing and lips that were venomous (Romans 3:13-14) to lips now kissed by the word of faith and mouths filled with the proclamation 'Jesus is Lord'. What a glorious contrast between feet that were swift to shed blood (Romans 3:15) and the beautiful feet that bring good news!

The end of the reading brings us our own commission to proclaim Christ, but we can proclaim only what we have heard, absorbed and experienced for ourselves. One of my most embarrassing failures in proclamation happened when I was on a student mission to Stockport in 1983. We were leading a school assembly and I was entrusted with the task of promoting a concert starring the young Martyn Joseph (see www.martynjoseph.net). My team members were aghast at my half-hearted efforts and the true fans distraught. The problem was that I had been sent to proclaim one I had never heard, so no wonder the pupils failed to believe and respond! Hopefully I did a little better at sharing my enthusiasm for Christ.

Thank you, Jesus, that you are always near me. Fill my mind, speak through my lips and live in my heart.

Paul for today

3 Grace talk: God-walk

Romans 3:21-31

Christ crucified and grace

Coming as I do from a context where being HIV positive or negative is usually, but erroneously, linked with how 'low' or 'high' one is on the scale of personal morals and religiosity, today's text offers a reassuring corrective that refills my spiritual supplies. For Paul emphasises that justification, acceptance and vindication in front of God (verse 24) are spiritual gifts given through divine grace; received through faith apart from works of merit (verse 22) and accessible to all of us, irrespective of our age, gender, religious creed, political persuasion, geographical location, sexuality or any other human identity-defining and differentiating characteristic.

The first reason why my HIV status cannot be a reliable measure to gauge my spiritual status is given in verse 23: 'For all have sinned ...' If this is so and the results from an HIV test were a reliable indicator to measure this 'sinning and falling short', then all of us should be HIV positive. Right? Thankfully this is not the case because 'spiritual righteousness' and 'safeness from disease-causing microbes and viruses' are not one and the same thing. Second, and probably equal in importance, this Pauline text tells us that all people, whether HIV positive, negative or HIV 'sero-status blind', are 'justified freely' by God's grace (verse 24). So no boasting!

Dear Lord, we give up our feelings of self-righteousness, our judgemental attitudes and our faulty beliefs. Open our hearts for change, love and forgiveness.

Notes based on the New International Version by

Gideon Byamugisha

Canon Gideon Byamugisha is an Anglican priest, theologian and public health activist who has lived and ministered openly with HIV since 1992. His ministry against HIV and AIDS stigma and discrimination has supported people living with HIV in more than fifty countries, earned him many friends worldwide and attracted many awards, including the 2009 Niwano Peace Prize and an honorary doctorate from the University of Botswana.

Foolishness and wisdom

1 Corinthians 1:18 – 2:2

When AIDS first appeared on the scene in the early 1980s, those who would test HIV positive would be referred to as 'AIDS victims', paying for their ignorance and licentiousness. Later, when treatment became possible, our counsellors and doctors delighted in using a very patronising term: 'our clients'. Now, the counsellors, medical experts and policy makers are much wiser: they refer to us as 'partners', after realising that there is unique knowledge and wisdom that people living with HIV bring to the table of HIV and AIDS prevention, care and management, coming out of our lived experience. That experience interrogates taken-for-granted paradigms, existing traditions and dominant research questions, helping, in the end, to extend boundaries of knowledge, values and science.

To Paul, the logic of locating wisdom and power in a 'crucified victim' appeared warped from the point of view of those who were stuck in the traditional paradigms of thinking about God, salvation, liberation and redemption (verse 18). Yet from the point of view of those who were willing to be open to the possibility, reality and experience of Jesus' resurrection, it was an acknowledgement that God could (and often did) turn the world upside down and reverse statuses (verse 25). Through divine empowerment processes and divine liberation arrangements, the oppressed, marginalised and humiliated can – to use a now popular phrase – 'talk back', making God's foolishness wiser than human wisdom.

Lord, in our search for safer, healthier and more peaceful living; give us new understandings of 'foolishness' and 'wisdom' and of 'weakness' and 'power'.

Newness of life

Romans 6:1-14

Paul continues his salvation theme of grace, arguing that, in Christ and by grace, the believer moves from 'works' to 'faith', from 'sin' to 'redemption' and from 'death' to 'life'. As Paul's readers of this piece of scripture will soon discover, such a presentation of the transformative effect of faith in God through Christ offers a practical and radical hope for unlimited breakthroughs against human sin (verse 2). New life for a believer is possible, minus the human propensity to sin. Isn't that transformation as wonderful as it is dramatic?

On the other hand, is there not a risk of oversimplication that could lead to chronic guilt, repeated depression and trauma, when believers fail to see that dramatic transformation in their lives? How new would 'new' be if people still see evidence of social, economic, political, cultural and personal sins in their lived experience?

From your reading of Paul, and from your own observations, is 'newness of life' a product of grace that has already arrived to a believer and to Christian communities and congregations, or is it still 'work in progress' until Jesus' return? How do we take the wonderful teaching laid down in verse 14 without at the same time creating 'first-class', 'club' and 'economy class' Christians who are judged so according to how they successfully avoid (or hide) sin both in personal lives and in the public square?

We thank you for the divine grace and newness of life promised through, revealed by, lived with, and hoped for in Jesus Christ.

Freedom is for freeing

Galatians 5:1, 13-26

To people facing various forms of slavery, like bonded labour, gender-based violence, racism or domination and bondage in their political, cultural, religious, spiritual and structural forms, this Pauline text will be heard, interpreted, applied and lived differently according to their different contexts. It is also a very rich text whose theological and spiritual fields can never be mined exhaustively.

My favourite verse in this passage is verse one, which gives me the spiritual energy to be 'me' in the battle against HIV and AIDS-related stigma, shame, denial, discrimination, inaction and mis-action (SSDDIM). Every time I read it, I visualise Jesus in front of Pilate and a religious crowd of self-righteous, finger-pointing and power-hungry leaders of that time: 'The chief priests accused him of many things. So again Pilate asked him, "Aren't you going to answer? See how many things they are accusing you of?" But Jesus still made no reply, and Pilate was amazed' (Mark 15:3-5). Jesus opts to take the freedom to be himself rather than being enslaved by the self-serving crowds. One young man who was promised freedom from jail if he could abdicate himself, his beliefs and his spirit refused the offer, saying he would rather die in prison than surrender all that defines who he is. Freedom is for freeing indeed! For what else can be said? Someone who chooses to die in prison, rather than being enslaved, dies free, and another, who chooses the cross rather than cheap popularity, not only dies free but frees others in the process!

God, may we not enslave but lead in a way that frees people to be the best they can be.

A different relationship

Philemon 1:1-22

Many of us in the HIV and AIDS prevention movement look at the continuing, but preventable and controllable, infections, illnesses and deaths, with two lenses. One lens looks at these realities as biological conditions that require biomedical interventions. The other lens, however, looks at them as symptomatic of things that have gone wrong in the way we relate with one another as humans in various spheres of life: for example, gender and sexuality, reproduction, trade, societal governance, religion and international relations.

A relationship can be 'life-defending', 'life-enhancing' and 'life-transforming' or it can be 'life-threatening', 'life-reducing', 'life-taking' and 'life-wasting'. Paul is looking for a different relationship between Philemon and Onesimus that falls into the first set of categories, even if it is countercultural to the Roman and Jewish context of that time – a context in which a runaway slave (and, some think, a former thief, from Paul's reference to Onesimus wronging Philemon and owing him money, in verse 18) would have been punished severely or even executed. In seeking that different relationship, Paul is at pains not to abuse his relationship with Philemon by commanding him what to do or threatening him with excommunication if he doesn't oblige. He chooses instead to use a transformative approach that could bring forgiveness and healing between Onesimus and Philemon, and a sense of justice to the wronged party, by promising to refund what was stolen.

This letter should help us all to review our own beliefs, attitudes and relationships that breed and sustain domination and other life-wasting practices.

Help us, Lord, to pledge ourselves to relationships that enhance life, health and peace.

Challenging empire

Romans 13:1-14

Paul is writing to a Christian community living within a context of imperial authority that could be brutal and lethal to anyone deemed 'not in line'. But it is very clear, right from chapter one, that his message is counter-imperial. Paul seems to be telling his hearers: Wisely, prayerfully and lovingly, submit to the gospel of Christ, not to Caesar's authority. In this gospel of Christ we are more than conquerors when imperial terror imposes on us hardship, distress, persecution, peril and sword (chapter 8). Whatever happens, we should not be conformed to this age (chapter 12), for the night is gone and the day is near (chapter 13). But, do not be naïve about the possible bullying, underhand methods and violence imperial power can employ to get the better of you – so submit to the authorities, not only because of possible punishment, but because of conscience and conviction to outdo the empire in living, demonstrating and modelling love (verse 10).

Two things challenge, relativise and subvert empire in this text. First, it is not Rome's virtue nor her gods that allow Rome to have the authority she is misusing. Second, reference to empire with words such as 'fear', 'wrath', 'violence' and 'bloodshed' is contrasted with Christ's community of 'love', 'blessing', 'care' and 'non-violence'. Is there a possibility that Paul is saying more than what meets the eye when he says 'Honour the imperial authorities'? Could it be another subversion of empire?

Lord, teach us to be as wise as serpents and as innocent as doves.

Gideon Byamugisha

The depth and breadth of love

1 Corinthians 13:1-8

One day I heard a sermon narrating a tradition concerning John, the disciple Jesus loved most. This preacher told us that Elder John grew to a very advanced age. In the circumstances, his disciples began beseeching him to give them the most important of the messages and life guides he had ever shared with them. Elder John obliged and motioned them to sit down and hear the message. 'Are you ready to hear my new message to you?' Elder John asked. They all replied in the affirmative. And the new message came: 'My children, love one another!'

The preacher told us that John's audience was totally disappointed. When their Elder asked why, they said it was because he had told them what he had always told them. They wanted something new, something deeper, broader and more potent. Elder John asked his disciples to give him a week of prayer and fasting that he might consult God about the message to give them. They agreed. When D-Day came, they surrounded his bed and waited. 'Are you ready for the new message?' Elder John asked. Then the new message came: 'My children love one another!' What do you think was the reaction of Elder John's disciples this time round?

In your opinion, is there anything in life that is deeper, broader or more important than love? And you and I, how do we score on the depth and breadth of the subject Paul is writing about in this text? Evaluate yourself by removing the word 'love' wherever it appears in this passage; replace it with your name and read the text again up to verse 8. What do you see unfolding as you read?

Teach us to love you, God, ourselves and our neighbours as we should. Forgive us when we fail.

Gideon Byamugisha

Paul for today

Notes based on the New Revised Standard Version by

Lori Rizzo

For Lori's biography, see p.213.

4 Living letters

1 Corinthians 1:10-16

You gotta have heart

Q: What do the church and Noah's ark have in common?

A: If it wasn't for the storm outside, you wouldn't put up with the stink inside.

It's one of those jokes where you laugh and simultaneously pick at a scab. Churches can be so disappointing. We expect the people inside them to love just like Jesus; turns out they are as insensitive and impatient as we are ourselves. There are plenty of parishes where Christ is worshipped and neighbour loved; however, the definition of church in current culture is an institution that excludes, judges and claims to know God better than the rest of us. As many say, 'I am spiritual, not religious' – religion sounds like the church, and who needs that!

Except that, as followers of Jesus, we are to love what he loves, and Christ gave his life for the church. All the people Jesus healed have died, but the church is his living work. Karl Marx is famous for saying, 'Religion is the opium of the people,' but few know the rest of the quote: 'It is the heart of a heartless world.' Even Marx understood that the church is our collective heart. In a world where human lives, God's greatest creations, are traded as commodities for profit, the church is called to recollect within us the truth of who we are in Christ. We need each other to keep the lights on until the dove comes back to the Ark with an olive branch, and we can walk all around God's heaven.

No camping

1 Corinthians 3:1-17

Paul lists the fruits of the Spirit as 'love, joy, peace, patience, kindness, generosity, faithfulness, gentleness, and self-control' (Galatians 5:22). It would make sense that 'communities of the Spirit' (churches) would exhibit these qualities. The sad reality is that when churches make the news these days it is more often for fighting than for generosity. I don't know what they're fighting about in your corner of the kingdom, but in the US we're fighting about sex. There are camps. I am part of one. I once heard someone from the other camp lecture on this issue. As he spoke, the sounds of people digging in behind their positions began to really concern me. I feared that someone was going to notice I wasn't purring along to the party line. Then he said, 'This is my position, but I could be wrong.' All at once, the entire room was against him. There was talk about excluding him from morning chapel services. I went up to him and whispered, 'I completely disagree with you, but I could be wrong.'

My wife and I were married this summer. We asked God to bless our union, so I must be pretty sure of the correctness of my position, but I could be wrong. I mean it. Thank God, my salvation is not dependent on being on the right side of this argument. Thank God, we will all be able to stand in God's presence because of the completed work of Jesus Christ on the cross, and nothing else.

Help me today, O God, to think less about how I am right and more about how your Spirit dwells within us all.

Whole food

1 Corinthians 11:17-29

I am an Anglican, so I have a high view of the sacraments, especially that weekly feast we call Holy Communion. When the celebrant speaks Christ's own words, handed down for two thousand years, they become a touchstone connecting us to every believer from the Beloved Disciple who rested his head on the Lord's shoulder as he dipped the bread, to the saints, to sisters and brothers near and far. My Eastern Orthodox friends call it 'the mystical feast', a meal that takes place outside human time. My working week takes me into some very sad realities. When Sunday comes, I am famished for a glimpse of life within God's dominion.

Paul uses strong words in response to the practice of the Corinthians. Their 'feast' is just business as usual: the rich wasting, the poor wanting. The notion that they can drag their worldly privileges and superficial titles into this fellowship is distasteful in the extreme. God will not bless disparity and, as a result, they're getting junk food. If you keep eating that stuff, you'll get sick.

The Eucharist is the ultimate wholefood because it heals what is broken inside us. Not by magic, but by communion. There are no individual tickets; the sacrament is always celebrated by a community that minimally includes those gathered around the table, but I think that, the broader we extend our communion to include the world outside our churches, the brighter will be our feast, the deeper will be our blessing.

Enlighten the eyes of our hearts, dear Lord, so that we can 'discern your body' in those around us, and so share your goodness throughout the world.

Communion

2 Corinthians 8:1-15

Consider Paul, principal theologian of the first-century church, taking up a collection for the poor. Shouldn't he be settling the law-versus-grace debate instead of passing the hat? But this collection is no mere task for Paul. There is a terrible famine in Jerusalem: widows and children who have depended on the church for charity are being turned away. The elders aren't fans of Paul's 'Gospel to the Gentiles', and the epistle of James (of Jerusalem) with its emphasis on works, is often set against Paul's epistles. Yet, on this point, both men could easily ask, 'If a brother or sister is naked and lacks daily food, and one of you says to them, "Go in peace; keep warm and eat your fill", and yet you do not supply their bodily needs, what is the good of that?' (James 2:15-16). No preacher has proclaimed God's grace better than a deacon giving away a bag of groceries.

The collection is about more than charity. Early Christians shared common rites to help them enter into the gospel story, but the power of the sacrament is not in their liturgy but their unity, around the table, but also to every other person who names Jesus as Lord. The love feast spills over, transcending walls, borders, cultures and class. The Corinthians enter into worship hungry for the Spirit, which is a good thing, but when worship unites you to people who are starving, you just can't walk away and say, 'Praise God and see you later'. If they desire the Spirit to be present amongst them, they must learn to love as God does.

God of my heart, let me love you, and all your children, in Spirit and in truth.

Lori Rizzo

Jesus is coming – look holy

1 Thessalonians 4:1-12

The Thessalonians were known throughout the early church for their generous hospitality, genuine conversion, and fervent expectation of Christ's return. They are a congregation that greets every morning wondering if this will be the 'day of the Lord'.

The city is always described as 'wealthy and fortunate'. It was considered a 'free state' as Rome had no army stationed there to enforce Caesar's rule. The church of Thessalonica was mainly Greeks who left the chaos of polytheism and were attracted by this story of a God who keeps his promises. They came to faith when Paul taught in the local synagogue, until he was run off as a troublemaker. This letter is the apostle's way to reconnect with them, to encourage and correct. In today's passage Paul is essentially asking, 'OK, so you get that the Lord can return any day now, what do you want to be doing when he gets here?' His counsel to them: to the best of your abilities, strive to keep your relationships clean. Don't take justice into your own hands. Live quietly, trust me and wait.

Evelyn Underhill used to keep the word 'Eternity' over her desk. It's a challenging spiritual discipline, but one I think we are lacking in the 21st-century church – this awareness that Christ could come in at any time and rock our world. Clearly, we would all care a lot less about how we measure up by the world's standards. Instead, we'd be busy preparing the world for his arrival.

Lord Jesus, allow me to live this day in expectation of your arrival, so that all I do is with you in mind.

Lori Rizzo

Share the gospel, share yourself

1 Thessalonians 2:1-12

This week in American sports, a famous player wrote 'John 3:16' on his face during a big game. As a result, millions of fans searched the verse online. That's one way of proclaiming the gospel! Paul had a different idea. He shared himself as a way to convey how very dear these Thessalonians had become to him. Consider the gift from their point of view. Paul is a well-learned Jewish rabbi, and they are gentiles, 'idol-worshippers', 'outsiders'. You are walking home one day, your arms full of too many packages. One slip and your potatoes are rolling all over the street. Out of nowhere, someone scoops them up and hands them back to you. 'Here you go, Rosa. I am sure you will make a great dinner of these for your family. Please say hello to your husband for me.' Huh? He's a rabbi and yet he bends down to help me? Knows my name?

I can read John 3:16 in Greek but I still don't get it. I agree that the gospel is most perfectly revealed in the fact that 'God so loved the world that he sent his Son', but it's hard to grasp. A little mitzvah breaks it down for me. It makes me wonder, 'If a stranger can show me such favour, perhaps it is possible that God could smile upon me.'

Another American, Anne Herbert, offers this challenge: 'Practise random acts of kindness and senseless acts of beauty.' You may not generate millions of Bible searches, but you might inspire some prayer.

Show me how to preach the gospel today, dear God, so that everyone may come to grasp your unfathomable love.

Lori Rizzo

Comforter

2 Corinthians 3:1-11

One way I pay bills is teaching maths to teenagers. They think the trick is to memorise everything. I agree when it comes to tables and rules but I insist they understand concepts. Maths problems can be crafty. If you can grasp the thinking, then you can follow their lead to the answer.

I've tried to memorise the Ten Commandments but I never get them right. I know the last one is against coveting, which is sticky. I am fairly certain of my capacity to avoid adultery with my neighbour's wife but I find it impossible not to covet their vacation. It is going to be really hard to listen to them tell me about all the great food and beaches. Left to my own devices, I'd avoid them till winter, except for this gnawing feeling from God that I am called to be present and pay attention.

This is why I always smile when I hear the Holy Spirit called 'the comforter'. 'Comfortable' is sitting alone sulking. Forcing me to love someone when I don't want to is not. When I think that Paul's critics accused him of making it too easy for the gentiles to join the faith, I have to laugh. Does anyone really think that having the third person of the Trinity living inside you is easier than obeying a list of rules?

The author of Hebrews describes God as a 'consuming fire' (12:29). How do you live with a consuming fire? You feed it until all that's left in your heart is that which only God can satisfy.

Dear Jesus, set my heart today where true joys are to be found.

Contested sites

1 Promised or stolen land?

Genesis 12:1-7

So Abram went

'There were four Christians, four Muslims and four Jews who went on a trip to the Holy Land.' It sounds like the beginning of a bad joke, but in November 2010 twelve of us set out from the UK sponsored by St Ethelburga's Centre for Reconciliation. We spent ten days sharing in each other's worship, visiting holy sites and exploring elements of the Israeli–Palestinian conflict. The following reflections are part of a continuing dialogue between two members of the group about the experience and the Israeli–Palestinian conflict.

In Genesis, Abraham is a traveller who leaves the comfort of home to journey into unknown territory. As I (Ray) entered into our journey, I felt I was continually challenged to lay down my preconceived ideas of what I was going to find. As a European Christian I found myself challenged to reflect upon how I related to the conflict, how easily words of condemnation had been part of my narrative. I felt called to sojourn the complexities and confusions, to be careful and thoughtful in my speech, to recognise I was in unknown territory, but also that in this journey was a promise that, if faithfully undertaken, I would more deeply understand the nature of God's healing and peace.

Use this interfaith prayer for peace during the week:

O God, the source of life and peace,
Give to us and help us strive for:
Understanding that puts an end to strife;
Mercy that quenches hatred, and
Forgiveness that overcomes vengeance.
Empower all people to live in your law of love.

adapted from a Pax Christi prayer card
(www.paxchristi.org.uk)

Notes based on the New Revised Standard Version and the Hebrew Bible by

Debbie Young-Somers and Ray Gaston

Rabbi Debbie Young-Somers is part of the rabbinic team at West London Synagogue. She has a background in interfaith work, and appears regularly on Radio 2's *Pause for Thought*.
Revd Ray Gaston is Interfaith Tutor and Enabler at the Queen's Foundation for Ecumenical Theological Education and the Birmingham District of the Methodist Church.

'Please let there be no strife'

Genesis 13:5-12

Abraham and Lot recognise there is a problem. They cannot continue as they are, and agree to a solution that will allow them both dignity and livelihood. Pesikta Rabbati (a homiletic Jewish commentary from around 845 CE) suggests that there was plenty of land to accommodate both the families; the problem was the fighting between the shepherds. The commentary continues that, when people cannot get along, even the most spacious land is not big enough. Sometimes, perhaps, we need to acknowledge when a relationship is beyond repair, and space is what is needed. In his pocket book *Help Us to Divorce* (Vintage 2004), Amos Oz makes this analogy with the current conflict in the Holy Land. He suggests that the Israelis and Palestinians are trapped in a marriage that has broken down beyond repair, and they need mediators and lawyers to help them divide up the family silver, books and CDs so that each can continue with their lives. There has been unacceptable behaviour from both partners in the relationship and it will probably take time for them to face each other again.

On the other hand, the total lack of contact between the two sides may also be exacerbating the problem, allowing each to dehumanise the other. Many charities are working to bring people together across the divide, while others are working hard to establish a two-state solution from both sides. One such charity, One Voice, surveyed both communities and found that over seventy per cent on both sides are willing to tolerate a two-state solution. Getting the balance right between knowing each other and having one's own space is tricky, in political as well as personal relationships, but important to get right.

'The water is ours!'

Genesis 26:12-22

This passage shows Isaac desperately trying to establish an encampment with accessible water and being bullied away by the Philistines. Resources remain an important element in many conflicts today, and in Israel and Palestine water is a key part of this. Water has always been an important and scarce resource in the Middle East and such resources are, of course, key elements in conflict resolution. When people have their basic human needs met (food, water, security, freedom of movement, employment), they are better placed to consider the humanity of others.

On our trip to Israel and Palestine last year, we all spent the night with Palestinian families near Bethlehem. On the one hand, I (Debbie) was surprised by the size of the homes we stayed in, with large TVs and hi-fis. On the other hand, these were the families that were capable of putting us up (many others were not), and the large homes encompassed three or four generations of one family. Our host was working two different jobs with no security, and none of us showered while staying there, as they hadn't had a water supply for six weeks. They had to purchase tanks of water, making this precious resource even more limited in its use. These scarce resources can be used almost as a weapon and, while Israel understandably wishes to ensure the security of her population's water supply, the Torah also reminds us many times that the stranger must be looked after too, not only your own kin.

What's been left out?

Genesis 31:1-3, 22-24, 45-33

No doubt you have read the selected passages from Genesis 31 set for today. Aren't you interested in exploring what's been left out of the story and why? How can we reflect on this complex engagement between Laban and Jacob without exploring the whole text? These are the questions that we wrestled with when given these texts. Our questioning of what was important in this chapter led us to reflect again on how seeking understanding of the Israeli–Palestinian conflict is so dependent on different interpretations of the same events and differing understandings of what is important in the history of the two peoples involved. It is also a reminder of our tendency to favour one narrative at the expense of another, which we can easily edit out entirely.

In our text, an uneasy truce is achieved by Laban and Jacob, who have both engaged in deception and trickery in their power struggles. However, such a limited settlement still seems to elude the contemporary conflict as negotiations towards a conclusive peace once again stutter and stall. So often we find ourselves becoming pro-Israeli or pro-Palestinian, adopting a narrative of one side or the other. But as Cornel West has pointed out: 'We must keep in touch with the humanity of both sides' (in 'Thoughts on Anti-Semitism' by Penny Rosenwasser, *Tikkun Magazine*, July/August 2002) even when we may be critiquing the particular actions of one.

On our visit we stayed at Neve Shalom /Wahat al Salam (Oasis of Peace). At this place, people live together as a binational community and the school curriculum helps children explore the narratives of both peoples. On a visit to the port of Jaffa, we took a 'two narratives tour' of the city, hearing each community's interpretation of particular events that had taken place there.

Where do you find your sympathies drawn in the Israeli–Palestinian conflict? How might you learn more of the narrative and thus 'keep in touch with the humanity' of the other side?

Wrestling with God

Deuteronomy 11:22-25

Biblical scholarship tells us that Deuteronomy was written by Israelites taken into exile by the Babylonians. It is important to remember that this is a text of a broken and defeated people, crushed by a vicious empire. The writer(s) are seeking to understand how this disaster has befallen them. And in exploring this they adopt a self-critical approach, 'We have not been faithful enough to God's way so we have lost the land', into which context the assertions of our reading today must be put.

Too often the Israeli–Palestinian conflict and discussion about it is fuelled by a way of reading scripture that owes more to biblical literalism than thoughtful exploration. I (Ray) recently watched a debate on Revelation TV between Christian Zionist Calvin Smith and an opponent, Stephen Sizer. This 'debate' consisted of the two men throwing biblical quotes at one another as they sought to assert divine sanction in support of their perspective. Very little light is generated from such an encounter.

At the heart of the texts we share as Jews and Christians is the name 'Israel', which means striving, wrestling with God. Too often we read scripture as a way to 'back up our argument' rather than allowing the text, and an understanding of the context in which it was written, to challenge our prejudices. The Bible also challenges us with numerous stories of God coming in and through the stranger and the outsider. God speaks to us in the challenge we face from those with different opinions and different understandings of faith from ourselves.

The temptation is to cut ourselves off from difference or to refuse truly to listen to others with different views, and simply engage in argumentation. It is important that we don't import that difficulty to the UK, that we don't cut ourselves off from those with different opinions and experiences of the conflict.

Mount Gerazim and Mount Ebal

Deuteronomy 11:29-32

Mount Gerazim, for blessing, and Mount Ebal, for curse, perhaps represent our human tendency to try to put things into neat boxes, black and white, blessing and curse, good and evil. Of course, the reality of human existence is far more complicated than this, however much we might wish it were otherwise. Whenever we try to simplify situations like the conflict in the Holy Land, we ignore real human pain and trauma, on one side or the other.

The two mountains might also represent other dichotomies, both in the lives of the Israelite tribes and in the ongoing conflict in the land today. Dichotomies such as politics and religion, which are often separated out and one side ignored, in reality generally walk hand in hand, or are entwined in invisible ways. In this political–religious dichotomy we regularly see Christian–Jewish–Muslim trialogues becoming mired, with different agendas from the different parties. Jews and Muslims may feel they must defend 'their' side and make defences they would never make in their own communities, while Christians feel they must pick a side (or an unmoving mountain) and become conduits of blind argumentation.

Our experience together travelling through the various narratives of the land taught us much. By listening to the many small and large conflicts, we were awakened to those whose stance was rigid and unmoving, like a mountain, as well as to those who were willing to be more open and flexible. We met many who understood how the political and the religious could both divide and unite; these were the ones living with deep complexities and nuance, and they showed us that it is rarely possible to make a simple division between good and evil, political and religious, us and them.

Against idolatry

Deuteronomy 12:29-32

We were standing on the rooftop looking out over the divided town of Barta'a: Muhammed, myself (Ray) and Debbie. Muslim, Christian and Jew. The sun had just set and we anticipated together, without speaking, that it would soon be the time for the Adhan, the call to prayer. The rest of the party had descended the stairs as we waited in silence. And then it began, a moment of unity, as the Adhan resounded from the minarets on either side of the border and this divided town, including the three of us, united in prayer. That was the beauty of our pilgrimage: the sharing of prayer, our mutual attraction to prayer; the experience of welcoming shabbat in an Orthodox synagogue in Jerusalem; being present at Eid prayers in a village in Northern Israel; sitting beside Sumaira, a Muslim woman, in the Church of the Holy Sepulchure as she helped me – a Christian – appreciate the beauty of the place.

The idols that are at risk of taking us away from 'diligent' faith are the easy political slogans, the ideologies that close our hearts to others. Sharing our spiritual practices helps us to move closer to each other and truly to worship God as we seek healing and peace. The late Krister Stendhal once said that we should seek to cultivate 'holy envy' in ourselves, a feeling of attraction to the best in religions other than our own.

In the land known as 'holy' can we come to an awareness of prayer uniting us in the heart of God, even though the necessity of boundaries and borders divides?

The All-merciful, may you create a bond of friendship between the descendants of Sarah and the descendents of Hagar.

From 'Thanksgiving after Meals', in *Forms of Prayer* (Movement for Reform Judaism, 2008), p.477

Contested sites

Notes on the Revised Standard Version by

Ann Conway-Jones

Ann Conway-Jones is an Anglican, living in Birmingham, involved in Jewish–Christian relations. She has completed a PhD thesis on Jewish and Christian descriptions of the heavenly temple.

2 'Neither on this mountain nor in Jerusalem'

2 Samuel 7:4-7, 11b-16

A time to plant

This week's readings feature construction and destruction. There is settlement and upheaval. The daily titles are taken from Ecclesiastes 3:1-8, which evokes 'a time for every matter under heaven'.

God travelled with Israel, and then settled with Israel. The desert tabernacle and the first Jerusalem temple (built by David's son Solomon) were designed to contain the uncontainable God. Solomon was well aware of the paradox: 'But will God indeed dwell on the earth? Behold, heaven and the highest heaven cannot contain thee; how much less this house which I have built!' (1 Kings 8:27). Judaism and Christianity have since developed as temple-less religions, and so we mistrust temple rituals, animal sacrifice in particular. But Christianity uses temple theology, the presence of God cradled within the material world, to describe the incarnation, sacraments and the church. We still live with the paradox of a transcendent God who draws near to us through our earthly reality of bodies and buildings. God may be everywhere, but we are not: individuals and communities meet God in particular places.

O God be near us, bless with your presence all who
travel, whether in hope or despair;
and all who seek to put down roots.

A time to gather stones together

1 Kings 6:1-13

For human life to flourish, and for the divine to be present, we need structure: material structures and structures of behaviour. Here the two are linked: the presence of God in 'the house of the Lord' (verse 1) depends on statutes, ordinances and commandments being kept.

The details of the temple building are not easy to follow, but the basic outline is clear. The house had two rooms: the nave and the inner sanctuary. A vestibule stood in front of them, and they were surrounded by various side chambers. This house was not for accommodating worshippers; they gathered in the courtyard outside. It was the dwelling of God, filled with 'the glory of the Lord' (1 Kings 8:11). The inner sanctuary was a windowless cube, for God was thought to dwell 'in thick darkness' (1 Kings 8:12). Inside it were two giant gold-plated cherubim (God's throne), and sheltering under their wings was the ark containing the tablets of the covenant (God's footstool). Only the high priest was to enter the inner sanctuary, once a year.

The temple building encapsulated the message that God is holy, beyond the grasp of human comprehension. Similarly, although our behaviour, relationships and worship provide structures for the presence of God, they do not guarantee anything. We cannot define and contain God; we can but offer a suitably welcoming space.

What structures provide your sacred space?

O God be near us, bless with your presence all who build,
who provide the structures within which communities
can flourish.

A time to mourn

2 Chronicles 36:15-21

The fate of people and temple are intertwined. Here destruction engulfs them both. In 597 BCE, King Nebuchadnezzar of Babylon captured Jerusalem, deported most of the ruling class, and stripped the temple. Ten years later, after an eighteen-month siege, he razed city and temple to the ground, carrying off the remaining temple vessels. What happened to the ark of the covenant has never been established.

These events can be explained in terms of the geopolitics of the region: a small vassal state caught up in the conflict between the Babylonian and Egyptian superpowers. But the authors behind Chronicles, probably compiled around three hundred years later, interpreted them in terms of the divine will. They hung on to faith by seeing the destruction as the wrath of God. The first temple was important to them, perhaps as a focus of unity for quarrelling factions in their own time. They described its vestibule as a tower 120 cubits high reaching up to heaven (2 Chronicles 3:4). Here they stress God's compassion 'on his people and on his dwelling place' (verse 15). But they have to explain the devastation, and do so in terms of punishment for the people's unfaithfulness.

According to 2 Kings 25:12, vinedressers and ploughmen were left behind to tend the land. Not so here: the land is left desolate, keeping a mournful sabbath. There is one faint note of hope: once seventy years have passed, might rebuilding be possible?

When has your life fallen apart?

O God, be near us, bless with your presence all whose lives have been devastated by war.

A time to cast away stones

Matthew 24:1-8

From one destruction to prophecy of another. The Jerusalem temple was indeed rebuilt. Under Herod it became one of the wonders of the ancient world. By the time Matthew's Gospel was written, however, it had once again been destroyed, this time by the Roman army. And once again people of faith were trying to make sense of catastrophic events. Matthew's community remembered Jesus prophesying that not one stone would be left upon another, and interpreting 'wars and rumours of wars' as birth pangs heralding the second coming. As time went by, Christians began berating Jews for putting their trust in a building rather than in God. Justin Martyr, in the second century, said that God foreknew that the Jewish nation would deserve expulsion from Jerusalem; and John Chrysostom, in the fourth, said that, after Christ died on the cross, he destroyed the city of those who had crucified him in order to teach that he was risen, alive and in heaven.

It is one thing to find lessons for one's own community in disaster, as Israel did after the destruction of the first temple; it is another to seize on disaster as a weapon, bludgeoning 'the other'. The destruction of 70 CE turned out to herald the birth of two communities: Christianity and rabbinic Judaism. Both learnt to find the presence of God without a temple. But the Christian rhetoric of blame has left a bitter legacy.

Who are the opportunists seeking to make political or theological capital out of today's disasters?

O God, be near us, bless with your presence all who fear for the future.

A time to embrace

John 4:4-7, 19-24

A Jew and a Samaritan meet at the well of Jacob, a patriarch revered by both communities. Jesus self-identifies as a Jew, which is unusual in John's Gospel. This may indicate that the story comes from the earliest layer of Johannine tradition, before its anti-Jewish polemic developed. Jesus is loyal to his people's traditions of worship ('we worship what we know', verse 22), and reflects the Jewish suspicion of Samaritan customs ('you worship what you do not know', verse 22). But this encounter with a Samaritan woman moves him forward, to a new level of understanding. He is enabled to see beyond the divisions and lack of comprehension, and look forward to a time when God, as Spirit, wild and free, will lead people into seeing the truth to be found in each other's worship. The woman joins him in his vision, trusting that the Messiah 'will show us all things' (verse 25).

Loyalty to one's own tradition does not preclude seeing beyond it. Beware of using verse 24 in a partisan fashion, along the lines of 'we worship in spirit and truth; your worship is idolatrous'. We are all necessarily constrained by the patterns of prayer that have shaped us, but we trust that there is a larger picture, in which all are valued. And it is often by meeting people who are different from us, whether we understand or agree with them or not, that we are drawn into a wider, more inclusive, vision.

Whose worship is foreign to you? How could you gain some understanding of it?

O God, be near us, bless with your presence all encounters across longstanding divisions.

A time to be born

2 Corinthians 6:16-18

In his letters, Paul never discusses the temple in Jerusalem, which was then still operational; but he does make use of temple imagery. Here is one example; others can be found in 1 Corinthians 3:16-17 and Ephesians 2:19-21. Paul takes longstanding traditions – here he alludes to Exodus, Leviticus, Ezekiel, Jeremiah, Isaiah and Hosea (the RSV gives chapter and verse in its footnotes) – and weaves them into a new pattern. We see Christianity coming to birth. The temple of God now becomes the Christian community: it is there that God will live and move.

Everything around a mother giving birth must be kept scrupulously clean, and Paul urges the community to keep itself separate. He quotes from Isaiah 52:11: 'touch nothing unclean' (verse 17). What might this mean in the context of faith? What must be excluded? Certain people, certain attitudes, certain ways of behaving? Is it God who needs protection, or the new fragile community? And as the community grows and becomes more confident, as it gains political power, does it still need to maintain an exclusivist attitude?

Keeping appropriate boundaries is never easy. How does one safeguard one's beliefs, one's standards, one's identity, without denying that all humanity are God's children?

What would you exclude from your holy place?

O God, be near us, bless with your presence all whose lives are moving in new directions.

A time for peace

Revelation 21:22-27

'I saw no temple in the city,' says John towards the end of Revelation (verse 22). And yet the whole book is saturated with temple imagery. In chapter 4 God is described as seated on a throne surrounded by four living creatures. This throne is the heavenly equivalent of the cherubim in the inner sanctuary of the earthly temple. (The equation of the living creatures carrying God's throne with the cherubim is made by Ezekiel; see Ezekiel 10:20.) The living creatures sing the Sanctus 'holy, holy, holy', the song revealed to Isaiah when in a vision the earthly and heavenly temples merged before him (Isaiah 6:1-3). In Revelation 8:3-4 we are told of a golden altar before the throne, from which rises the smoke of incense. And the inhabitants of heaven wear white robes (e.g. 4:4, 7:9), copying the linen garments worn by the high priest for his yearly entry into the inner sanctuary (Leviticus 16:4).

Perhaps 21:22 says that there is no temple because God's glory no longer needs to be contained: it shines across the city, and the gates will never be shut. And yet its holiness still needs to be protected: nothing unclean is to enter. Falsehood and abomination have no place. Maybe we can envisage the fierce light of God's glory stripping away all that is false in each of us, so that our true selves are made ready to live in God's presence.

What is your vision of heaven?

O God, be near us, bless us with your presence, and may your glory infuse our lives.

Contested sites

3 God's vineyard

Notes based on the New Revised Standard Version by

Monica Jyotsna Melanchthon

Monica Jyotsna Melanchthon is a Lutheran minister from India, currently teaching Old Testament Studies/ Hebrew Bible at the Uniting Church Theological College, Melbourne, Australia. Her involvements and theological reflections are driven by the conviction that the Christian gospel should meet people at the point of their needs and struggles. She has strong commitments to the marginalised, who, in the Indian context, are the poor, women and Dalits.

Ecclesiastes 2:1-11

Partnering with God

There is the story of a hard-working farmer who toiled and turned an arid piece of land into fertile soil with varied flowering plants. His pastor, seeing the blossoming field, admired and praised God's glorious creation. The farmer shot back, 'Padre, you should have seen this place when God had it all to himself!' The farmer had grasped the truth. We are the vineyards, for God is our farmer. But we are also farmers; co-creators with God; our vineyards, our institutions and churches reflect our leadership, our fruits. We are simultaneously the farmers and the vineyard.

In today's text, Qoheleth speaks of the futility of material greed, total dependence on human ingenuity and individuation or the human tendency to totalise individual experience. The ones who believe that the world is entirely for them will not find happiness or joy, for people's value is not determined by their toil for individual gain. Instead, there is value in cooperation with God in cultivating the vineyard, for this enables us to grasp wisdom, come into the consciousness of the Other, into knowledge of God and a better understanding of the self and the world.

Do you really believe that human toil is futile?

Gracious and merciful God, give us wisdom to recognise the connectedness we share with you and with those around us. Bless our partnerships, that together we might grow in knowledge of you and the world and its people. Let kindness and cooperation flourish between all human beings.

The cost of resistance

1 Kings 21:1-16

A king covets another's land, his wife plots, and a group of corrupt elders cooperate and together kill a man and take possession of his ancestral vineyard, and seemingly get away with it. The agenda of the king is accomplished at the expense of justice for Naboth.

The experience of Naboth resonates with the Dalit struggle to hold on to their land, for at the root of caste violence is the issue of land. Like Naboth, who resisted by saying, 'The Lord forbid that I should give you my ancestral inheritance' (verse 3), they too resist in various ways. But resistance is costly and many have lost their lives and property doing so.

The story is unsettling and discomforting. But that is its intention, to disturb us. By doing so it helps us recognise similar incidents happening in the world today where individuals and systems of power engage and employ deceit, the power and machinery of the state, and even religion, to cheat and disenfranchise the poor and the powerless. With the prophet Jeremiah we too have probably asked, 'Why does the way of the guilty prosper? Why do all who are treacherous thrive?' (Jeremiah 12:1). And God responds as God always does, through us, God's created beings and agents, to address and confront such oppressive incidents and find ways to resist them. When injustice becomes the rule, intervention becomes a duty. It is our responsibility and we go forth in courage, empowered and fortified by God's sustaining power.

Dear God, I pray for strength to resist unfairness and prejudice wherever I see it, and for all people who struggle and toil diligently against all forms of dehumanisation. May your nurturing Spirit uplift us all and breathe life into us, so we may never be too tired to resist.

Justice delayed is justice denied

1 Kings 21:17-27

The injustice done to Naboth receives attention from the Lord, who calls upon Elijah the prophet to meet with Ahab and pronounce judgement. One wonders why such delayed intervention? Could not the Lord have saved Naboth from death? Elijah pronounces judgement against Ahab and Jezebel. Although the vineyard is at the centre of the controversy, in this section of the chapter the attention is now on Ahab and his repentance. In response, the Lord relents and the punishment on Ahab's household is delayed, to be implemented on his sons. Jezebel, however, is given no opportunity to repent. It is not told if she heard the judgement. But she is a foreigner and an idolator and, in the writer's eyes, not worthy of redemption!

The unsettling aspect in this story is that the judgement does not include any restoration for Naboth nor does the repentance of Ahab include the return of the land to Naboth's household. The land remains with Ahab. There are many in my part of the world who struggle and resist and yet are denied justice and continue to live lives in the midst of injustice.

How do we, or can we, the more privileged, partner with those who struggle for justice?

Lord of justice, help us respond to your call to change the world, wherever we are. Help us bring justice and peace and reconciliation into a world that is hurting and crying for your justice.

Sweet and wild grapes

Isaiah 5:1-7

The vineyard is a common venue for epic conjugal meetings in ancient West Asia, and today's text identifies itself as a love song. It begins with a list of the many things that the farmer has done for the vineyard, yet it has borne only wild grapes. The love song has turned into a song of scorn; a song that addresses a nation and her God.

When you read this text, whom do you identify with? The vineyard or the farmer? We might, along with the farmer, condemn the vineyard and in so doing witness to our own misdeeds. By condemning the vineyard, we condemn ourselves, because we are the vineyard. The farmer did everything possible, but perhaps there were other factors beyond his or her control that impeded the production of sweet grapes. As we recognise this possibility, we are also encouraged to figure out which part of the problem is within our control. If there are problems in the world, we need to ask what our role has been in causing it to be so and move toward the creation of a better world. This might require destroying the field and starting anew. It requires that we break down, choke, and starve every notion, attitude or tendency within each of us that contributes to the building up of walls that separate, dehumanise and subjugate. To experience transformation at the personal, interpersonal and social-structural level, it is vitally important to be willing for our lives to be unmade and remade.

Give us, O life-giving God, the strength, the courage and the will to let go of all that hinders us from being a sweet grape. Help us to bear fruits of justice and righteousness in our lives.

Engagement and disputation: ingredients of active hope

Isaiah 36:13-22

This speech of Rabshekeh, the field commander of the Assyrian army, is a propaganda campaign that seeks to intimidate the residents of Judah and shake their faith both in Hezekiah their king, and in Yahweh their God. Rabshekeh lures them into submission with promises of rewards in the form of plenty; of ownership of fertile land and water resources (verses 16-17). Noteworthy are his provocative questions in verses 18 to 20, but particularly, 'Have they delivered Samaria out of my hand?', for Samaria was the northern kingdom that also trusted in Yahweh. Judah will soon be conquered. The response of the Judahite listeners was one of silence, dejection and despondency.

Conflict, war, famine, poverty and an endless life of hardship and struggle, where resolution to one's everyday struggles seems distant, create the craving to be in a better place. The lure of the West and the good life that it seems to offer is the bane of many impoverished communities, leading to legal and illegal migrations and their many constituent challenges. How does one generate hope among such communities? Not an unrealistic hope that engenders human passivity but an active one that leads to human action and trust? Hope can be sustained only by engagement and disputation rather than by acquiescence and submissiveness, so that people may be empowered to enter into the situation as active agents with the ability to survive, to envision a future that protects their dignity, their identity and their faith.

Help us, Lord, to live a life of consciousness, to see beneath the surface of things and discover your grace, our hope and strength, so that we might enter into the fray and participate in the struggle for life and dignity.

The land on loan

Mark 12:1-12

This parable offers a counter image to the kingdom of God, and is subversive and explosive in its intent. The tenants in the parable abuse the trust put in them and attempt to take over, to control; they inflict injury and death upon the messengers sent by the owner. The owner therefore has no recourse other than to 'destroy the tenants and give the vineyard to others' (verse 9). The violence is unmistakable, perhaps on both sides. We are used to hearing stories of the owner abusing the tenants. But this parable reflects the experiences of many colonised peoples, the adivasis (the original inhabitants) of the land, such as the Dalits, who have been evicted from their lands by tenants who have raided, abused, killed and exploited the colonised, often driven by greed.

On another level, the parable calls to mind the creation narrative and God's command to humanity 'to fill the earth and subdue it' (Genesis 1:28), a text that has been grossly misunderstood and abused. This world in which we live has been given to us 'on loan'. We are all tenants! And yet we seem to be unaware of the inextricable connectedness between humans and the land. In our abuse of it, we abuse its original owner, God, and are disrespectful of our creator.

How do we live lives as 'tenants' and what are our responsibilities to God?

Help us, O Lord of the earth, to develop a sense of perspective, of our place on this earth. Teach us to acknowledge the preciousness of the earth and its people, and show us how to live with respect and reverence to each other and to you.

Acting out one's belief

John 15:1-8

The way we were raised makes us who we are. We are also products of our faith or lack of faith. Our lives and how we live them, our commitments and involvements, reflect our God, our faith and our upbringing. Today's text conveys the fact that an authentic relationship with God in Christ becomes evident when we participate in the works that Jesus does. This connection is powerfully expressed in the allegory of the vine, which conveys two harmonising truths: that we bear fruit when we abide in Jesus; and that, when we keep the commandments, we abide in Jesus and in God. This is similar to the prophetic contention that our knowledge of God is authenticated in the doing of justice. Our true identity as Jesus' disciples is confirmed when we do what he commands: to love the neighbour; to care for the poor, the widow and the destitute; to respect the woman; to nurture the child; to pray for others; to seek the welfare of all.

The intimate relationship between belief and praxis, between theological truth and action, is at the heart of the parable. God's love, holiness, righteousness, justice, reconciling and redeeming action must be appropriated and given tangible expression in human life and society. God's forgiveness mediated in and through Christ must be shared and lived out in transformed lives and relationships. Periodic self-interrogation and reflection on the message that is being transmitted through our individual and corporate lives is essential.

O God, help us fulfil your commandments, continually reflecting your love, your grace and your mercy to those around us.

Navigating Numbers

Notes based on the *Tanakh* (Jewish Publishing Service); Liberal Judaism's prayer book *Siddur Lev Chadash;* and the original Hebrew by

Pete Tobias

Pete Tobias is rabbi of the Liberal Synagogue, Elstree, Hertfordshire. His latest book, the second of a children's series, *The Question of the Hidden Matzah* (Liberal Judaism), was published in 2012. Pete features regularly on BBC Radio 2 and is a devoted fan of Watford Football Club!

1 Taking stock, counting heads

Numbers 1:1-4, 17-19

Making ourselves heard

'A voice in the wilderness': a phrase that describes someone with a unique message, a vision of the world that perhaps isn't shared by others. It's certainly a voice of one brave enough to speak out. And it's a voice that, so often, people don't want, or choose not, to hear.

Well, right now, there are lots of voices in the wilderness. Voices belonging to people with experiences similar to mine, who were slaves like me, who, along with me, followed that man Moses out of the land of Egypt, out of slavery and into ...

... into the wilderness. And here we are. Hundreds and hundreds of us. Each of us has a voice, a memory of what has happened to us, a sense of why it happened to us, and an understanding of what it means.

But how can I make my voice heard? Here in this place where silence usually reigns is a babble of thousands of voices, all vying to be heard. Who am I and what is my vision? Will my voice in the wilderness be heard?

In our modern world, we often feel alone. Our crowded streets, roads and transport systems make us feel more isolated. Like the Israelites, we stand alone in a wilderness, surrounded by hundreds and thousands of others, trying to be heard. 'Out of the depths I cry to you, Eternal God; hearken to my voice' (Psalm 130:1).

Help us, Eternal God, to find our voice, to find our place in our own wilderness, and enable us to become who we can be.

Numbers

Numbers 2:1-34

And now we begin to discover something more about who we are. Each of us is part of a tribal group, according to our family. Moses and Aaron, who led us from Egypt, are telling us to organise ourselves. But unless we are twenty years old or over and male, our voices still won't be heard in the babble in this wilderness.

And now we know that there are at least 603 550 voices. That's not counting the ones who are teenagers or children or women. So many people, so many voices, so much noise, so little chance of being heard.

How can I work out who I am, how can I tell others who I am, in the deafening sound of this wilderness? Surrounded by so many voices, how will I be heard? How will I hear myself?

'We stamp many coins with one seal and they are all alike; but God has stamped all human beings with the seal of Adam, yet none is like the other' (Mishnah Sanhedrin 4:5).

Although we can sometimes feel overwhelmed by the numbers of people that surround us, let us learn to celebrate the diversity of human life and recognise who we are and the unique relationship we have with our God. As the Rabbis said: 'When you see a great multitude of people, say "I praise You, Eternal God, Sovereign of the Universe, to whom the innermost secrets of every one of them is known"' (Midrash Numbers Rabbah 21:2).

Allmen are equal ...

Numbers 3:1-11, 14-20

And now we discover that out here in the wilderness, where all of us are equal in the eyes of God, some of us are more equal than others. Perhaps it is so in every group of people. Who put this Moses and Aaron in charge of us? And now they want us to believe that their tribal group, the tribe of Levi, should be treated differently from the rest of us.

And this inequality is extended: Aaron is a Levite, but he is a special Levite who has particular privileges and responsibilities. Does one have to be a son of Aaron to be able to have one's voice heard? Or at least one of the other sons of Levi, one of those permitted to work in the service of the Almighty? Can these specially appointed ones help me to understand my place here, help my voice in the wilderness be heard?

The world in which we live is filled with inequality. Some have achieved rank and status by their own merit; others are there through no effort of their own. May we learn to accept our place and to strive for inner achievement, knowing that God recognises goodness, wherever it is found. 'I call heaven and earth to witness: whether a person be Gentile or Jew, man or woman, male or female servant, solely according to their conduct does the holy spirit rest upon them' (from 'Seder Eliyahu Rabbah', chapter 10).

God says: 'Although I have appointed for you heads, elders and officers, yet you are all equal before Me'.

Midrash Tanchuma Nitzavim, 2

Chosen to be special

Numbers 4:1-20

'The Universe was brought forth by an inexhaustible creative Power; fearful and wonderful, mysterious and terrible, sustaining and destroying. By that Power, matter came forth out of chaos. Time passed, time beyond imagining; matter crossed a boundary and became life, and life gave birth to us' (Siddur Lev Chadash, p.163).

Here in this wilderness where so much is difficult to understand, and where so little makes sense, a way has to be found to approach the mysterious power that has led us to this place. Perhaps there are those who can both help us approach that mystery and protect us from it. After all, it has enormous and terrible power: it destroyed Pharaoh and his troops; it caused terror to rain on the Egyptians, allowing us to escape. And it will guide us through this place, leading us to a new life, a new hope.

But only if we treat it with reverence and respect. And so it is right that this awesome power be approached with caution, with proper preparation and with special furnishings. And we do this by establishing boundaries, to make special preparations and presentations, and to put in place a group of people whose role it is to minister to this power and manage it on our behalf. Otherwise we could be exposed to it and find ourselves consumed by its awesome and fearsome might.

'When I look at the heavens … what are we that you are mindful of us, we mortals that you care for us?' (Psalm 8:3-4). Help us, Eternal God, to sense your presence and to approach you with reverence and respect.

Making ourselves heard again

Numbers 4:21-33

What is the purpose of all these ritual items? Is there not a danger that we will become obsessed with the fire pans, the curtains, the frames and the poles, the costumes and the people who use them and wear them?

The people in the wilderness seem to respect the work of the Levites, their different responsibilities. And they seem to acknowledge the authority of Aaron and his sons, Israel's priests, who intercede for us with this frightening force that dwells in the mysterious Tent of Meeting.

But what of the voices of ordinary Israelites? Who is prepared to hear my voice, to listen to my experience, to help me make sense of the terrifying and wonderful things that happened to allow us to escape from Egypt, the astonishing revelation at the mountain, the miracle of the food that sustains us here, the sheer loneliness of this place? All these special people and all these special items leave me feeling excluded and distant from the possibility of God hearing my voice.

Sometimes in our places of worship or in our homes, we assemble items to remind us of our devotion and to help us focus on God. But these things are to help us – they are human, not divine. For God is everywhere and has no need of such symbols: 'In every place where I cause my name to be remembered I will come to you and bless you' (Exodus 20:21 or 24 in some Bibles).

'Commune with your own heart upon your bed, and be still' (Psalm 4:5).

Choosing to be special

Numbers 6:1-8

Perhaps the answer is to become like them, to make myself holy and special. To dedicate myself to the service of that mystical power just as Aaron and the Levites have done: not as a consequence of my birth, but by choice – a conscious decision to serve the Almighty. I might adhere to the rules that will set me apart, just as they set apart the priests and the Levites. There is a discipline, a structure, here that might enable me to make my voice heard in the wilderness and that might let me feel God's presence, receive God's blessing.

For it is lonely here in this crowded wilderness. Surely there must be ways that I can approach God just as the priests do? There must be a way to encounter God with the same proximity that is granted to the special ones, God's ministers and servants. I too want to be a servant of God, I too want to feel that proximity.

But my fear, my lack of standing and the quietness of my voice, drowned out by all the thousands of voices around me, inhibit me from taking those steps.

At times, we might consider ourselves inadequate or unworthy to approach God, sensing that others around us are more privileged, closer to God than are we. But God is always waiting for us: 'When you seek me you will find me, if you search for me with all your heart' (Jeremiah 29:13).

'May the words of my mouth and the meditations of my heart be acceptable to you, O God, my rock and my redeemer' (Psalm 19:14).

We are all special

Numbers 6:22-27

Perhaps some of the priests enjoy the power they exercise over the people. Maybe some of the Levites consider themselves to be holier than us ordinary Israelites. It's possible that my fellow Israelites, here in this overcrowded wilderness, place too much faith in the fixtures and fittings, the ritual and the ceremony. Perhaps those of my fellows who have dedicated themselves as Nazirites believe they occupy a more privileged position in the religious hierarchy. It's a hierarchy that seeks to silence my voice in the wilderness, that seems to prevent the word of the Eternal One reaching me.

But finally it all makes sense. For at the heart of the worship ceremony over which the priests preside is the blessing that comes directly from God, passing through the priests to the people, reaching out to us wherever we may be standing, with our voices ready to speak out and to be heard. No matter how small, insignificant or unheard we might be in this wilderness, God's blessing touches us all, enabling us to be reached and to be heard, to know and to be known.

Every effort we make to commune with God, even in isolation and loneliness, will find its reward in a sense of righteousness, comfort and peace. Every religious tradition teaches us how we can experience God in our own wilderness; may these teachings bring us peace. 'All your children shall be taught about God and great shall be the peace of your children' (Isaiah 54:13).

May God bless you and keep you.
May God's face shine upon you and be gracious to you.
May God's face be lifted up towards you and bring you peace.

Numbers 6:22-27

Navigating Numbers

2 Journeying on

Notes based on the New Revised Standard Version by

Chris Bedding

The Reverend Chris Bedding is an Anglican priest in Perth, Western Australia. His passions are social justice, ministry in the first third of life, and liturgy. He is also an actor, director and comedian.

Numbers 7:1-11

Stuff and nonsense

Human beings are obsessed with stuff: acquiring it, using it, keeping it in good condition. Some of us can't get enough stuff, and spend our time in covert jealousy of other people's. We're mad for it, driven mad by it, and often taught to eschew it if we are to be more 'spiritual'. Yet God, at least in this week's readings from Numbers, seems very interested in stuff. Lampstands and wagons, oxen and razors, trumpets, meat and babies – all are given significant attention by God.

Many of us would be suspicious of a God who is interested in details. Surely the Creator of the universe is more interested in lofty ideals and profound truths than in the minutiae of liturgy, meals or relationships? Yet the great paradox is that the God revealed in the scriptures is deeply concerned with gritty reality. Our actions and thoughts have value for God. So as we journey with Moses through innovation, challenge to authority, despair and fatigue, let us consider the details of our own life. The little decisions, the big challenges. The seemingly petty acts, the major life changes. Each of them says something about our faith, and each has value in the eyes of God.

God of bits and pieces, of things and stuff and matter,
make your presence known to us:
in pettiness, in detail, in how we organise.
That all our work may be your joy,
all tasks theology, all movement worship.

Routines and regulations

Numbers 8:1-14

One can imagine God arriving at the tent of meeting like a patriarch to inspect the family and ensure that they are up to standard. The God of the Israelites, it seems, requires the Levites to have a full body shave, a bath and clean clothes. The lampstand is to be arranged correctly, and everything is to be in order. The ceremonies are to be 'just so', and then God will be happy!

But what if these requirements are not for God's benefit but for our own? What if the layout of the tent and the presentation of the Levites is not God's demand on humanity but a human response to God's presence? The details about stuff are not God's checklist requiring obedient adherence but the means by which humans can learn and communicate the fullness of God. When we arrange the lampstand as an act of devotion, we preach powerfully about our awareness of God's light. When we prepare our bodies to serve God, we proclaim our thankfulness for the creative Spirit that dwells within. These disciplines, and their modern equivalents, shape and form us, but they must first arise from a knowledge of our identity as the people of God.

This week, try imbuing a routine with new significance. Make sweeping the floor an act of prayer, or brushing your teeth a spiritual discipline. See what happens when the ordinary takes on sacred value.

Lord, we feel unworthy for you to come into our midst, as if our homes are grubby and you are the sneering guest. Yet we are the guest, and yours is the home, and our worthiness flows from you.

Passover customs

Numbers 9:1-14

Keeping the Passover is a privilege, but it's more than that. It's a blessing, but more than that. Keeping the Passover is how the Israelites know who they are. So, whatever your circumstance, you still do it. Because, if you don't, you forget who you are.

Recounting and reliving the escape from Egypt could easily become a hollow bit of play-acting. Retelling and celebrating God's providence could easily become a shallow ritual. But accompanying the observance are two powerful signs. First, those who are ritually unclean are to be included. This subversion of the purity laws is, to a Christian, a foretaste of the message of Jesus. God made the rules, God can break them, and does! Second, the resident alien is to be included in the feast. For a people so fiercely tribal and protective of culture, this is a major departure from the norm. Once again, God's inclusive character is demonstrated as part of this most central act.

Those of us who have shared in a seder know the power of the ritual meal. No sterile 'going through the motions' – all Jews who keep the feast journey with their forebears out of Pharaoh's clutches and into the land of freedom. The *agape* meal of the early Christians perhaps preserved this sense of shared meal and shared story. One wonders how much has been lost in the stylised and fussy celebrations of the Eucharist so prevalent in the West, and to what extent the 'unclean' and the 'resident alien' have been excluded.

Welcome us to journey with you, God, out of the land of slavery and into the land of promise. Spread our arms wide to gather the outcast and forgotten, the unclean and unnoticed, and join us in the feast.

The big picture

Numbers 10:11-36

This must be some kind of joke. If this story was true to form, the Gershonites would be delayed by a couple of days because they missed the memo, and the company of Dan would have set out first, then complained that nothing was ready when they arrived. Yet here it is: the Israelites have an effective, repeatable system for moving people from one place to the next. And not just people: this whole process ensures that the tabernacle receives proper care. One company goes in advance to prepare the way and another company acts as rearguard. The tabernacle is set up and ready when the holy things arrive, and all these vital objects are kept under guard. Among the Israelites, the holy things are treated with dignity and keep their proper place in the midst of the people.

Do our systems and processes serve to keep the presence of God at the centre of our journey? We spend a lot of time concerned with minutiae (like the colour of paint), and relatively little time on big-picture issues (like long-range financial planning). We get so concerned about the details that the system in which those details exist never receives scrutiny. Yet here the Israelites provide an example of a system that is both effective and sacred. It's true – with God all things are possible!

What systems and processes in your life or church need to be refined and de-cluttered so that service and worship of God is central?

We are unfinished, Lord. A work in progress. Direct this process, that we might know the value of detail yet forget our obsession with minutiae. Help us see both the big picture and the vital elements, bound up in your wholeness.

Whinging and complaints

Numbers 11:1-15

People having a tantrum are often faintly hilarious. There's something about a person losing control that brings on the giggles. Now, we're probably not supposed to laugh when God's anger is kindled, but the absurdity of God's anger singeing the edges of the camp is deserving of a smirk at least. It's just the sort of thing that militant opponents would use to poke fun at theism, and understandably so. And what has caused this rage? The menu is simply not up to scratch, complain the Israelites. Fish and melons are what we want, not manna day after day! The people are angry, Moses is angry and God is angry. About food.

Now this is pretty funny but also entirely understandable. Everyone who has ever organised an event knows that the best speakers and workshops in the world cannot make up for dodgy catering. Likewise, congregations will put up with dreadful preaching so long as there's a good spread at morning tea. Food is important for communities. It defines our identity and provides the context in which we relate to one another.

So it's no surprise that food is the catalyst for Moses' deeply moving lament. No leaders could read this without projecting their own experience on to it. It is so poignant, so authentic that it defies analysis. It's raw, it's real and it's in the Bible. Thank God.

Why, God? Why the whingers and complainers, the naggers and naysayers? Why not constant positivity and cheerful optimism? Come to us and defeat our despair, through Christ who cried over his people.

Morality tale?

Numbers 12:1-16

Leprosy as punishment for criticising the leader reads like the sick fantasy of a megalomaniac. Miriam and Aaron may well be jealous of Moses, and may well be out of order, but to afflict Miriam (but not Aaron) with a skin disease seems unusually capricious. This is, without doubt, one of the Bible's texts of terror. A vengeful God doling out arbitrary punishments is distasteful to modern sensibilities. We really don't know what to do with it. How often, for example, does this story feature in Sunday school curricula or preaching schedules? Yet, there it is in our Bibles, demanding a response.

We could turn it into a moral lesson about jealousy, or respect for prophets, or good manners, and perhaps that was its original intent. Perhaps this story and others like it are simply morality stories about how to relate to one another. But perhaps there's a key also in the description of Moses as 'very humble' (verse 3). Moses has married a foreign woman and upset his inner circle and, presumably, the other Israelites. When he is the target of an angry confrontation, he does not fight back. Most of us would respond to jealous critique with defensiveness and anger. But not Moses. It is God who dispenses justice, God who punishes, God who teaches lessons. Perhaps Moses' humility, acceptance and non-violence are the true morality lessons here. We need not respond to every attack upon us – ultimately it is God who will judge.

When we are attacked and confronted, and anger is at hand, drench us in humility. Enable us to stand strong but not proud and, through our weakness, defeat envy and malice.

Possess the land or not?

Numbers 13:1-2, 25-33

The promised land is nearby after years of travelling and it turns out to be inhabited by strong tribes who live well off the land. Only Caleb and Joshua think that the land is worth invading; the other ten spies are afraid. Of course, underlying this story is the reality that the promised land was the home of the Canaanites. It was not *terra nullius*, there for the taking. The land had to be subdued and conquered. War was the only possible path.

Yet Moses and the Israelites decide against it. God punishes their lack of faith by making them wander in the desert. Despite the fact that this was the land that they had been promised, the Israelites get cold feet.

On the one hand, this is a lucky reprieve for the Canaanites. On the other, it is an unfortunate decision based on the faithlessness of Moses and the chosen people. Caleb and Joshua, however, may be an example to us. They go into enemy territory, see the danger and decide to fight on. This kind of courage, some would say foolhardiness, seems to be common among those who put their trust in God. Sometimes we simply need to see the land that God has prepared for us and be prepared to travel there, whatever the cost.

You hint, Holy Spirit, and tease us with glimpses of the land you have prepared. Some see clearly, others dimly, and many live in fear. Lead us on, great Spirit! Stock our packs and strengthen our muscles to follow where you lead.

Navigating Numbers

Notes based on the Jewish Publishing Service *Tanakh*; Liberal Judaism's prayer book *Siddur Lev Chadash*; and the Hebrew by

Pete Tobias

For Pete's biography, see p.262.

3 Beyond the plains

Numbers 14:1-25

The chronicles of Amram

These are the Chronicles of Amram, recorded in Egypt, the desert of Sinai and in the wilderness of Kadesh. Amram and Yocheved had three children, Miriam, Aaron and Moses. Miriam, Aaron and Moses led the children of Israel out of the land of Egypt, out of the house of bondage and into freedom. And each of the children of Amram and Yocheved served the Israelites in the wilderness, each of them achieving greatness.

Miriam led the people to water in the desert, followed, it would seem, by an everlasting fountain. Aaron ministered to the people and interceded with God on their behalf. And Moses led them to the borders of the land that God had promised to their ancestors. Yet all of them, all the children of Amram and Yocheved, would die in that wilderness.

Sometimes our lives feel directionless and without purpose. But everything we do and everything we say is recorded in some invisible account of our lives: we all leave our mark on this world and make for ourselves a place in eternity: 'Birth is a beginning, and death a destination. And life is a journey, a sacred pilgrimage – to life everlasting' (Rabbi Alvin I Fine, quoted in Andrew Goldstein, *Siddur Lev Chadash*, (Union of Liberal and Progressive Synagogues 1995), p.201).

Rabbi Zusya, said 'In the world to come if they ask me: "Why were you not Moses?" I will know how to answer. But if they ask me: "Why were you not Zusya?" I will have no excuses.'

based on Martin Buber, *Tales of the Chasidim*, quoted in *Siddur Lev Chadash*, p.227

Dealing with disagreement

Numbers 16:1-22

And how did the sons of Amram and Yocheved, this Aaron and Moses, leaders of these troublesome people journeying from slavery, respond to their rebelliousness and their challenges? They fell on their faces! But what else might they have done? How does one deal with a challenge to one's leadership that is so defiant, so cruel and so harshly expressed? By raising one's voice in anger? By resorting to violence and weaponry? There must come a point in any dispute where the time for words is ended and the time for action must begin. But what should be the action?

Surely the action should be a search for compromise, a recognition of the humanity that is shared between all those who take part in a quarrel. And, having recognised that common human bond, can one human being then continue to fight with another? One might wish to continue the struggle. What then must the other do? Fall on his face to demonstrate humility and a desire for peace.

We all have our own opinions, which means that there will always be times when we disagree or argue with one another. There is nothing wrong with this – it's part of our nature. What is important is the way we treat the people we disagree with, during and after the argument. 'In a place where no one behaves like a human being, strive to be a human being' (Pirkei Avot 2:5).

'When two quarrel we see which one becomes silent first then say, "This one is of nobler character"' (Babylonian Talmud Kiddushin 71b).

The death of a daughter

Numbers 20:1-21

Miriam died in the wilderness at Kadesh. And there was no water for the Israelites to drink. For, when Miriam died, so too did the waters of life. And much more besides. Will Miriam, who danced and sang at the shores of the sea, raising the spirits of the weary, giving voice to the relief and joy of the redeemed, be remembered? Will the sound of her timbrel, the beauty of her song and her gift of living water to her people be recalled at the end of this wearing journey through the parched wilderness? Or will Moses, her brother, whom she watched over and protected in his infancy as he floated on the Nile, strike rocks to achieve what his sister could do without effort? And will Miriam's life, her love, her joy and her devotion, be omitted from the record of this desert struggle, her death narrated in one sentence, unnoticed and unmourned?

Where are you, Miriam, sweet daughter of Amram and Yocheved? And where is your story in the tales of our people? To us you will never be forgotten; for you bring new life to the children of Israel every day. Liberal Judaism seeks to acknowledge and remember the role of Miriam and other women in biblical history whose voices are silent and unheard. Let us recognise the contribution of all individuals to human development and progress.

Miriam the prophetess, strength and song are in her hand.
Miriam will dance with us to strengthen the world's song.
Soon, and in our time, she will lead us to the waters of salvation.

Andrew Goldstein and Pete Tobias,
Haggadah b'Chol Dor va-Dor
(Liberal Judaism, 2010) p.10b

The death of a son

Numbers 20:22-29

Then Aaron also died in the wilderness. And the children of Israel mourned for him for thirty days – thirty days more than they mourned for his sister. What does this tell us about the children of Israel and our children, the sons and daughter of Amram and Yocheved? It speaks of the disregard of the role of women. It speaks of inequality. It speaks of ingratitude.

The role of Aaron the priest was truly noble: there was the nobility of his bearing, the importance of his ritual presence, the need for a connection with the God of Israel who led Israel through the wilderness. But our daughter, our precious Miriam, played a role in their lives that was no less vital. She brought water to the people, sustaining them on their journey, giving voice to their joy and their celebration of freedom. Where are the records of what women did for the children of Israel, for the people of the world? Are they, like our Miriam, buried silently in the desert?

Let us work to ensure that the contribution of women is properly recognised and valued. 'A woman of value, who can find? Her worth is far beyond that of rubies ... She is clothed with strength and dignity; she looks to the future with joy. Her mouth is full of wisdom, her tongue with kindly teaching' (Proverbs 31:10, 25-26).

'Hold no one insignificant and nothing improbable, for there is no one person who does not have their time and nothing that does not have its place' (Pirkei Avot 4:5).

A lament of Moses after the death of Miriam and Aaron

Numbers 21:1-9

Eternal One of Israel, now I am alone. My work is done, my people are free, and here they are before you complaining, protesting, demanding to go back. And I am alone. No sister to watch over me in the river. No brother to speak for me to Pharaoh. Alone in this wilderness with six hundred thousand men, their wives, their children and a mixed multitude besides, but no Miriam, no Aaron.

And God said, 'Make a serpent of bronze and place it on a pole. And when you look upon it your loneliness will be cured.' And Moses looked and found healing and found hope.

The bronze serpent has become a symbol of physical healing and wellbeing. The following oath is often recited as a promise by doctors who commit themselves to preserving human life, but its words serve as a guide to all who seek to help those in need, alone or in distress: 'The eternal providence has appointed me to watch over the life and health of God's creatures. Grant me the strength, time and opportunity always to correct what I have acquired, always to extend its domain; for knowledge is immense and the human spirit can extend indefinitely to enrich itself daily with new requirements. Oh, God, you have appointed me to watch over life and death; here am I ready for my vocation and now I turn unto my calling' (Maimonides).

'Some lose their way in trackless desert, unable to find their way to others; Let them cry out in their trouble to God, who will rescue them from their distress' (Psalm 107:4, 6-7).

The book of the wars of Yahweh

Numbers 21:10-20

So much of our history, the story of our civilisation, is one of conflict and struggle. So many of our achievements are born from our attempts to find ever more ingenious ways of making war with our fellow human beings.

When, O God, shall we turn our genius and our skills to making peace? When, Eternal One, shall we learn that our true destiny, our way out of this endless wilderness of conflict and discord, is to seek to understand one another and live in peace together?

May the words that are written to chronicle our own journey through the wilderness bring light to us and our world. 'May it be your will, O God, that war and bloodshed shall vanish from the earth, and that a great and glorious peace may reign for ever in the world. Let every human being understand that we have not been created for strife and discord, hatred and envy, but only so that we may come to know you to whom all praise is due for ever' (Nachman of Bratzlav).

They shall beat their swords into ploughshares,
and their spears into pruning-hooks.
Nation shall not lift up sword against nation,
and never again shall they learn to make war.

Isaiah 2:5

Following in the footsteps

Numbers 27:12-23

And so the journey ends. Or rather, this stage of the journey; for in truth the journey has no end. Each of those who made this journey, who travelled from slavery to freedom, from Egypt to the promised land, has a story to tell, a heritage to pass on. And, although at such times many argue about inheritance and speak only of material possessions, there are greater riches to be transmitted, nobler values to be passed on. And, while sons and daughters might grapple over their parents' possessions, each of them, regardless of their age or gender, receives something infinitely more precious: the wisdom, love and guidance of those who have gone before them.

And so it is also with those whom leaders choose to succeed them. Each of us can make only a limited contribution to humankind's journey: we struggle to make our voices heard and pray for guidance and direction. We should live our lives in order that those who come after us may carry forward our beliefs, our hopes and our love. When we hand on the responsibility of continuing the journey, let us tell those who take over from us that their duty is to build on our achievements, and that they honour us best when they live as we would wish, and strive to fulfil the hopes and dreams we cherished.

'You are not required to complete the work, but neither are you at liberty to refrain from it'.

Pirkei Avot 2:16

Mothers

1 God at the birth

Notes based on the King James Version by

Sibyl Ruth

For Sibyl's biography, see p.41.

Genesis 3:20 – 4:2

Not your children

I'm more used to novels than the Bible. In fact, I tend to approach scripture as if it were a novel. One written in two parts, with lots of authors and a massive cast. In Part One the main character is Yahweh. Yahweh is as potent, as unpredictable, as any hero of romance. His women are subjects, bit players with cameo roles.

The way books are marketed has become increasingly gendered. (If it's got a sparkly cover it's for girls.) By these standards, I'd say the Bible was a blokes' book. However, at times women do manage to get a look in. Strong female characters emerge in brief fragments. Across the millennia, they speak loud and clear. Take that exultant cry of Eve's, 'I have gotten a man from the Lord.'

I know Part Two of the Bible best. The nativity story was read to me each year when I was small. It's interesting to go back and discover that Part One holds many more astonishing birth stories. The *Daily Mail* might splutter about teenage mums, women who are too old to have babies, fathers being sidelined. We've been here before. It's all in the Old Testament.

Even now, when so much is known about human biology, conception still seems miraculous. As a child, I was a sceptic. But now I'm adult it feels reasonable to regard Yahweh as the giver of life. Because, as Khalil Gibran said:

Your children are not your children.
They are the sons and daughters of Life's longing
for itself.
They come through you but not from you...

Khalil Gibran, *The Prophet*

All that hear will laugh ...

Genesis 21:1-7

I'd have been five when my mother bought me a pair of books featuring Old Testament stories. Many of the tales seemed as harsh as anything out of the Brothers Grimm. I used to worry about these narratives. Were they true? Could they be real? Even so I dipped into the books regularly. I liked the illustrations. They used bold, strong colours – gold, red and black – that seemed to fit alongside the savage, primal narratives. I looked at my unabridged Bible with its black cover, its one thousand tissue-thin pages, much more rarely.

The story of Sarah conceiving at the age of 90 is one I remember from the story books. Even though at the time *all* grown-ups seemed impossibly old. The birth of my younger brother, just before I was six, was a major disruption. Now I am going back to Genesis at a point when, though I'm younger than Sarah, another baby would definitely be miraculous. This time I am working with the full 1611 text, so I'm able to read how Sarah marvels at God's ability to carry on performing miracles. With divine help, she's not just conceived and had a successful delivery; God has also enabled her to feed her new son. 'Who would have said ... that Sarah should have given children suck?' (verse 7).

Work on translating the King James Bible would have happened while Shakespeare was writing his tragedies. There's an echo here of Lady Macbeth, reminding her husband 'I have given suck, and know/ How tender 'tis to love the babe that milks me.'

For the first time I am able to see that Sarah's story is about laughter. This version has her say, 'God has made me to laugh' (verse 6). Which could mean, that it isn't just Isaac's arrival that is a source of celebration. Perhaps, despite our misfortunes, everyone was created for the expression of joy? And, when something good happens to one of us, 'all that hear' should join in the celebrations.

Do the right thing

Genesis 29:31-35

It's not just the Song of Solomon that is a love story. There's romance in Genesis, too, when 'Jacob served seven years for Rachel: and they seemed unto him but a few days, for the love he had to her' (verse 20). However, the best romantic fiction (Jane Austen comes to mind) also involves moral choice. As an Old Testament heroine, Leah has less room for manoeuvre than Elizabeth Bennet. She needs to do what her dad tells her. And Laban has chosen to marry her off to Jacob, even though Jacob prefers Rachel.

But this isn't a soap opera or an escapist story about courtship. This is a serious account of the resolution of problems *after* marriage. It's bad enough for Leah that her husband prefers someone else. But it is worse not knowing what Yahweh thinks about Laban's shenanigans. Maybe Leah herself has fallen out of favour? It's not easy for deities and mortals to converse. But the two of them manage via a kind of sign language. Yahweh flags up his meaning with conceptions. Leah talks back through the naming of children.

I am better with English literature than Hebrew, so I turned to a Torah website, www.torah.org, for help. It explains how the symbolic names of the children show Leah realising that marriage to Jacob doesn't cut her off from Yahweh. The alliance is part of a greater plan.

Leah is 'looked upon' by Yahweh. She continues to be heard. Having played her part in mothering the future tribes of Israel, Leah can, at last, secure Jacob's affection. Having achieved all this, her fourth child is an extra blessing.

I could say this is folklore. Or part of Jewish history of doubtful relevance in an age when women can pick their own partners, take control of their own fertility. Yet Leah's story can't be dismissed that fast. There are times when we're all forced into compromises; when we struggle to keep different people happy. And when, like 'tender eyed' Leah, we could do with reassurance that yes, we're doing everything we can.

Hidden heroines

Exodus 2:1-10

Who is being hidden in this story? 'Moses' is the obvious reply. This is his book. It's all about his lineage. His near magical escapes. But there is another answer. What about that anonymous woman who 'conceived and bare a son' (verse 2)? We know her as Levi's daughter, the hero's mum. Not having a name obscures her, makes her seem less of a person. The other female characters here aren't named either. Is Exodus a work in which female strength and resourcefulness are duly acknowledged? Or do women get less than their due? The verdict could go either way.

The book begins by giving the 'names of the children of Israel, which came into Egypt, every man and his household' (Exodus 1:1). You have to be masculine to be a child of Israel. The women are like chattels. But chapter 1 does identify two midwives, Shiphrah and Puah, who play a vital role. They disobey Pharaoh's orders to kill baby Hebrew boys as soon as they're delivered. Men might hold sway on earth, but these women's first responsibility is to God (or possibly to medical ethics). And they can talk themselves out of a corner. It's all because of the 'liveliness' of Hebrew women who give birth before they arrive.

The mother of Moses doesn't speak out like Shiphrah and Puah. She simply keeps her son as long as she dares. She does an excellent job in constructing the ark. And then she gets her son back, nursing him in Pharaoh's household. (The woman is both DIY expert and secret agent.) Her name, Jochebed, appears later half-buried in a genealogical list. Despite this inconspicuous placing, this name is important. She is the first person in the Bible whose Hebrew name contains the divine element *yah*. This is a shortened form of YHWH, the name of God.

This could signify a specially close relationship between God, who nurtures us then sends us on our way, and motherhood. Or just that in ancient times, as now, women have to wait that bit longer to receive the recognition we deserve.

All's well that ends well?

Ruth 4:11-17

Mostly, the Old Testament seems more concerned with fathers (or Fathers?) than mothers and wives. It's as macho as any Hollywood action film. Nonetheless it offers, whether accidentally or on purpose, glimpses of the lives of women and their dealings with one another. These are not always stories of sweetness and light. As marriage contracts are made by men, and husbands can take more than one wife, the bonds between women are not ones that they themselves have chosen. No wonder that their relationships are so often based around suspicion, not collaboration.

Against this background Ruth is remarkable. It's as if we've wandered into another movie (a chick flick?) with a different scriptwriter. The only thing that's not right is its title. Shouldn't it be called Ruth and Naomi? Or better still, Naomi and Ruth? Either way it is the story of two unlikely buddies from different backgrounds and different generations.

Perhaps it's because she's the older woman that I particularly identify with Naomi. Though it could just be that her role has what scriptwriters would call a strong narrative arc. At the opening, it is a tale of death: 'And Elimelech Naomi's husband died ... And Mahlon and Chilion died also both of them' (Ruth 1:3, 5). Naomi is severely tested. And I admire her refusal to make light of what's been lost, the way she dares to ask big questions. If we are defined by the men in our lives, who are we when those men are no longer with us? And if the Lord can bless women, enrich them, give them children, can't he also do the opposite as well. ('I went out full, and the Lord hath brought me home again empty', Ruth 1:21).

But there is a happy ending, thanks to Ruth. Those earlier promises she made were not hollow ones. Ruth's pregnancy becomes their shared blessing. Obed's birth gives new life to Naomi. He will be better to her than seven sons. When the infant is 'laid in her bosom' (verse 16), she is a mother once more.

Gifts and loans

1 Samuel 1:20-28

It's not surprising that I gravitated to Hannah's story. Like her, I am married and no longer young. My husband had an earlier marriage, so there was another wife, with children, in the picture. When I became pregnant, I felt profoundly blessed. But, despite knowing that a willingness to make sacrifices is important, I didn't like the part where Hannah gives up her child.

Hannah may have petitioned the Lord to 'give unto thine handmaid a man child, then I will give him unto the Lord all the days of his life' (verse 11). But isn't that like one of those clauses in a contract, excessive interest charges, for example, that should never be enforced? Did Hannah herself think she'd promised too much? Perhaps that's why she delays returning to the temple until Samuel is weaned. Or is she doing her absolute best to stick to the bargain, by ensuring she hands over a healthy child?

Although Hannah's dilemma might seem of little relevance today, don't all parents need to ask who their child really 'belongs' to? When my own daughter was just weeks old, I was struck by a sense that she was separate and would end up going her own way. I wrote about this in a poem:

At times it seems you're only here on loan,
not mine.
One morning I'll nip out.
Just to post a letter on the corner
or fetch milk from the shop,
turn round
and find you gone.

Now that my child's a teenager, I often find her gone.

Maybe it's time to take another look at Hannah's story. Hannah juggles logic and emotion and promises to comply by *loaning* her son. 'I have lent him to the Lord as long as he liveth' (verse 28).

Departed glory

1 Samuel 4:19-22

'Glory' is a fantastic word. I've always relished being able to say it. The word remains powerful in a secular context. Like the poetry of Wordsworth. In 'Ode: Intimations of Immortality' he repeatedly harks back to the gloriousness of being young in an apparently unfallen world. Glory isn't easy or pretty. So giving birth can be glorious, especially when you hold a baby in your arms, and start looking forward to the future.

This was not the experience of Ichabod's mother. Having heard shocking news, she went into labour prematurely. The description of her plight is vivid. 'She bowed herself and travailed for her pains' (verse 19). The word 'travail' is related to the Latin words for 'torment' and 'torture'. Earlier passages have involved good fortune, miraculous pregnancies, the joy of a child's arrival. But this section of the Bible is about reversals, misfortune. And there is a bleak realism here. In a time before blood transfusions and antibiotics, mothers died. Babies too. So it is something that Ichabod survived. Perhaps a name that means 'the glory has departed' is fitting for a boy who will grow up with no parents, no grandfather – perhaps even without God? Not knowing what happened to Ichabod adds to the bleakness. I found myself wanting to carry on the story, inventing a new life for him.

Recently I listened to excerpts from a memoir by Jeanette Winterson, who was adopted. She recalls a social worker explaining that her birth mother had breastfed her for several months. This was a significant gift. I should like to think of Ichabod being given his gift, the story of how determined his mother was to name him. Maybe in the end he, like Wordsworth, resolved that:

Though nothing can bring back the hour
Of splendour in the grass, of glory in the flower;
We will grieve not, rather find
Strength in what remains behind.

William Wordsworth,
'Ode: Intimations of Immortality' from
Recollections of Early Childhood

Mothers

Notes based on the New Revised Standard Version by

Annie Heppenstall

Annie Heppenstall writes on Christian spirituality from a perspective of environmental and social justice concerns, exploring feminine and natural imagery about God. She lives in a culturally diverse area of Birmingham where she enjoys deepening friendships with people of many faiths and none. Annie writes and presents reflective worship in a Celtic Christian spirit, which she finds offers a way to connect with God and scripture through the natural world.

2 Mothering continues

Genesis 16:1-16

To see God and live

Just as 'Father' is valued as a key to understanding something of God's nature, Mother too, *the* most profound and fundamental of relationships, reveals something to us of God. In the passages this week we encounter mothers each of whose stories offers a window on to God and our relationship with God.

Hagar is the epitome of exploited humanity, her choice restricted to risking death in the desert by running away or enduring life as a sex slave. Yet, for all her suffering, Hagar is blessed among women and gentiles because she meets, speaks with and names God. In a culture where child-bearing often increased a woman's status, something that has already led to animosity between herself and her mistress, Hagar surprisingly makes no response to the angelic news of a son. It is her encounter with God that completely absorbs her in that moment, filling her with awe. In the ups and downs of our own lives, can we too become so immersed in God's presence that all else takes second place? Is it right to be so engrossed in God? Jesus says it is: our love for others does not diminish through such devotion to God, it increases.

O God who sees all, give me vision that I may recognise your presence with me, and insight, that clarity may transform my inner confusion. Strengthen me to face the challenges of my life, touched by your mercy.

Letting go with a blessing

Genesis 24:28, 53-61

There is a strong sense of letting go, even though it hurts, in this account. Rebekah's mother must surely be torn between trusting her daughter to a stranger, rich though he may be, and keeping her close and safe. She is a single parent with responsibility, authority and love for her child, whom she has brought up to function successfully as an adult in that society. She has always known her daughter will one day have to leave in order to fulfil her own life and that this life will revolve, like her own, around marriage, mothering and home-making. Although she cannot know the details of her daughter's future, she knows the shape it is likely to take and Rebekah is equipped to step into the unknown with confidence.

Parents know the selfless, sacrificial nature of this essential nurture and letting go, as children become young adults and seek their own independence. Surely this reflects something of our God-given state of free will, which inevitably leads us on a path of seeming separation from God. Each life has to unfold. We have to mature and step into the unknown, free. All hopes, all fears are contained in the journey away from the mother who watches us go, but there is always a blessing to hold on to and a memory of love for comfort. But in the mother's heart there is an undying love, whether her child is present or not, and a longing for reunion. So it is, surely, with God.

O God who nurtures us and lets us go, help us to use our freedom wisely. Help us to step with courage into the unknown, knowing ourselves blessed by your word and held in your motherly love for ever, wherever our lives may lead us.

True reconciliation

Judges 17:1-6

It is quite likely that Micah was due to inherit his widowed mother's wealth one day but, unlike the prodigal son in Jesus' parable, he had not even bothered to ask for an advance, he just took it. Part of the woman's distress on finding it missing was surely the grief that she would have nothing to leave her son. Although she blesses Micah when she discovers the truth, this is not simply a story of cheap grace. It seems she recognises that he needs some help in order to change for the better. We may raise our eyebrows at the image she makes with the silver, but what effect does it have? Imagine its presence enshrined in his house – will it not serve as a constant challenge to his conscience? Is this not the mother's veiled call to self-reflection? Will the sight of the effigy finally bring Micah to the repentance and thanksgiving that seemed to be so distinctly lacking earlier in the story?

Repentance is the essential step towards true reconciliation with God and one another: remembering the prodigal son again, remorse finally turns his face back towards home, and then his father comes running out to him. The good news is God's grace, the forgiving parent. Just as the idol is taken away later in the story, so too is our shame. Perhaps Micah's mother is the agent of wisdom who helps her son to search his soul.

Forgive me, O God, for my moments of waywardness, when I take liberties with your love. Guide me, challenge me to find true humility in my heart, that I may learn to value the generosity of your grace.

Finding the love in our hearts

1 Kings 3:16-28

We might first engage with this account as outsiders. In the 'real' mother, we might see a model of divine love, desiring life for her child to the point of utter self-denial. Her self-sacrifice, we might also observe, is juxtaposed by the other woman who claims loving relationship but really has self-interest at heart. But this is not just a moral tale presenting us with a picture of godly versus ungodly attitude. It calls for personal engagement: it asks us whether there is anything of God's love in our own hearts for these characters. In many ways, perhaps it is easier to judge them than to love them. They are both prostitutes for a start. One is a liar and a child-snatcher. Solomon seems callous and domineering. But the women are victims of their own society. Solomon's response, seen negatively as indifference, or positively as detachment, simply allows truth to emerge – a touch of God's wisdom.

My question is, how can these women possibly go back to living together having suffered this breakdown of trust? Truth might be established, justice done, but where is the healing? Here the work of love begins, for there is a woman who is bereaved and a woman who has lost a friend, and the restoration of the child is not the end of the story. Solomon establishes truth, but what of love? Without judging, without trying to solve all their problems for them, how do we step into their brokenness as a compassionate presence?

O God, free me from the temptation to pass judgement on others. Give me instead the gift of love, that I may learn to bring your healing peace to this hurting world, this broken mother earth and her children.

Annie Heppenstall

Shalom and Shekhinah

Leviticus 24:10-23

This account is set in an ancient, emerging society in a hostile environment. A law has been instituted that sets the parameters, protecting the vulnerable and establishing accountability and limits to behaviour. The man who has infringed the agreed law is accountable, whether we feel uncomfortable about the penalty or not.

Looking for God, we should search beyond the law. The law, while of divine origin, is not God. The Hebrew Bible tells us often that God has, among infinite other qualities, steadfast love, mercy and compassion. The feminine word *Shekhinah* came to be used by the rabbis to describe God's presence. Melissa Raphael, in *The Female Face of God in Auschwitz* (Routledge, 2003), talks about the Shekhinah as compassionate presence, personified by real women sitting with others in their death. She says it is this presence that makes an otherwise bleak death 'good'. I would suggest that the mother's loving presence makes a difference in this way to her son's experience of death and, even, that she represents the Eternal One's continuing love (*hesed*) for the man even though he is subject to the instituted law. As though in confirmation, we are given the mother's name, rather than the man's. It is Shelomith, which is related to the word for true peace, shalom.

We might ask where the Shekhinah is to be found today: the compassionate, feminine presence of God. Is she present in our own hearts as we witness (and are caught up in) the violence of the world?

O God, break open my heart that I may be truly moved by the suffering around me, and by your grace express compassion in the face of despair and true peace in the face of violence, that your love may be made known in the world.

The One who yearns for us

Luke 7:11-17

At one level in this account, we see the familiar figure often described in sermons: a woman in a society where widows depend heavily on their sons to provide for them, that is, a woman in desperate need. It is often suggested that it is her vulnerability, her hopeless situation of destitution, that Jesus sees and responds to; he gives back her source of livelihood. This may be true, but she may in fact be perfectly able to provide for herself, like Micah's mother in Judges 17.

Economics aside, there is something else here, if we reflect on the event as a metaphor for our own situation. The account is about a separation that has occurred, and separation points to our own state of alienation from God. The mother's deep yearning for her beloved son can be seen as a reflection of God's yearning for us. We live with a sense of separation from our source, our God, who longs for us to awake and realise the love that is there for us. God longs for living relationship with us like a mother cherishing the thought of her absent child.

What do we read in Isaiah 49:15? God promises that, even if a mother might ever forget her own child, God will never forget us. Jesus calls us back to life and reunites us with the one who loves us. He is the agent of our restoration to the one who yearns for us: God, our Mother.

O God, touch me and wake me to the reality of your unending love, that I may come back to you with all my heart.

The call to ever-widening love

Mark 7:24-30

It is possible to feel a little disappointed with Jesus in this story, and to start making excuses for his apparent unfriendliness because he is tired and in need of time alone. Some have suggested that the woman brings about a shift in him, where he realises his mission goes beyond the 'lost sheep of the house of Israel'. There is something else in this account, however, that we find when we ask ourselves where and how God's presence is revealed. First, the mother's request to the man Jesus is a call for help. But it mirrors the divine call to all humanity ever to widen the outreach of love. Her call stirs something in Jesus that overrides his human fatigue with the irrepressible compulsion of the Christ to be the agent of that love.

In Jesus, both fully human and fully divine, we see the triumph over normal human weakness, in obedience to the divine call for mercy. In our own acts of mercy, it is the Christ waking in us and working through us, overriding our human inclination to avoid unwelcome demands. So, there is an interplay between the mother and Jesus that is both earthy and sublime. How often are we too called out of our weariness and withdrawal, and out of our prejudices, to extend compassionate love ever wider by, through and in the God of love who calls to us in such unexpected and unwelcome voices?

O God, open the ears of my heart, that I may hear your call. May Christ wake in me, stirred by voices I would rather ignore, to serve and to love with divine generosity until all the world knows itself loved and made whole by you.

Facing death

1 Facing death in the Old Testament

Notes based on the Hebrew Bible and the New Revised Standard Version by

Renato Lings

Kjeld Renato Lings is a Danish translator, theologian and writer. He has published a number of articles in English and Spanish and is currently preparing a book based on ten years of biblical research.

Genesis 21:15-18

Women and children in the wilderness

Hagar's tears of helplessness reach the ears of God. An angel leads her to a well that saves her life and that of her son Ishmael. Their desperate situation in the wilderness has contemporary parallels. As I write, thousands of Hagars and Ishmaels face starvation in the Horn of Africa. For women and children, the combination of natural disasters such as drought and manmade disasters in the form of armed conflict and anarchy is lethal.

In the affluent West, some women and children are exposed to violence in their homes. Women may be beaten up by their husbands or partners while the children watch. Some are killed and others escape. Many major cities have set up shelters offering protection to these modern-day Hagars and Ishmaels with nowhere to go.

For a number of years, young women from eastern Europe, Africa and Asia, looking for a better life in western Europe, have ended up as forced prostitutes. Once trapped in that situation, they are unable to break their chains. They literally live as prisoners struggling to survive in an urban jungle. Moreover, a growing number of unaccompanied children arrive as asylum seekers in the West from countries ravaged by war. What dangerous wildernesses have they had to traverse?

Exodus 22:21-23 reveals that God is moved to anger and compassion whenever defenceless women, children and migrants are mistreated.

God of compassion, let me be mindful this week of oppressed women and children facing danger and death.

The death of Jacob

Genesis 49:29-33, 50:1-3

Both Abraham and Jacob survive into peaceful old age. Abraham buries Sarah at the cave of Machpelah and he himself is laid to rest by his sons Ishmael and Isaac. As death approaches, Jacob charges his sons to take him to Machpelah so that he may be 'gathered to his people' (verse 29). To Jacob the idea of physical proximity to his kin is important even after dying.

In the rural community where I grew up it was customary for families to be buried together in one place. However, in contemporary Denmark, that habit is disappearing. Today families live dispersed and most people are buried near their place of residence. Still, many people are laid to rest next to their partners or spouses.

In most countries, being surrounded by loved ones when death approaches is regarded as normal. Most people want somebody trustworthy to be near them. Unfortunately, to some groups this privilege is denied. In a number of countries in which same-sex partnerships are not legally recognised, hospitals do not grant lesbian and gay people visiting rights as spouses when they apply for permission to be with their dying life companions beyond normal visiting hours. This can cause unimaginable distress.

Nowadays, many women and men in the Western world are single, divorced or widowed. It is not unusual for people to die in solitude. I sometimes wonder what my dying circumstances will be like. My mind echoes these words by Leonora Speyer: 'Let not my death be long, but light as a bird swinging' (in Elizabeth Gray Vining, *Facing One's Own Death*, Wider Quaker Fellowship, Philadelphia, 1994, p.3).

Pray for any who will die alone, or separated from loved ones, this day.

Moses dies

Deuteronomy 34:1-12

Following a long and sometimes tumultuous life, Moses breathed his last in the land of Moab, in Transjordania. He was not allowed to enter the promised land but died at peace with God and himself. His mission was accomplished, having led the people of Israel out of slavery in Egypt and through the desert to a new, very different, life in Palestine.

Many people do not have peace of mind in the face of death. Those who are anxious about dying often feel something important in their lives has been left undone. Perhaps they never managed to resolve old pain or past conflicts. Perhaps they realised too late that significant opportunities had slipped through their fingers. Some may regret that they did not develop and use their natural talents sufficiently. Perhaps they always dreamed about making a difference and never really succeeded. Broken dreams, unfinished plans and smouldering conflicts make it difficult to accept the fact that life is coming to an end.

I hope to be able to speak during my final days. I hope there will be a trustworthy person near me who can listen and understand. I will want to talk openly and freely about my life, successes and failures, joys and sorrows, hopes and wishes. And I will find it important to share thoughts about death, the afterlife, and God.

I will both lie down and sleep in peace,
For you alone, O Lord, make me lie down
in safety.

Psalm 4:8

The death of Saul

1 Samuel 31:1-13

In his final battle against the Philistines, King Saul is wounded and unable to flee. He prefers to die rather than have the approaching Philistines 'penetrate' him. The thought of painful humiliation at the hands of victorious enemies is more than he can take. Death is better than disgrace. So Saul commits suicide.

In the modern world, the issue of suicide is not as rare as some people think. Mental disease may drive patients to such despair that they take their own lives. Insecure teenagers bullied by peers are at great risk. Among the elderly, loneliness and widowhood may cause chronic depression. In many such cases, adequate counselling or treatment is crucial for preventing suicide attempts.

The story of the death of Saul raises further issues, including loyalty. After the mutilated bodies of Saul and his sons are put on public display in the land of the Philistines, they are stealthily retrieved at night by a group of faithful Israelites from Jabesh-Gilead. They bring the corpses back to their territory to be buried with dignity. Similarly, following the death of Saul's son Jonathan, who loved David as his own soul, David recites a passionate lament for his most intimate friend. After becoming king of Israel, David remains true to their lifelong covenant by taking Jonathan's crippled son Mephibosheth into his own household.

God of faithfulness, have mercy on those who take their own lives.

David mourns his son

2 Samuel
18:31 – 19:1

Losing a child is heartbreaking for any parent. On two occasions, David disconsolately mourns the death of a son. In both cases the Bible places responsibility for the tragedy squarely at David's feet.

David is a human being with a number of strengths. First, in antiquity, being a successful warrior is regarded as a blessing. Second, David behaves generously vis-à-vis his enemy King Saul. Third, after Jonathan's death, David remains faithful to the covenant established with his beloved friend.

However, David's weaknesses are notorious. His fatal affair with Bathsheba causes two deaths, namely those of her husband Uriah and the newborn baby. Furthermore, he is a disastrous father. Following the rape of his daughter Tamar, David does nothing. This causes deep resentment in Tamar's brother, Absalom, who takes revenge. As Absalom kills the rapist and stages a rebellion against his father, David and his household have to flee. However, as soon as Absalom loses the battle and dies, David declares himself in mourning.

The uncanny contradictions in David's life make me ponder the stark contrast between those who mourn the death of a child and certain Christian parents who reject their lesbian and gay children. This tragic situation is described in the documentary *Better Dead than Gay* (1996). Faced with the hostility of close relatives, many vulnerable youngsters are helpless. Not surprisingly, the suicide rate among young lesbian and gay people is considerably above average.

God of reconciliation, enable us to face the uncanny contradictions in our lives.

Teach us to count our days

Psalm 90:1-12

Like the psalmist, countless generations of poets have pondered the mystery of life on planet earth, in all its brevity. Two Danish poets have approached the theme from different perspectives. In one of her compositions, Grethe Risbjerg Thomsen has inverted the usual logic of the way we humans think of life and death. Here is my English translation of the poem 'Perhaps a Night in March' (*Måske en martsnat*, 1948):

I'm dying just a little
As seconds tick away.
My death I have to carry
Throughout the years of life.

Some balmy night with showers,
Perhaps it will be March,
Into the dark I'll wander
And leave dying behind.

For his part, Christian poet and songwriter C Richardt has pondered the ways in which human beings may learn wisdom and serenity from the cosmic forces governing nature. Here is an excerpt from his song 'Evening Star' (*Lær mig nattens stjerne*, 1861, translated by S D Rodholm). It reads almost like a prayer:

Mighty ocean, teach me
To do the task that needs me
And reflect, as days depart
Heaven's peace within my heart.
Mighty ocean, teach me.

Available at www.danamerica.com
/ibsen_cultural-values.pdf

Facing mortality

Psalm 103:13-18

Poet Karin Boye is much loved in her native Sweden. A library has been named after her, and at her statue in Gothenburg people regularly deposit flowers. During her lifetime, it was difficult for a woman to love another woman. Lesbian relationships were regarded as unacceptable. Karin Boye took her own life in 1941. While her days came to a tragic end, she fortunately blessed posterity with an impressive literary production. One of her best-known poems is 'Indeed It Hurts' (*Ja visst gör det ont*, 1935). Here she imagines the pain felt by buds as they burst, and she describes the anxiety experienced by water drops on a branch before falling to the ground. In Boye's universe, the fear of death and the unknown is mixed with the longing and attraction that are essential to the birth pangs of life.

In 1991, Danish poet Inger Christensen published an intensely beautiful collection of sonnets dedicated to the ephemeral lives of butterflies. These extraordinary poems speak of tensions between light and darkness, clarity and opacity, fullness and emptiness, transformation and permanence. There is intriguing attention to local detail coupled with breathtaking cosmic awareness. Amid the overall picture of exuberant natural life on a hot summer day, the notion of dying is subtly present. In the final sonnet, it is death with its own eyes looking straight at the poet from the wings of a butterfly.

Heavenly Creator of flowerbuds, water drops, butterflies, and human longing, may your name be glorified!

Facing death

Notes based on the New Revised Standard Version by

Jennie Hurd

Jennie Hurd is a presbyteral minister of the Methodist Church. For the past four years, she has been a full-time postgraduate student at the Queen's Foundation, Birmingham, engaged in doctoral studies in Practical Theology concerning pastoral care in death, dying and bereavement. Having served in three appointments in England and Wales, she returns to full-time ministry this autumn.

2 Facing death in the New Testament

Matthew 2:16-18

'It's all in here!'

As a teenager, I belonged to a youth fellowship group. Sometimes, the leader would wave his Bible at us, declaring, 'It's all in here!' I was sceptical: my life was far more complex than in biblical times, so how could these ancient texts say anything to me, many years later? Yet the Bible tells of people who, like us, experience the full range of all that it means to be human. Nowhere is this truer than in relation to the fundamentals of birth and death. Truly, 'It's all in here!'

The death of a child is a terrible tragedy. Herod's evil tyranny and paranoia, threatened by a baby boy, led to brutal murder and inconsolable grief. Jesus was as much in danger from Herod as the other little boys of Bethlehem because, from infancy to adulthood, his divine incarnation did not bring any additional protection from the vulnerability he shared with all humanity. Yes, he escaped death then, but to the risky life of a refugee rather than to safety. Thus the relevance of the wise men's gift of myrrh, used for embalming, was revealed sooner than anyone might have imagined. Even in his birth, Jesus embraced our human death.

Jesus, born of Mary, sharing our human life and death, you know our vulnerability and the risks and challenges we face. Be with us, in the power of your incarnate love, as we journey through life and death, and hold us always in your strong embrace, which is eternal.

Care and caring makes the difference

Luke 7:1-10

According to the old adage, death is the 'great leveller'. Maybe, but the same cannot be said about dying. Social and economic inequalities often persist until life's end, today as in the days of Jesus. End-of-life care in the UK, for example, is a world away from that which may be offered in the developing world. Wherever you are, if you are poor and disadvantaged, your dying is likely to be very different from that of someone who is rich and privileged.

There could hardly have been more disadvantaged or underprivileged circumstances for anyone during New Testament times than those of slavery. Bought and sold, denied their freedom, at the mercy of those who owned them, slaves were generally regarded as subhuman, no more worthy of compassion in their dying than they were in their living. The centurion's slave could easily have been in this position, had it not been for the fact that his owner 'valued' him (verse 2). This value could have been economic, emotional or both. Whichever (and the text seems to suggest the latter of the two), the centurion's caring about his slave in his dying enabled Jesus to show he cared.

Knowing that we are cared for can make all the difference to how we face death. For those who know this reality for themselves, to show God's care for one nearing the end of life is precious gift. It can be conveyed by something as simple as our presence and our prayers.

Jesus, compassion of God, you show God's love for those suffering and dying. Help us not to turn away in the face of death but to draw on your compassion to show your care. Be with us, in our living and dying. Enfold us, too, in your loving care.

Costly discipleship

Matthew 14:1-12

Another wicked and unjust death, another Herod. The Herod who ordered John the Baptist's killing was a son of the one who had commanded the slaughter of the infant boys of Bethlehem. Like father, like son, it's said: tyranny ran through the family like letters through a stick of rock. John's prophetic proclamation of God's kingdom and his ethical stance were too much for this Roman puppet ruler. John's execution was cowardly, pathetic and unnecessary.

Yet there was a terrible inevitability to it. John's personal integrity put him at enormous risk of death from one who was so corrupt himself. Like his father, this Herod was threatened by innate truth and goodness. John's death resonates with the deaths of Bethlehem's baby boys, thirty-odd years before; it resonates to the future, and the death of his cousin Jesus, and it resonates further still, to the deaths of the saints and martyrs of the centuries who could do nothing else but speak and live their faith in Christ. The powers that killed Dietrich Bonhoeffer, Oscar Romero and countless others, to this day, were more like the Herods than they might like to think.

Death can come sooner than it should for any who strive to live with faith and integrity. Stress and strain can take their toll on health; reduced economic circumstances, and the consequences, may come from living for the truth. There is a very real cost to discipleship, even unto death: is it one we would be prepared to pay?

Jesus, brother of all, you faced death throughout your life. You shouldered and suffered the consequences of being integrity personified. When following you with integrity demands the same, give us courage and faith. May the day of your justice come soon, and such untimely death be no more.

Life before (and after) death

Luke 16:19-31

Some years ago, the development agency Christian Aid had the slogan, 'We believe in life before death.' The words grab attention by contrasting with the Christian belief in life after death. In this parable, we have an evocation of both, with an added dimension. At the beginning, we meet poverty-stricken Lazarus, who endures a living death, and Dives who, in his affluent ignorance of Lazarus, indulges in deathly living. When both die, Dives becomes the one suffering deprivation akin to Lazarus' earlier situation, while Lazarus himself finds fullness of life. Their roles are reversed as the message is delivered.

Similar stories are found in the Egyptian and Jewish folk-tale traditions, and the version that Jesus told has always been popular. It has been falsely used by those with much in common with Dives to tell those who know what it's like to be Lazarus that it will all be all right: there'll be 'pie in the sky when they die'. While latter-day Dives types have been able to eat, drink and be merry, it's been convenient to forget those who, like Lazarus, would be glad of scraps from overladen tables. The parable demonstrates, however, the coherence of life and death in our relationships together. To show active, practical concern for the life of all can bring life to all, including ourselves, within the whole of eternity. When we deny life to others, we deny it to ourselves, eternally. This is tough teaching to receive from Jesus: death, or life.

Jesus, word of God, your words speak clearly in a world where so many face death before they die. Inspire and enable us to challenge the affluence and ignorance that allows this to happen and, in challenge and change, to find the life that is your will for all.

The resurrection, the life, the Messiah, the Son

John 11:17-27

I have lost count how many times I have stood before a coffin on the threshold of a church or crematorium chapel and declared the words of Jesus, 'I am the resurrection and the life.' Jesus himself spoke them as his journey to Jerusalem to face his own death drew ever nearer; they were spoken to a woman facing the grief and distress of the death of her beloved brother. For those who have followed the coffin of a loved one into a funeral service, they can bring painful reminders of sorrow and pain, as well as the reassurance of God's promised comfort and hope. These words resonate deeply.

The response these words provoked in Martha is remarkable. Martha, the activist, the practical sister; Martha, who demonstrated her love for Jesus by giving him the warmest welcome she could; Martha, who would no more have sat at the feet of the teacher than fly, responded to his question about her belief in his statement with a profound theological truth: 'you are the Messiah, the Son of God'. From the depths of her distress, facing the reality of death, Martha made a confession of faith as real as the disciple Peter's, without the experience of continuous months in Jesus' company.

The pain of facing bereavement and the death of one whom we love can be indescribable but, even in this, God may teach us something precious and new. Born in the facing of death, such insight can bring us life.

Jesus, bringer of life, comfort us with your presence when grief is real and raw. Help us as we face the pain and parting of death to put our trust in you. Teach us again that you are the resurrection and the life and, in that, give us hope.

United in uniqueness

John 13:33-38

On this All Saints' Day, we find ourselves in the company of Peter, upon whom Jesus said he would build his church. Peter is seen to be an impetuous character as we read the gospels. Possibly, in his declaration that he would follow Jesus to his death, laying down his life alongside him, he was responding immediately to the new commandment that Jesus had just given his disciples. To Peter, it may have seemed that the best way to show his love for Jesus there and then was to go to his death alongside him.

Jesus' death was unique, exceptional. However, it is true to say that everyone's death is unique. No one else can die our death. It is ours alone. Not only did Jesus know that Peter's desire to die alongside him suggested a promise he would never be able to keep, but it was also the case that Jesus needed to die his death uniquely. Peter's accompaniment of him in death would have been a distraction from the work that was Jesus' – Jesus' alone.

When we find ourselves alongside others as they face death, this scenario may give helpful insights. It's not good to make promises we cannot keep and, although we may long to, we cannot die another's death for them. However difficult it is, the faithful presence of those at the cross gives a model for us to follow. In giving loving support to those who face death, we learn more how to face our own.

Jesus, lover of all, we thank you for all your saints. We remember those present and those who have gone before. Help us to learn from their example how to live and die, so that, as we face death, we may never be alone, and know ourselves uniquely loved.

Facing death in the depths of despair

Matthew 27:1-8

A prison chaplain friend asked me to sponsor her for a fundraiser for the Samaritans. She explained the vital part this telephone listening service plays in prisons, supporting offenders whose despair brings them to want to take their own lives. Having someone available to hear them, unconditionally, can make the difference between death and life.

Judas' remorse at betraying Jesus was evidently real. He repented his crime and confessed to the religious leaders, the Sanhedrin. Having got what they wanted, they had no concern for his feelings or future. Racked with guilt, rejected, Judas chose to face death. In his isolation, it seemed the preferable option. For many, it is impossible to imagine the despair that compels people not just to think about killing themselves but actually to do it. Judas was at the lowest point a human being can reach.

Compare his situation with that of Peter, whose own betrayal of Jesus immediately precedes this passage. He also felt bitter remorse. The brash, impetuous man who had promised to follow Jesus to the death was reduced to weeping by his part in the fate of Jesus. Peter, however, managed to return to the disciple group. In John 21 we find him heard and reconciled by the risen Christ, his threefold betrayal replaced by a threefold declaration of love. Peter went on to live, fully.

It can be hard to understand someone who deliberately faces and chooses death. Being met and heard in deep isolation, however, can be a true life-saver.

Jesus, hope of the hopeless, we pray for those who betray and are betrayed. In the depths of despair, when to choose death seems the only option, bring your compassion and your love. Take away isolation, let feelings be heard and make it possible again to choose life.

Facing death

3 Facing death with God on our side

Notes based on the New Revised Standard Version by

Paul Nash

Paul Nash is Senior Chaplain at Birmingham Children's Hospital, where he heads up a multi-faith team. He served his curacy in Aston, Birmingham. He is also a part-time tutor at the Midlands Centre for Youth Ministry at St John's Nottingham, where he teaches ethics, practical theology and ministerial formation. In his spare time he enjoys writing, playing golf, watching films and is always theologically reflecting.

Psalm 71:17-21

So who's got you?

This week's readings are about God and death. Where is God when we die? What does God have to say about approaching death? There is a wonderful story about a man who has fallen down a cliff and is about to be rescued. Someone reaches down over the ledge; all the man can see is this arm reaching out of nowhere. As his hand is grabbed and he is swung off the ledge, a voice says 'Don't worry, I have got you.' The man replies, 'Yes, but who has got *you*?' The answer, as we shall see, is that, when it comes to our death, God has got us.

The Jews of the Hebrew Bible had a very different view of the afterlife from that of us Christians. On the whole they believed they would live on not in heaven but in the lives of their children. That is why generations are so important. Our verses today implore God not to forsake the writer in old age. My wife and I do not have children, so we do not have the comfort of the thought of their looking after us when we get old, frail, sick or dying. This is where I must trust God to be with me.

What are your fears of ageing? Which are the areas where you find it hard to trust God?

Are there bits of you that God hasn't got?

Creator God, help me to trust you in those times and places where I find it hard.

The wise on the hill

Psalm 121

Where does my help come from? What a great question. There are so many places we can look for help: family, friends, money, work and the ubiquitous internet search! God can sometimes be an afterthought for us, but not to the psalmist.

The hills in our reading today are the hills on which Jerusalem was built and, more importantly, the temple. The Jews reciting this psalm were looking up to the temple, where they knew God resided. They were not looking to some nice view; they were not even looking upward to heaven – they were looking towards the place where they believed God could be found. It was on such a hill, Mount Moriah, that Abraham went to sacrifice Isaac, a story that would be familiar to the hearers of the psalm, who would know how God watched over Abraham and provided a lamb. They would expect God to watch over them too.

Over the past ten years I have read this psalm more than any other. I find it a challenge and a comfort. I have used it in times of loss and bereavement and know it will continue to provide comfort even in death.

Do I look to God's presence for comfort or am I distracted to look to other places for help and hope?

I thank you, Lord God of the hills, that I can look to you for help always and that you watch over me for ever.

Too good to be true?

Luke 23:39-43

We are often warned, when we hear a really good offer, that if it sounds too good to be true then it probably is! This is how it must have seemed to the criminal being executed with Jesus. We do not know what this criminal did but let's imagine the victims of the crime(s) overhearing the conversation. What would they have thought? We might think they would have been justified in feelings of revenge, anger and hatred. 'An eye for an eye' is still a philosophy many people hold. But God has a different perspective.

This paradise, or garden, is the same place mentioned in the story of Lazarus and the rich man in Luke 16:19-31, where Lazarus is found in the bosom of Abraham, a place referred to in the Talmud as a place of comfort and rest between death and resurrection.

Who do we expect to be in heaven? Mass murderers, rapists, fraudsters? However we understand this place, the promise is that it is never too late to turn to God and to be welcomed by God. When we reflect back on our life there may be many things we are ashamed of, and as we approach death we may be very grateful for this gracious response of Jesus, a response that can bring comfort and assurance.

Sometimes that really good offer *is* true.

Gracious God, please remember me, and help me to keep turning to you.

Befriending death

John 14:1-7

I have recently worked on a book called *Sam and His Special Book* (Christian Education, 2011) about a child who has a life-threatening illness and cannot be cured (cheerful, I know). Sam hears this story in John by Jesus and starts thinking about what his room will be like. He begins to draw rooms for himself, his family and his friends. The book finishes by saying that, although Sam does not know what his room will be like, he does know that he will be with his friend Jesus.

What Sam is doing is 'befriending death', making death and heaven his friend. For some this is a very difficult thing to do. I describe myself as a 'friend of death'; I know death, and death knows me. This is a liberating place to be and helps me to be present and minister to those who are facing their own death or the death of a loved one.

It can be easy to let our heart be troubled, to fear what we don't know and can't see. But we need to live now, with all our worries, aches and troubles, in a place where our hearts, minds and spirit are not disturbed, but at peace, comforted by the promises of Jesus. He has gone ahead of us and prepared a place for us, so that you and I and Sam will always have a place where we belong.

Loving God, you know that I sometimes get anxious about what is beyond this life. Help me to have hope and assurance in your word. Help me to understand what it means to face death with you at my side.

That's just greedy

John 14:18-27

What do you mean, you want even more than Jesus? What else could we possibly need apart from the Son of God? Well, Jesus seems to think we need something, or should I say someone else, as well.

As his death was imminent, Jesus was focusing on the needs of those he was leaving behind. For some of us, our own death isn't too difficult to think about, it's being left behind by someone we love or leaving them behind that is harder. It is reassuring to know that in those difficult circumstances the Holy Spirit will be close to us and those we love. It is encouraging to think about the wild goose, the Spirit, teaching us and reminding us of all Jesus has previously promised us about death and the life beyond. We need not be afraid or troubled; the Spirit assures us of heaven.

It may be helpful to think of the image of the Holy Spirit as a dove, the dove of peace, emblematic of shalom, the promise of wholeness that will be ours in the life to come. In the midst of our death or the death of a loved one, we have the promise of Jesus that he has left a comforter for us.

Think back to your childhood. Did you have a comfort blanket or toy? If so, remember how it made you feel. Ask God to help you have that same sense of security through the Holy Spirit's presence with you. What symbol acts as a reminder of that presence today?

Gracious God, help me to be open to all the counsel and comfort your Holy Spirit wants to give me.

It's a hard choice ... sometimes

2 Corinthians 5:1-10

They say the trouble with getting old is that your body feels a hundred but your mind tells you you are 22! I can still do most of what I could do thirty years ago, just not as fast! In this passage, Paul seems to give us permission to complain about our bodies and lives now. It is okay not to be satisfied with this frail, physical body.

The trouble is, most of the time I rather enjoy this life. Most of the time it's fun, a pleasure and privilege, to serve God. I have not experienced many of the hardships and difficulties that the apostle Paul did in his life, although I can imagine that if you find life hard then you would long to be with God.

I have a bucket list, a list of all the things I want to do before I die. Two of the things I have crossed off are seeing the Grand Canyon and playing golf at Pebble Beach – both beautiful places, perhaps a glimpse of heaven on earth, my sort of heaven anyway! We live by faith and not by sight and my faith is in what God has promised and my actions are those I hope are pleasing to God. I may not understand everything now but I try to live in the light of what I do understand.

Which do I want more, my earthly or heavenly body? Why? What in this passage is hard to grasp? How can I have an attitude that is more like Paul's?

Lord, help me to live a life pleasing to you in this body and my heavenly one.

Hard comfort

Revelation 21:1-7

In my work as chaplain in a children's hospital, there is not much one can say when a child dies. 'I am so sorry for your loss', is sometimes all I can say. To jump in with all God's promises of peace and assurance is inappropriate, insulting even, even if it is true.

One parent told us, 'Don't worry about saying the wrong thing, whatever you say can be no worse than what has already happened to us.' The comfort many of these families find, some quickly, some in time, is that their child is no longer suffering. Although their hearts break at their loss, and they wish the child was with them still, and they would give their own life for that of their child, the promises I make to them that their child is in a place with no more needles, operations or pain are like words of balm to their broken souls. This is our final promise of the week: we can look forward to a place with no more death, or perhaps even more comforting, no more dying.

'The end' – there are so many times when we look forward to those two words, but how do we feel about them in relation to our own death? How do we understand the idea of a new Jerusalem? Is it part of what we are hoping for? What is it we are looking forward to most in heaven?

Thank you, God, that your promises of a place where there is no more dying, death, grief or suffering will be mine one day.

Facing death

Notes based on the New Revised Standard Version by

Susan Hibbins

Susan Hibbins is a freelance writer and editor who endeavours to apply the Christian faith to everyday living in the 21st century. She is especially interested in history and choral music, and is secretary of a local community choir.

4 Facing death and beyond death

Matthew 27:45-54

Jesus' death on the cross

There is a tendency today to celebrate Palm Sunday and Jesus' entry into Jerusalem surrounded by cheering crowds, and to hurry past the events of Good Friday to reach the joy of Easter Day. Instead, we need to spend the hours of Good Friday at the foot of the cross, and look steadily at the figure on it. Jesus died. His death was one of the most agonising ever devised; his body was savagely beaten and then broken, for us.

We know that this was not the end, that the resurrection awaits. But none of those watching the crucifixion, their terror mounting as darkness deepened over Golgotha, knew that Jesus would rise again. All they knew was the dreadful torment of watching their Lord and friend die in agony and, perhaps worse, feeling separated from his heavenly Father. His anguished cry, 'My God, my God, why have you forsaken me?' (verse 46) must have torn at the disciples' hearts, who had heard Jesus speak so often of his Father's love. Even the words of the centurion confirm it: 'Truly, this man was God's son' (verse 54). Jesus' life was over. To understand fully the miracle of the Resurrection, we need to keep vigil with the disciples at Calvary.

Help us, dear Lord, never to forget the sacrifice you made for us on the cross. Dying, you enabled us to live.

He lives!

Mark 16:1-8

Shock and fear follow anguish and grief for the women who visit Jesus' tomb to pay him one last service. Their emotions must already have been at breaking point, and to be confronted with an empty tomb and a 'young man, dressed in a white robe' (verse 5), telling them that Jesus was not there, would have felt almost too much for them. Unable to take it in, perhaps fearing a cruel hoax, they run away and tell no one. Did they stop and think, later on, and begin to remember Jesus' words to them, that he would rise again on the third day? Then did they start to believe?

The dread and horror of Good Friday have gone, to be replaced by a heart-stopping joy. Jesus has conquered death. He is alive again, and whole. And his promises begin to make sense to us too: 'I am the resurrection and the life. Those who believe in me, even though they die, will live, and everyone who lives and believes in me will never die' (John 11:25).

The last time I heard these words spoken was at my mother's funeral. Just like the women at the tomb, words meant to convey good news to me did nothing, just then, to make me feel any joy. Although I was relieved that my mother's suffering was at an end, my belief that she was yet alive was something I felt only with my head, because I read the words. I didn't know it in my heart for some time. Maybe it is just too wonderful for us to take it in. Because, if Jesus' words are true, then there is no need to mourn. Eternal life for us is a fact. It started at dawn in the hush of a garden, and it will continue for all time.

To die for our faith

Acts 7:54-60

Stephen is the first in a long line of Christian martyrs. Like Jesus before him, Stephen prayed that those who killed him might be forgiven for their sin.

In the early days of Christianity and right through its long history, countless Christians have been killed for their faith, sooner than deny it. One of the most moving sights in Rome, for me, was the simple cross that stands in the Colosseum, a memorial of all those Christians who died terrible deaths in the arena for the amusement of the Roman crowd and ruling elite.

In more modern times Christians have been silenced for standing against injustice, and for refusing to be intimidated. Martin Luther King, leader of a high-profile campaign for civil rights and equality in the United States, a passionate speaker for the marginalised, was gunned down in 1968. Oscar Romero, speaking out against the oppression of the poor and the persecuted in El Salvador, was assassinated in 1980 while celebrating Holy Communion.

We may never be placed in a position where we face death for speaking out for our faith. But do we stand up for our Christian belief if it is being ridiculed? How do we react to racist jokes? To blasphemy? Are we prepared to face ostracism or to lose face among our work colleagues, for example, because we refuse to join in general laughter at someone's expense? Do we have the courage of Stephen, and of all those other men and women who died sooner than deny their Lord?

Sometimes, Lord, I find it hard to find the courage to stand up for what I believe in. When I find myself with the chance to proclaim you as my Lord, help me to speak up bravely, trusting the consequences to your unfailing love.

Storm at sea

Acts 27:9-26

This story might have been written yesterday. Sailors everywhere have faced the same choices. Stay or go? Chance it and hope for the best? The passage reminds me of scenes from the film *The Perfect Storm*, in which the captain and crew of a fishing vessel decide to try to push through a huge storm at sea rather than lose their catch, and their money. Catastrophe follows and all aboard are lost. First- or twenty-first-century sailors who fail to respect the sea pay a high price.

We can imagine the rising panic on Paul's ship as the storm increases, and as the crew tries and fails to stabilise the ship. Nothing works and, after they have run out of ideas and the storm continues to batter them, the sailors abandon themselves to their fate.

Yet in the face of possible drowning, Paul was able, by force of his own personality and the demonstration of his faith, to hold the crew together long enough to ride out the storm and eventually reach Malta (Acts 28:1). Clearly Paul's belief that it was God's will that he stand before the Emperor in Rome, and that therefore he and those with him would be safe, was such that he did not give the threat of death another thought.

We may never face shipwreck at sea but our lives may be threatened by other 'storms'. Illness, frailty, accidents: all bring our mortality uncomfortably close. Have we the faith to trust the outcome to God?

Dear Lord, help us to entrust our days, however long or short, to your unfailing care.

No separation

Romans 8:31-39

Paul might have been thinking of his own experiences of hardship, distress and peril (verse 35), and yet his faith in Christ is such that he can state unequivocally that nothing at all, whatever it might be, can separate us from God's love. Not even death can. It is a thought worth hanging on to every morning when we awake.

Many people fear death. The idea that life will one day be over for us, that the world will carry on without us, is not something we want to think much about, let alone accept. We fear too the manner in which death might come, perhaps with great pain or intolerable anguish; we fear we might die alone.

In dying and defeating death, Jesus comes to take away our fear of death. There is no circumstance, no part of life, where God's love in Jesus will not be available to us. There is no situation that might arise, no experience he has not known before us, nowhere we can go but we will find him there. Psalm 139 reminds us: 'If I take the wings of the morning and settle at the farthest limits of the sea, even there your hand shall lead me, and your right hand shall hold me fast' (Psalm 139:9-10). And if it should happen that physically we die alone, we will not be alone, for his hand will be in ours, waiting to lead us into a greater life.

When we feel afraid for the future, Lord, help us to remember your great promises through Jesus Christ. In faith help us to live, and to remember your promise that nothing can separate us from you.

Where, O death, is your sting?

1 Corinthians 15:51-58

Losing our loved ones is among the hardest things that we will face in our lives. However much we try to make sense of a death, seeing it perhaps as a blessed release for someone very ill or aged, nothing can make up for the fact that our beloved ones are no longer here. We cannot hold their hand, give them a hug, hear their voice or say all those things that we wished we had said. The silence they leave behind them is hard to bear. Yet Paul's words reassure us that that silence is not the end. Life has the victory, not death.

When my mother died, I felt numb. The pain in my heart took many months to heal. And yet, even in the darkest time, I would sometimes feel a tremendous sense of joy. It is hard to put into words, yet it seemed that for a moment the door of heaven opened just enough to show me the glory that lay beyond, and to reassure me that my mother was safe, and at peace, and beloved. Fanciful, you may say. Delusional, many would certainly say. Those moments did not take away my grief but they made it bearable, gave me hope that the sadness would one day pass. Death's sting has been translated into hope, and hope into victory.

Be with all who grieve today, Lord. Comfort their sorrow with your presence, and reassure them that death is not the end, but a beginning for all who dwell in your love.

The victory of Jesus

Philippians 2:5-11

We end the week's readings where we began, with the death of Jesus on the cross. Here, though, we see Jesus 'in the form of God' (verse 6), one with the Father, before his coming to earth in human form. Reading these words we are reminded that Jesus entered our human life voluntarily, went to a broken world to redeem and restore it, and us, to a right relationship, with God. In obedience to that choice, all his life was directed to that one end. To those who would listen, he spoke the word of life that stayed in their hearts. When people would listen no longer he went to the cross and died for them. In doing so he defeated death, for no power could destroy the love that took him there. As risen Lord, he is exalted with 'the name that is above every name' (verse 9).

In Jesus' coming to be one of us, we see a glimpse too of the nature of God. Some people today still see God, even unconsciously, as an angry parent who has to be appeased somehow, by our being on our best behaviour. But the fact that God in Jesus came to earth to win us should tell us something about the nature of God's love for us. What did it cost God to watch Jesus suffer as he did? There is nothing God does not know about sorrow and grief. Yet love has the final word, and Jesus' victory over death is complete.

Help us to be aware of your great love for us, Lord, that for love of us Jesus took on our human life and went to the cross and died. Help us to know that your love for us will never change, in this life or in the life eternal that awaits us.

Readings in Luke (2)

4 Jesus the teacher

Notes based on the New International Version by

Eun Sim Joung

Eun Sim Joung is a research scholar at the Queen's Foundation, Birmingham. She holds a PhD from Birmingham University, published as *Religious Attachment* (Cambridge Scholars, 2008). She is involved in lay ministry with international women in Birmingham. She has been a visiting lecturer teaching women's studies and leadership at a number of universities in Korea.

Luke 13:1-9

The portrait of the teacher

In the gospels, one of the portraits of Jesus is as a teacher who possesses great teaching skills. He asks intriguing questions to invite people to engage in deep dialogue. His teaching is usually twofold: he tells stories and parables to help people understand the truth, and at the same time this very method conceals the truth from others. Using images from nature is one of his most common methods. Whatever the method, the lessons of his teaching are very challenging.

Many people asked questions of Jesus, with different motivations. Some asked genuine questions while others asked merely to trick him. Whatever the motivation of the questioner, they were amazed by his answers, which were seldom comfortable for the questioners.

This week's readings from Luke 13 and 14 illustrate Jesus' teaching on several occasions. In today's reading, Jesus perceives the questioner's mind and asks if the people killed by Roman soldiers were worse sinners than any others. He answers his own question with a firm 'no' (verse 3). The lesson is clear. In God's eyes, all are equally responsible and all are offered the same chance of repentance. The parable of the fruitless tree and the mercy-begging gardener demonstrates the compassion of God who is always willing to offer another chance.

Lord, our great teacher, help us to become good teachers like you.

Two kinds of teacher

Luke 13:10-21

Chang was caught by a teacher and taken to his tutor for breaking a school rule by climbing a tree in the playground to pick chestnuts. He knew that a boy in another class who had done the same thing was severely told off and smacked with a baseball bat by the boy's tutor. At the office, Chang was trembling with fear while waiting for his tutor to arrive. His tutor, Ohkii Kim, came, smiled at him and tapped his shoulder, saying 'Don't do it again.' The teacher's name and address were engraved on the doorpost of his room and also in the boy's heart. Thirty-five years on, he still remembers the tutor's name and address.

In today's passage, two kinds of teacher appear: Jesus and the synagogue ruler. Jesus saw and responded immediately to the woman's needs, while the ruler imposed a lifeless, abstract principle. What makes Jesus' teaching different from that of the Pharisee? Jesus was able to read the questioner's needs and also relate the text to the context. His teaching was focused on giving life.

His teaching in the synagogue on the Sabbath concludes with a parable. Why this parable of the mustard seed and yeast? The kingdom of God will flourish like that.

Life-centred teaching is also like planting a mustard seed that will grow in pupils' hearts. It is like mixing yeast into flour that will influence and transform pupils' lives.

Think of an experience of being a teacher or a learner. What elements, whether positive or not, make you remember it? In what way has it inspired or informed you?

'Make every effort!'

Luke 13:22-30

This saying from verse 24 reminds me of a video clip. Some leading university students in Korea run a website called 'god of study'. They support high school students by uploading video clips giving mentoring, information for studying and tips for preparing exams. 'We will do everything except studying for you. Do not worry about anything else but just make every effort in studying!' it says at the end of the speech in one of the video clips.

'Make every effort!' Jesus knew that it was no use wondering how many people would enter the kingdom or sitting back as if they were already saved. Jesus wanted his hearers to *do* something, to participate in their own salvation. This does not mean that deeds save us.

What does he mean by 'Make every effort' (verse 24), then? Verses 26-27 are quite interesting. 'We ate and drank with you, and you taught in our streets' (verse 26). This points to those who had come around Jesus but were not genuinely interested in his teaching. 'Away from me, all you evildoers' (verse 27), Jesus responds. Pretending to be engaged or being preoccupied with other things may be a form of evil that separates us from the loving action of God. It is, in fact, acting untruly and doing evil.

Lord, you gave everything to save us but we thought and acted as if we were self-justified. Forgive our arrogance and evildoing. We know that we need only to open our hearts and listen to your words. Help us to make every effort to do so.

'You were not willing!'

Luke 13:31-35

Jesus is told by the Pharisees to leave Jerusalem, as Herod wants to kill him. Were they actually concerned about Jesus? Jesus laments, 'O Jerusalem, Jerusalem … how often I have longed to gather your children together, as a hen gathers her chicks under her wings, but you were not willing!' (verse 34) The first chapter of John's Gospel states the same, 'The light shines in the darkness, but the darkness has not understood it' (John 1:5). 'He came to that which was his own, but his own did not receive him' (John 1:11). We catch a glimpse here of the divine desperation, deepest sorrow and heart-aching grief that compassionate love must bear.

At some points in their lives, many teachers and parents identify with this portrait of a lamenting Jesus. Twenty years ago, I taught at a high school in the outskirts of Seoul. Many pupils were not self-motivated. They were not willing to learn. Some had no textbooks, pens or notebooks. Some boys were distracting the class by making noises. A few girls were daydreaming. One boy put his shoes on the desk and was polishing them. Nowadays they would be texting and watching videos on their telephones.

Nothing is truly achieved unless you are earnestly willing. Fortunately or not, I did not remain long with these pupils. Jesus, however, stayed with the people who rejected him. He did everything that he could do, even giving his own life.

Lord, you sent so many signals to teach us, but we did not recognise or understand them. Forgive our unwilling and unresponsive hearts. Thank you for your unconditional love and sacrificial teaching. Help us to be willing to open our hearts and accept it.

Having many eyes and ears

Luke 14:1-11

Teachers were highly respected in former days in Korea. Royalty, teachers and parents were regarded on the same level. Teachers had absolute authority and were regarded as mystical figures. In my school days there was always at least one naughty pupil in the class trying to trick the teacher, yet the naughty pupils' plans were never successful, even though they carefully watched the teacher and planned their tricks. The teacher said, 'You didn't know I had many eyes and ears!'

Jesus was carefully watched by Pharisees wherever he went and whatever he did. But they too were watched by Jesus. Jesus observed people closely in order to teach, carefully watching human nature and teaching about human desires, tendencies and habits.

He knew that the Pharisees were watching how he would react to an ill man on the Sabbath day. Jesus, however, asked them, 'Is it lawful to heal on the Sabbath or not?' (verse 3). They remained silent. Their careful plan was exposed by his counter-question. Ingenious! Jesus also noticed that people tended to pick the places of honour at the table. He taught, however, that being humble was the only way to receive honour. He had many eyes and ears in his body. The eyes can perceive the inward truth of the mind and soul. The ears can listen to deep desires, pains and needs.

Lord of deep vision and hearing, we know that we cannot hide from you. Teach us how to be humble.

Seeking the poor in spirit

Luke 14:12-24

Cheolsu always wore a yellow shirt during most of his school days, as his family could not afford to buy many shirts. In his art class, he applied himself with diligence, although he was not good at art. The teacher said, 'Nobody did as well as the boy with the yellow shirt.' From then on, the teacher called him 'the boy with the yellow shirt'. The shame that he had previously felt for wearing the same shirt every day turned into pride.

When missionaries first came to Korea about 150 years ago, they started mission schools. People, particularly the ruling class, did not approve of this because it challenged their educational privilege. Now women, servants and those from the low class were invited and took full advantage of the free education provided by the missionaries.

'Blessed are those who will eat at the feast in the kingdom of God' (verse 15), said one of the privileged who were invited to the dinner in the house of a prominent Pharisee. This man spoke as if he was already at the feast of God. Jesus told the parable of the great banquet in response. I wonder who would be more grateful for the banquet: the privileged who thought they had a right to be there, or the outcast who did not think they were worthy enough. Who is truly blessed?

Lord, give us wisdom to appreciate what we have, but let us long for what you have still to give us generously in your grace. Teach us how to be poor in spirit.

Provocative teaching

Luke 14:25-35

Today's passage is somewhat puzzling. Why did Jesus suddenly turn to the large crowd and speak all these teachings concerning the high cost of discipleship? Then, after the hard teaching, why did he finish his teaching by saying, 'Whoever has ears to hear, let them hear' (verse 35b)? When it is difficult to understand his teaching, how do we apply it in practice?

In fact, Jesus' teaching is quite often twofold. It is a teaching for those who are willing to wrestle with it, and also for those who have ears to listen. Jesus knew that in a large crowd someone's identity could be easily hidden and one could be less committed. Perhaps he foresaw that the large crowd would cheer him on the way to Jerusalem, and shortly afterwards would turn into a cruel mob. Jesus' teaching is particularly offered to provoke individuals to wrestle with it.

We are not wrestling with something if we are not committed to it. When I was at university, I was the only Christian among my closest friends. We often discussed and wrestled with some ultimate questions about God, Jesus, the universe and humanity. Twenty-five years on, they all became active Christians and committed their lives to Jesus, much more than I do now.

Lord, you seek our full commitment to you. Forgive our tendency of wanting to hide in a crowd and avoid your calling with all sorts of excuses. Restore in us our full saltiness so that we are fully committed to you.

Readings in Luke (2)

Notes based on the New Revised Standard Version by

Paul Kybird

Paul Kybird has worked for the Methodist Church in London for the last twelve years in adult education, with a particular concern for the training of local preachers, and mission consultancy for churches and circuits.

5 The kingdom is among you

Luke 16:1-9

Wake up to money

At 5.30 on weekday mornings, on BBC Radio Five Live, you can listen to a programme called 'Wake up to Money'. To the financial expert it is no doubt helpful and informative but, to the ordinary listener, stories of fortunes won or lost, market prices, global financial meltdown and threats to pensions are disturbing. It's not the way to start the day – an apocalyptic moment just when you don't need it! However, as we approach Advent, that time of reckoning, 'Wake up to money' sets our theme exactly. At every point we hear Jesus dealing with money issues. We glimpse great wealth, grinding poverty and people driven by the desire and need for money. With the skill of a great teacher, Jesus calls us to 'Wake up to money!'

This is the sort of story that would make the lighter moment on 'Wake up to Money'. It has all the essential ingredients. Handling money is the cause of the problems and their solution, and it's a bit of rascally dishonesty that a very rich master can take in his financial stride and even be amused by, so no one gets hurt. Maybe the disciples waited with interest to hear Jesus condemn this scandal. If so, they were disappointed. The world of money has trained the steward to see the danger, plan ahead and take action. In this story, decisive use of dishonest wealth is what secures friendship and the future. What will secure the disciples' relationships and destiny?

Lord, wake me up to money, and wake me up to what really gives life.

'Money, money, money!'*

Luke 16:10-13

The harsh language of this passage springs from the ghastly economic context of slavery. The slave would know better than anyone the meaning of having one master whose every whim was law, and the impossibility of serving two.

What responsibility does the slave have? Just to obey orders, any orders – no thought involved. Better not to think, just act. Like slaves given orders, our cultural habits can be so strong that we can be entirely unaware of what we do or what is driving us. Such is the subtlety of the way people let money master relationships, decisions and values that it may not be at all easy to see or hear clearly who is the master we really obey.

Throughout history, Christians have found motives shaped by the need and desire for money a dreadful challenge. Hindsight teaches us clearly the mistakes of earlier generations, but how well do we know ourselves and our motives? Motivation is crucial and Jesus struggles to bring it to a conscious level for the people. His stark words aim to help them understand themselves and the impact on their lives of obsession with money. And for us? It really is time to wake up to money and begin to examine our attitudes towards money and how it shapes our world.

How do we face the challenge of escaping money-driven values in a world (often unknowingly) obsessed by them?

Lord, again we ask, help us to wake up to money and to our true service of you.

* This week's headings are quotations from songs by Abba and Paul Simon (Universal Music Publishing Group/EMI).

'If I had me a wealthy man'

Luke 16:14-18

Money provokes the fiercest arguments, and this shows how deeply we care about it. The Pharisees have something to say to Jesus and in strong language! Jesus' language is as strong in return and raises the most fundamental and sensitive matters, not the economic world of master/slave, but the Law and the great movement of God that began with the Advent figure of John the Baptist. However, the context of this passage shows the risk we take if we leave money behind at this point. Perhaps we need to ask what the Law has to say about money and its power and its use. Can the Pharisees with their wealth-driven values still hear fully what God commands?

Maybe the saying about adultery that seems rather out of context here nevertheless still pertains to financial issues. Was the Law capable of manipulation in cases of marriage and divorce if money was at stake? Is that why it must not change? Maybe there were ways of dealing with people then as now that valued them only for financial profit. It is always surprising what cannot be changed with carefully rationalised justification by skilful and determined minds, if the rewards are great enough! And what rewards more than money? All too easily God's most dedicated servants can slip into hypocrisy. The questions of anti-capitalist demonstrators camped outside St Paul's Cathedral as I write are vital for the health of the church and wider society.

Teach us, Lord, to understand our deepest motivation and so save us from hypocrisy.

'so lonesome I took some comfort there'

Luke 16:19-31

Here we are in a broken world of extreme wealth and desperate poverty. Jesus describes an everyday sight that is all too recognisable in our own time. Does the vision of the afterlife where roles are reversed lift the mood? And is the vision of the beggar finding comfort and the rich suffering what we mean by justice? Should the beggar be content that things will get better? And the wealthy challenged to be more generous? How would that impact the yearning to build an economic system fairer to all? Jesus pictures the fears of and for the rich.

Habits of money die hard. When people can be sent to do another's bidding (slaves, beggars or any who might be useful), there are signs of money-corrupted relationships. Then we catch a glimpse, on the rich man's lips, of what might truly make the difference, the power of resurrection. As Christians, we know that possibility in the core of our being; we have lived with it for many centuries. But the poor, and super-rich, are still with us. Wealth and its complexities are a mighty power. Faced with them we do not have to look far into our hearts to sense failure of nerve when it comes to trying to make a difference. The story ends with a gloomy realism that would rob us of hope if it does not serve to remind us that there is battle to be joined.

Lord, give us courage to know and to battle in the power of your resurrection.

'If I had a little money'

Luke 17:1-10

Just how intimidating could Jesus be? The disciples' anguished cry for faith shows the impact he was having as he continued to expose the corrupting spell that money can cast over the integrity of even the dedicated disciple.

Verse 4 exposes a context where numbers are carefully monitored, contingencies budgeted for, accurate records kept, investments anticipated. But the beautiful gift of forgiveness is not to be measured, rationed or bargained for. The echoes of such calculation can be heard too behind Jesus' strictures on leadership. The precious calling to care comes with responsibilities that stretch human potential to the full, not as something to be accrued as a source of self-esteem.

Only faith can help, but money can still cast its corrupting spell. How can dependence on and openness to the Father be measured? The glorious graceful relationship of faith – is it, too, subject to investment and profit? For human beings, the temptation to calculate is always there. Jesus shatters it with his angry words. Calculation is the antithesis of grace.

The fate of the slave ends this passage. This dehumanising and possession-based image is evoked realistically, not to advocate the habit of grinding self-denial and humiliation that can become part of some spiritualities, but to set in perspective the temptation (albeit unconscious because so habitual) to respond to even the loveliest of God's gifts with a profit/loss calculation. Yet such gifts are beyond price: care, forgiveness and the gentle self-offering of faith.

Give us joy, O Lord, in your gifts of care, forgiveness and love.

'Thank you for the ...'

Luke 17:11-19

At last we meet a moment of light in these grim passages and a glimpse of faith for which the disciples longed. Yet the story begins unpromisingly, in geographical and social margins among lives isolated by the terrible fear of incurable, infectious disease, at the mercy of charity and compelled to keep distant from normal society.

The disease of leprosy knew no remedy, except perhaps in the stories they had heard of the healer. The lepers' distant prayer was answered. They set out on their journey back to society. After all the harsh words so far this week, here is Jesus the compassionate, healing and restoring people to the community. And of course his orders are clear.

What makes one of the men different? Just a little culturally more distant, maybe he had a sense of freedom the others lacked. The others, understandably rigid with anxiety lest something go wrong and the cleansing be lost, maintained a relationship based on orders, a pattern of behaviour with which human superstition would be all too familiar. The one man discovered faith, and faith made him well. Spontaneous gratitude overwhelmed everything else and set him free from habits of calculation, fear or superstition. Faith breaks the rules of anxiety. The gift that money cannot buy is returned. Falling at Jesus' feet, there is no more distance to be measured. 'Get up, go on your way' – the fruit of faith is freedom.

O Lord, we pray for gifts of thanksgiving, freedom and faith, that we may be well.

'I work all night, I work all day'

Luke 17:20-37

A grave danger with money and the attitudes it inspires and makes habitual is the distance it creates between us and the realities of the kingdom. The Pharisees, ostensibly in a search for clarity, show this same habit of mind as they use an otherwise positive process, the asking of questions, to create distance in the face of Jesus' overwhelming awareness of the immediacy of the kingdom. No doubt many of us have experienced those committees where eminently reasonable questions are asked that all too easily divert attention from vital decisions. For Jesus, so urgent is the moment that the question provokes not only a clear and disturbing answer, but a stern warning to his disciples about such tactics. There is no time. So crucial is the moment that questions, along with other routines of distancing – the sheer busyness of everyday life – must not muffle thought and senses to decisive response.

Jesus' apocalyptic tones of cosmic crisis, pain and the irresistible change of natural disaster are laden with impending judgement. We hear them, and may be tempted to bring to bear upon them a money lens, based on patterns of finance, records and account sheets, credit and debit columns. If we do so, we lose sight of the judgement that is based on understanding, compassion and the passionate love of the kingdom – divine judgement, which is the source of our hope in the face of fear. Calculation and spontaneity, anxiety and thankfulness are again in tension here. We, like the original hearers, have to make our own choice.

Lord, awaken us to the presence of the kingdom and to the hopefulness of its judgement.

Isaiah 56 – 66

Sunday 1 December
(Advent Sunday)

Notes based on the New Revised Standard Version by

Keith Riglin

The Revd Dr Keith Riglin is an Anglican priest serving in the Diocese of London. He has served in Baptist and United Reformed congregations, in university chaplaincy and in theological education, including two years in Jamaica. He maintains a strong connection with Ghana, travelling regularly for teaching and church work.

1 Soon my salvation will come

Isaiah 56:1-5

Do what is right

The readings this week come from a time of uncertainty. The prophet speaks to a people who've experienced exile and look forward to a salvation that will come. But what will it mean? And how are we to live? Each day's reading addresses some of the issues faced by Isaiah's hearers, issues still faced by his readers of today.

After my mother had her hip replacement, the temptation was to stay in the chair! What was really needed, and thankfully happened, was exercise and maintenance.

Today Isaiah speaks to those who've returned home after the harshness of exile in Babylon. The challenge is not to let the experience damage them or make them afraid or bitter, not to stay in the chair. Rather they're called to 'maintain justice, and do what is right' (verse 1). Don't let what you've been through overwhelm; don't lose sight of what's important – 'maintain justice'.

In the busyness of getting ready for Christmas, let's not lose sight of what God calls us to: 'justice' and doing 'what is right'; to welcome the stranger ('the foreigner', verse 3), and to 'keep my sabbaths' (verse 4). May God give us grace to be as inclusive of others as God, in Christ, is of us; and may we always have time for God's rest.

Gracious God, as we prepare for the coming of your Son, strengthen us to live as you would have us live, to welcome as you welcome us in Jesus, to work for your realm of justice, and to know your generous sabbath rest.

Room for all

Isaiah 56:6-8

The experience of those who came to England from the West Indies during the 1950s was not always one of welcome. Arriving for Sunday worship in their local churches, they found themselves often treated as foreigners (which they were not) and as unwelcome strangers. Whoever we are and from wherever we come, I doubt there are many of us who haven't experienced that sense of not being welcome, not being part of the crowd.

Isaiah's hearers had every reason to feel that they were special. As the people of Judah, now called 'Jews', they had their own ways, their own traditions, their own beliefs. But, having been delivered from oppression and exile, the prophet's challenge is not to land that same exclusion on others. The prophet calls his hearers to see what God sees and to hear what God hears: 'their sacrifices will be acceptable on my altar; for my house shall be called a house of prayer for all peoples' (verse 7).

Think of the welcome; remember the times you have felt excluded simply because of who you are, those times when you have felt 'foreign'. God tells the prophet that he will 'gather the outcasts of Israel', the prophet's own kith and kin, but also 'I will gather others to them besides those already gathered' (verse 8). And think of the welcome God asks us to give, even as the Christ of God welcomed and welcomes all.

Pray that God will give us open hearts and open doors for all, as we make room for the Christ-child who made room for us.

Not out of this world

Isaiah 57:15-21

It's only the first week of December but some are, I'd imagine, already singing Christmas carols. One of the most popular is Charles Wesley's 'Hark! The herald angels sing', with its penultimate line, 'born to raise the sons of earth'. The promise of God, in Christ, is of a Saviour who 'lays his glory by', whose coming means humankind no more may die, that all those made in God's image shall be 'raised' as God's children: daughters and sons of grace.

Centuries earlier, the prophet gave his fellow returned-exiles a vision of God as one who dwells 'in the high and holy place' and yet also 'with those who are contrite and humble in spirit' (verse 15). To a people who had experienced exile, who are now seeking to build and rebuild their society – one inclusive of all – salvation was their desire. But note how the salvation of which Isaiah speaks is that of restoration and renewal, 'I will heal them; I will lead them and repay them with comfort' (verse 18), rather than deliverance. Not a rescue from the world but rather a renewal of it; a kingdom of God.

Preparing in Advent for the salvation soon to come, consider the prophet's model. Remember the words of the carols we rehearse, not of a fleeing from this world to some other, but of a God who comes to heal, comes to us right where we are, alongside us: Emmanuel, God with us.

In what ways do the activities of your church speak of rescue from the world, or of the world's renewal?

God of grace and glory, as we prepare to celebrate your coming among us in Jesus, raise us to new life and, as you promise to restore all things in him, equip us to be your servants of renewal in the world, through Jesus Christ our Lord.

Live it and show it

Isaiah 58:1-5

Fasting has been a part of most religious traditions for as long as anyone can remember. For the people of the prophet's day, seeking to reassert themselves now that they're back in the Holy Land, things that all could see – feasts and fasts – seemed to hit the mark. Remember, though, Jesus' challenge to those who make a show of their religion: let it 'be seen not by others but by your Father who is in secret' (Matthew 6:17).

Notice how the prophet condemns those who serve only their own interests by their religion, or who think nothing of the state of their world, their society, whilst they busy themselves in church (verse 3).

There's nothing wrong with ordered worship, truly offered. But 'liturgy' (originally meaning 'the work of the people' or 'public duty') is only truly worship when expressed in transformed lives and communities. As a Baptist minister I knew used to say at the dismissal, 'the worship is ended, the service continues'.

A prophet of our own day, Desmond Tutu, reminds us of the truth of all our observances: 'There is nothing you can do that will make God love you more; there is nothing you can do that will make God love you less.' As we continue our looking to the salvation soon to come, remember the call to worship God, in Christ, in truth; and the call to live transformed and transforming worshipful lives, not to earn God's favour, but as our response to grace.

Most loving God, guide us in our worship, strengthen us in our service, and confirm us in transformed lives that, seeing our salvation drawing near, we may be those who follow your Christ, whose words and deeds were one, Jesus Christ our Lord.

Sunrise

Isaiah 58:6-9a

There are days when I cannot sleep and get up early. There are other days when I rise to greet the dawn. I remember, years ago, rising early and meeting friends to experience dawn over the South China Sea. Somehow, being in an unfamiliar land, seeing the sun shining its light afresh, life was reaffirmed and hope renewed.

Having challenged his people to 'fast' in transforming ways, now Isaiah speaks of such a rising: 'Then your light shall break forth like the dawn, and your healing shall spring up quickly' (verse 8). And, if a fearful people cry out, God will answer, 'Here I am' (verse 9).

For some, such words reflect but a pious hope. And so they could be, unless we grasp their conditional character. For the light that 'shall break forth like the dawn' is the light shining from people's lives. The response to the cry for God's presence is answered by God's 'Here I am' in the healing (the 'salvation') embodied in transformed and transforming lives.

Jesus' glorious claim, 'I am the light of the world' (John 8:12) is expressed and lived out today in the lives of his disciples, to whom he gives the charge, 'You are the light of the world' (Matthew 5:14). God's call to us is to heed Isaiah's challenge, to be those who are God's very presence for all we encounter today – a breaking dawn in a world in need of healing.

Why not get up early tomorrow to watch the sunrise? Think about shining for God in the world.

God, whose glory fills the skies, may we spring up quickly to illumine goodness and challenge injustice, and greet our risen Lord, the Sun of Righteousness, Jesus Christ the Saviour.

Being Father Christmas

Isaiah 58:9b-12

The original Santa Claus, St Nicholas of Myra, the fourth-century bishop, is commemorated today in some churches. He is famously remembered for his acts of charity, especially his generosity to a poor man who couldn't afford a proper dowry for his three daughters. Nicholas decided to help the man in secret, and on three consecutive days threw purses of gold coins through an open window into the man's house (in one version the third purse is dropped down the chimney). When confronted by the man, initially affronted by such generosity, Nicholas says that the man should not thank him, but God alone.

As well as providing origins for the stories of Father Christmas associated with St Nicholas, the incident resonates with Isaiah's words: 'If you satisfy the needs of the afflicted, then your light shall rise in the darkness and your gloom be like the noonday' (verse 10).

Notice, however, that the prophet also condemns a judgmental spirit, 'if you remove the pointing of the finger, the speaking of evil' (verse 9). It was hard for Nicholas' charity not to be questioned by that poor man, questioning the saint's motives; we too can be threatened by such kindness when shown to us.

The new realm envisioned by Isaiah and realised in Christ is one where all serve all, then shall we be as 'a watered garden, like a spring of water' (verse 11).

Think of how you could be an anonymous benefactor this Christmas.

Consider the hymn, 'Brother, sister, let me serve you' by Richard Gillard (611 in *Singing the Faith*, Canterbury Press Norwich, 2011); how can you be a neighbour today?

Pray that God will not only strengthen us to be generous in our words and actions, but also have the grace to receive from others.

Work, rest and play

Isaiah 58:13-14

We may not all be able to explain Archimedes' Principle, but climb into a full bath and, as the water level rises, we understand that the volume displaced is equal to the volume submerged. Try it out!

The challenge of the prophet today is to try out the sabbath. And just as it was easy to turn active faith in Isaiah's day into the strictness of rules and the sabbath into a struggle, so we may slip into equating a faithful response to God with hard labour, and Sunday as a bind.

The prophet challenged his hearers to build God's realm of justice and welcome, of generous service and gratitude. And that's why their approach to the sabbath was so important, for the way they treated 'the holy day of the Lord' (verse 13) spoke of how they saw the practice of their faith. How do we treat Sunday?

The salvation that's drawing near is fulfilled in Jesus, who said that we need no longer carry 'heavy burdens', that he is 'gentle and humble in heart', that in him 'you will find rest for your souls' (Matthew 11:28-30).

A well-known confectionery bar was once advertised with the words that it would help you 'work, rest, and play'. In this season, let's not just talk and explain, let's try it out afresh: to know the work to which we're called, but also experience the rest, and even the play.

Glorious God, give us grace this season to delight in the hope you give us, to work for your realm of peace, and to dance and play in your love, through Jesus Christ our Lord.

Isaiah 56 – 66

Notes based on the New Revised Standard Version by

Jennifer Smith

The Revd Dr Jennifer Smith is a Methodist minister serving in West London. Originally from the USA, she has lived in the UK since 1993 and travels annually for teaching and church work in Nigeria.

2 Your sins have hidden his face

Isaiah 59:1-8

A dollar short and a day late

When a friend claims to have something to tell me 'in love', it usually means I am going to get a telling off. Too easily my defences go up and I get ready with justification. Of course I am secretly relieved to stop running away: my actions or approach may well have hidden me from my friend's comfort and help; defensiveness surely does. The readings this second week of Advent take us 'in love' through just such a deep examination of our relationship with God: our collective sins have hidden God's face. Though uncomfortable, the relief of God's love awaits.

Our public conversation finds lots of excuses to avoid responsibility for hard things. Increasing inequality of wealth? Blame the bankers! Rising illiteracy and unemployment? The selfish youth of today, or lazy teachers. In the US we describe someone who always has an excuse as 'a dollar short and a day late'. The prophet cuts across the conversation: has God become so weak as not to even hear the cries of the people? No, we all share responsibility for the effects of our way of life. We are all 'a dollar short and a day late', and we will not see God until we know it.

Ever-present God, when we fill our prayers with defensive striving, deal gently with us; lead us again into the way of peace that we may hide from you no longer.

Justice and righteousness get stuck in traffic

Isaiah 59:9-15a

Some seventeenth-century theologians wrote by way of dialogue between personified virtues. 'Peace' would argue to quiet 'Truth', who might in turn be haranguing 'Mercy' for all she was worth. The writer would try to tease out ethical conflicts by means of a veritable soap opera of relationships between the virtues. Each character was assumed to be functioning as God's emissary, each with a mission in a healthy society.

Today's passage is a lament about the sin of the whole society impeding the function of these virtues: because truth 'stumbles in the public square' (verse 14), justice is turned back and righteousness keeps well away. Justice includes the protection of the weak and foreigner; righteousness is God's desire to see justice prevail.

Without honesty about our oppressive thoughts and self-serving instincts, justice and righteousness will be forever stuck in traffic. Until we tell the truth about those groups excluded by the way our society functions, we will be left to 'growl like bears' (verse 11), stumbling along in the darkness as if we were dead, while 'the vigorous' (verse 10) seem to walk freely all around us. The good news is that God will not suffer righteousness and justice to be kept in gridlock for ever: truth will stand up again and walk.

Is it always right for the 'truth' of a situation to be known, for reconciliation of aggrieved parties? Think of your own life journey for examples.

May truth walk safely in our homes and hearts, and stand witness to our love. Send justice to us quickly, and turn us again into paths of righteousness, for your name's sake.

Flash flood justice

Isaiah 59:15b-19

Few of us would want to be caught in a flash flood, having seen the chaotic destruction they can bring in news reports and pictures, or first hand. One second a country lane is dry and quiet next to a trickling stream, the next a torrent of water crushes people, livestock, buildings and cars. Children can be snatched from parents' arms, trees uprooted. These floods are so destructive exactly because they cannot be anticipated. Even if a general warning is given, a flash flood may take only minutes to build up and destroy a whole area. It should alarm us then, to have the prophet describe God's coming justice like a 'pent up stream that the wind of the Lord drives on' (verse 19). This imagery is not unique to Isaiah: Amos too calls for justice to 'roll like waters, righteousness like an ever-flowing stream' (Amos 5:24).

The readings for today and tomorrow mark the end of the prophet Isaiah's lament over the sin of the people, and the beginning of God's fightback. What we cannot do for ourselves, God will do for us, by forceful means if necessary. God will not let the vulnerable, the weak and the foreigner remain without justice; God will neither let oppressors rest without salvation. God is willing to go to war to renew the righteousness of God's people.

Many Christians today struggle with the military imagery used in our scriptures, and rightly so. It has too often been used by governments or empires to authorise violence in God's name. We need not step away from the images in today's readings, however. In context, they speak of God our great protector, who will confront evil and overpower it. They do not authorise the military might of one nation over another, but describe a God who will fight to protect the vulnerable. Would that every army was clothed with such weaponry, and that wrath and vengeance should always serve the cause of righteousness!

Words on the tip of the tongue

Isaiah 59:20-21

It can be uncanny, the way even a very small child will use a turn of phrase or gesture that so resembles an aunt or grandparent as to make us laugh in recognition. It might be the way the child holds her head, or the gestures of a hand, but we see particular phrases handed down across the generations. They are 'words on the tip of the tongue' that we might not be able to predict, but which link the generations.

Today's reading is about the spiritual 'word on the tip of the tongue' that God promises will follow our children and children's children. Like the 'word on the tip of our tongue' we cannot quite remember, there may be times when we lose awareness of it, but it will pass to those who come after us nonetheless. The word in question is that God will come 'to Zion as Redeemer' (verse 20). It is as if this promise will be underneath all the other words we say, binding us to God's future in Christ. God will write this language deeply in our mouths. The promise to the people is that the days when their sin hides the face of God are coming to an end.

What did you learn about God as a child that you would want to pass on? Are there any lessons you learned about God as a child you would be happy not to pass on?

God who came into the world in the child Jesus, protect all children in our world. Allow them to grow and develop, and give them loving adults to guide them.

Winning the lottery of life

Isaiah 60:1-7

Most of us have at one time or another fantasised about what we would do if we won the lottery, even if we have never bought a ticket. Part of the hook that keeps us watching the draw on TV is the drama of the numbers' revelation. At three numbers we are assured of a thousand pounds, at four, ten thousand, then a hundred ... until the full glory comes upon us. Confetti falls, people cheer, and a bottle of champagne is shaken for the photo. Except the winner only gets the money.

That's enough, we might say: those who have always had enough (even if only just) should be wary of dismissing the importance of money in a world where many suffer great hardship in its lack. But the joyful revelations demonstrating God's favour in today's reading go far beyond mere money. We see children gathered, abundance of sea and land, and gifts beyond imagining. The prophet tells us we will 'be radiant,' that our 'heart will thrill and rejoice' (verse 5). This is indeed good news, coming to the people whose sins 'had hidden God's face' (Isaiah 59:2).

But the one receiving this revelation also receives a command: arise, shine. Show God's glory in the world that is still covered in darkness. If Advent is a time for deep examination of our own sin and barriers to relationship with Christ, it is also a time to hear this command. We are never to hole up safe with our store of grace, but to shine.

Loving God, may I today shine with the love of Christ wherever I may find myself. May I meet each one with kindness, and know myself secure in your love.

Christmas lists

Isaiah 60:8-16

The litany of gifts God will bring to the redeemed people continues in today's reading. Not mere things, but the abundant promise of restoration: God promises the future to a people who have known loss and oppression. If Advent is about examining ourselves in preparation for the coming of Christ, and today's reading about the promise of gifts, it is worth asking, what do you want?

What do you really want: not what you ought to want, or the useful pair of socks or gloves, scented soap (however welcome) that many of us will be happy to receive at Christmas, but what would you really want, if you knew that God promised you abundance as part of the whole redeemed creation?

My authentic Christmas list might look something like:

1. Every missed chance to be taken.
2. Every bit of heartbreak, if not avoided, then repaired.
3. To have enough not to worry, and to share.
4. To finally live out-loud, fully alive to the glory of God.
5. To anticipate my sin, and avoid it so I never lose sight of God's face.

Not to be too pious, the real list would also include a gorgeous leather satchel that never slipped off my shoulder. What do you want?

Make a Christmas list. Include everything. Pray over each item on your list, and let God show you which things are most important.

Generous God, you have given your people every blessing. Help me to recognise the gifts you put in my way, that I may feel truly wealthy in your grace.

Directed by peace and righteousness

Isaiah 60:17-22

I have a slightly old, usually reliable satellite navigation system that I faithfully stick on the dashboard of whatever car I am driving. Because I do not have the best sense of direction, I treat it both as my overseer and taskmaster, and do what it says. Helpfully, the commands are clear: 'Right turn ahead,' or 'turn around, when possible'.

In this final reading from Isaiah 60, we hear that Peace shall be our overseer, and Righteousness our taskmaster. The language of our reading anticipates the imagery of the Revelation: no sun nor moon to shine, but 'the Lord will be your everlasting light' (verses 19, 20). I have a sense that the oversight and direction given by Peace and Righteousness may not be as immediately clear as that offered by my satnav, however. The same God whose face is hidden by the sins of the people does not redeem us as robotic devotees. God gives us the gift of discernment and then expects us to use it.

Today's passage comes just before the scripture that Jesus will read in the Nazareth synagogue (Luke 4:18): 'The spirit of the Lord God is upon me ... he has sent me to bring good news to the oppressed, to bind up the brokenhearted, to proclaim liberty to the captives, and release to the prisoners' (Isaiah 61:1). This is the kind of direction given with Peace as overseer and Righteousness as taskmaster: right relation with God will be based in right relationship with our neighbours.

Lord, do not hide your face from us, but show yourself as we navigate through life. Set Peace over us; guide us in Righteousness; bring us closer and closer to the Christ-child coming. In Jesus' name we pray.

Isaiah 56 – 66

3 Good news to the oppressed

Notes based on Today's English Version by

Vincent Manoharan

Vincent Manoharan is an ordained minister of the Lutheran church, a lawyer and a Dalit human rights defender who has campaigned in his native India for many years. He has recently completed his doctorate in Dalit liberation theology.

Isaiah 61:1-4

Good news ensures freedom and new life

Good news is absolutely contextual and liberational. This week challenges us to reflect upon what 'good news to the oppressed' is; and our responsibility to become the carriers of that good news, for the freedom of the disadvantaged. For Dalits like me, good news is nothing but a life freed from the horrendous caste system that denies human dignity, equality, justice and peace to me and my community. The same is the case for those who suffer from racism, patriarchy and other analogous forms of division, discrimination and suppression.

Today's text reminds us of Jesus' Nazareth manifesto (Luke 4:18-19). While Isaiah encourages the Israelites to envision their deliverance from captivity and exile, Jesus proclaims that his good news is to provide liberty and freedom for those who are in distress and suffering oppression. The good news of Jesus embodies worldly sufferings like poverty, broken-heartedness, sickness, blindness, captivity and all forms of exploitation and oppression. Alongside imagining deliverance from such, Isaiah envisages the effects of freedom: the freed people will enjoy gladness, praise God and flourish like the aloe tree planted by God (Numbers 24:6). The good news ensures both freedom and a prosperous life to the oppressed.

Today's text calls us to ponder and respond to the call of God to become the carriers of God's good news to the oppressed.

Our God, our mother and father, provider of freedom and a life of joy, equality, justice and peace, help us to carry your good news for the deliverance of the poor and the oppressed.

Good news ends shame and disgrace

Isaiah 61:5-7

The pernicious system of slavery was outlawed and abolished but the shackles of modern slavery remain in hidden forms. Violence and persecution continue against migrant workers, prisoners of war, refugees, repatriates, indigenous people and daily-wagers all over the world. In South Asia, Dalits live like strangers on their own soil, forced to live outside the villages and compelled to undertake all the filthy and disreputable jobs such as manual scavenging, gutter cleaning, garbage removal, clearing carcasses, cremating dead bodies, sweeping and cobbling. They are not allowed to enter Hindu temples and their rights over land have been infringed by the Brahmanical codes. They are put to shame and disgrace by the untouchability practices of the non-Dalits.

Into such a reality, today's text offers comfort that the shame and disgrace faced by all the oppressed will be put to an end. It provides hope that they will regain the status of sons and daughters and enjoy the right of ownership of the land and natural resources of the nation. They will have the freedom to worship their God and lead a joyous life for ever.

But how can these disadvantaged people inherit such rights and fulfil their needs unless they are encouraged, supported and protected by those who are in privileged positions? Therefore, today's text challenges those of us in a better position to stand by the victimised. It reminds us of our responsibility to enable the disadvantaged to assert their rights and needs.

Our God, give us strength to wipe off the shame and disgrace of the victimised by granting them their rights and needs.

Vincent Manoharan

Good news brings reward and blessing

Isaiah 61:8-11

Today's reading speaks of the reward of enjoying an eternal covenant with God and the blessings of salvation and victory. These are intended particularly for the oppressed who have undergone such disgraceful persecution and suffering at the hands of the mighty and wealthy. God loves justice and hates oppression, says the prophet (verse 8). Another way of putting this is to say that God is against those who practise injustice and who hate others. While the oppressed sprout and grow by their reward and blessing, the oppressors become infamous and condemned.

We live in a bipolar world packed with the affluent and the deprived, the powerful and the powerless, the arrogant and meek, the dominant and weak, the good and bad. Isaiah's words are reaffirmed in the warning of Jesus, that those who have a privileged status will find it difficult to enter the kingdom of God (Mark 10:25). This does not mean that it is necessarily wrong or a curse to be affluent or in powerful positions. However, by virtue of their privileged position, the rich and mighty often tend to distance themselves from the suffering of others and sometimes to commit injustices. But when they love the 'poor', by sharing their wealth and standing up for the justice of the disadvantaged, then they are equally eligible to gain the reward and blessing of God.

Loving God, our mother and father, teach us to share what you give us with the poor and to stand for the justice of the other.

Good news means no longer exploited

Isaiah 62:6-9

Exploitation is not always exercised by invaders, captors, colonial masters and overseas companies. The Israelites may have been exploited by their invaders (the Romans and Greeks) but, in the contemporary world, exploitation may come from elsewhere: from the greedy designs of people and companies in our native country, as well as from corporate giants who cross continents to amass wealth. When extensive usurpation of land, water and other basic resources takes place, ordinary people face acute starvation and even death. Many countries are rich in natural resources but their people are poor, facing malnutrition, killer diseases and untimely death.

God is against the exploitation of people's labour and of creation itself. God's creation is for all and God gave responsibility to human beings to administer it (Genesis 1:27-30), not to destroy or exploit it. The good news, according to Isaiah, is that God will appoint sentries to watch over the creation in order to fulfil the promise of protecting people, land and cities. There will be no starvation or death; people will harvest what they sow; their land and the products of cultivation will no longer be appropriated by others. Although this good news was originally addressed to Israel, it applies universally to all humankind. It offers hope to the exploited while issuing a warning of punishment to the exploiters.

Lord, deliver us from the temptation of exploiting fellow human beings and natural resources. Appoint us as your sentries to protect humankind and your creations.

Good news brings the status of God's people

Isaiah 62:10-12

What will be the joy of the oppressed when God releases them from oppression and makes them God's holy people? In today's reading, Isaiah joyfully encourages the people in Jerusalem to go and build roads to receive the Lord, the saviour, as well as the people returning from exile. According to Isaiah, the good news for the oppressed Israelites is not only that they will be released but also that they will gain the status of becoming God's people.

How many pains and persecutions do oppressed people undergo owing to their class, caste, race or patriarchal divisions and discriminations? Yet if we believe Isaiah's words, if the oppressed cry, God will release them and make them God's people. They will thus gain a precious status, a status more honourable than anything the world can bestow. As Peter says, 'at one time you were not God's people, but now you are his people' (1 Peter 2:9-10). This good news is incredible.

As a lawyer, I remember vividly a Christian Dalit rights activist shouting at the top of her voice in court, 'God, you have proved I am your child!', when the judge acquitted her of a murder charge concocted by vested interest groups. Being released from persecution and bondage, and realising we are part of God's people is an amazing experience.

God, help us to get rid of all bondage, including sin, and accept us as your people.

God's time to save the oppressed

Isaiah 63:1-6

Today's reading helps us to think about the importance and certainty of God's timing in saving the oppressed and punishing the oppressors. Isaiah portrays the Israelites being saved by God from their captivity when God's time came. Paul also reminds us of God's time to listen, show favour and save people (2 Corinthians 6:2). We read in scripture that, when the time came, the mighty God listened to the cry of the Israelites and killed the Egyptians in the Red Sea (Exodus 14:28). There is a time for God to act, but no one knows when God's time will come. As God says, 'my thoughts are not like yours and my ways are different from yours' (Isaiah 55:8). Jesus also says, 'No one knows, however, when that day and hour will come – neither the angels in heaven nor the Son' (Matthew 24:36).

These texts emphasise that there is a time for God to save the oppressed and punish the oppressors. Therefore, the oppressed need to remain faithful in prayer and in crying out to God (Matthew 21:22). And the oppressors should stop their cruelty against the oppressed. As Isaiah warns, when the time comes, God will crush the oppressors like grapes: 'I have trampled the nations like grapes'. Today's text teaches us to comfort the oppressed and warn the oppressors, reminding ourselves of God's good time.

God, quicken the time when you will save the oppressed and change the sinful ways of their oppressors.

Prerequisite for eternal protection

Isaiah 63:7-9

Isaiah talks about the suffering of Israel as the reason for God's eternal protection. God says, 'They are my people; they will not deceive me'; in his love and compassion he rescued them (verse 8). These words of blessing have a prerequisite and also a sting of warning to the oppressed. As scripture says, Abraham was a nomad and God chose and blessed him and his descendants as God's people (Genesis 12:1). God listened to their suffering in Egypt and rescued them. When the Israelites rebelled against God in Canaan, they were punished and sent as captives to live in exile. Again when they cried, God saw their suffering and saved them. Thus God is not neutral but always takes sides with the sufferers and the oppressed, granting them eternal protection.

However, to retain this status, the oppressed need not remain oppressed for ever. They could be released to enjoy a freed life. Yet, once released, the oppressed should remain simple, humble and pious, loving God and loving their neighbor, not, as so often happens in history, becoming oppressors of others. If they become oppressors, this amounts to deception, and they will no longer be entitled to remain God's people. Therefore the main prerequisite for sustaining God's love, compassion and eternal protection is to remain righteous and non-oppressive. Today's reading calls us to be non-oppressive in order to gain the eternal blessings and protection of God. We are called to share this message.

Loving God, teach us to be worthy of enjoying your everlasting love and eternal protection.

Isaiah 56 – 66

Notes based on the New Revised Standard Version by

Nathan Eddy

Nathan Eddy is a writer and minister at North Lowestoft United Reformed Church. He has worked previously as a university chaplain and as a journalist, and is ordained in the United Church of Christ (USA). He lives in Norwich with his wife Clare, an Anglican priest, and their two daughters.

4 You are our Father

Isaiah 63:10-19

Look down and see!

The last chapters of Isaiah show the reality of rebuilding a society after disaster, in this case, the Babylonian exile. Walter Brueggemann has called Isaiah the pre-eminent urban document in the Bible (*Using God's Resources Wisely: Isaiah and Urban Possibility*, Westminster/John Knox Press, 1993), and in our age of global financial crisis the end of Isaiah is a good companion. Here we find God's promise but also lament, anger and realistic assessment of the challenges that face people of faith who seek to rebuild society. And in the midst of it all we discover God's astonishing delight. May God speak to our times, and to your heart, through this poet and prophet.

One Christmas, my family and I went to a massive shopping centre where a huge Santa towered over the car park. His arm waved slowly; he was distant, vacant. Sometimes God feels like this. *Work! Consume! Die!* is the name of a recent book by UK comic Frankie Boyle (HarperCollins, 2011). For how many people is this simply reality? 'Look down from heaven!' says the poet to God. 'Where are your zeal and your might?' (verse 15). Even in lament, the poet remembers God. Our disciplined praise, too, is the grit that reminds us that despair is not inevitable, and will not have the last word.

God, our hearts break for your presence. In the Advent night, light a candle of hope in our world and in our hearts.

Tear open the heavens!

Isaiah 64:1-7

The poet's lament is urgent: we desire more than rhetoric, we need fire or earthquake! We know our God is not uncaring or blind to injustice; yet God is hidden (verse 5). God's face is turned away (verse 7). We can't live a day longer without the living God. Tear open the heavens, God!

I work as a half-time minister in Lowestoft, the easternmost town in the UK. The town has been hard hit by the loss of the fishing industry and other industries, in the last forty years. On the street I hear the poet's lament regularly: 'Times have changed … the politicians don't care … the town has had it.'

In these verses rises the dull ache of a memory of deeds done on our behalf (verse 3); of gracious dwelling with those who seek to live justly (verse 5). God's face has not always been turned away. What is it like when turned towards the world, God's creation? From it shine life, joy, power, love, forgiveness, acceptance, energy. God's face will not be hidden for ever. Come, Lord! Let your light shine on us and through us!

The Ignatian tradition (based on the writings of Ignatius Loyola) invites us to be with God simply by imagining God's loving gaze on us. God's face is not always turned away. What does God feel towards you? What does God feel towards your town or city? What would you like to share with this God?

God, look at us. Do not forget us. Be close to us.

And yet! You are our Father

Isaiah 64:8-12

In the film *Of Gods and Men* a group of monks decides to remain in war-torn Algeria despite acute danger to their lives. One of the brothers has a deep crisis of faith, yet in prayer realises God is profoundly present. In a remarkable scene he prays, arms gripping his own torso in embrace: 'You envelop me, hold me, surround me. You embrace me. And I love you.'

In the dark of our Bethlehem night we, too, realise God is present. 'Yet, O Lord, you are our Father' (verse 8). What hangs on that 'yet'? What reserves of strength and memory, what radical openness amid despair, are needed to utter it? Yet: you are our potter. You formed us. You are with us.

But we don't control God. We are left with the haunting question of verse 12: will you punish us so severely? The question is genuine; Israel truly does not know the answer because, as Brueggemann has observed, God cannot be summoned mechanically, as the Santa atop the shopping centre can (*Isaiah 40–66*, Westminster John Knox Press, 1998, p.237). For Isaiah, Israel's history itself is 'ragged,' open like a wound. Our history, our lives, are no tidier. Global warming, financial crises, terror; whether there will be more local jobs. The future is highly uncertain. Scripture shows us how to put the question to God rather than assures there will be no suffering. And yet … and yet! God is our potter. God is with us.

God, you are my potter. Hold me, surround me and embrace me, and those whom I know to be in need this day.

The Lord delights in you

Isaiah 62:1-5

My wife taught for a year in a school in the Eastern Highlands of Zimbabwe. God led her through the experience to ordained ministry. More than fifteen years later she can still see her students' faces: Blessing, Rumbidzai (Shona for 'Praise the Lord'), Kudzai ('Love'), Tatenda ('Thank you').

The names given us, and the names we call ourselves and others, are important. In God's new creation, opened to all the world in Jesus' birth, we are given new names, alternative futures and healed pasts. We have cried with Isaiah, with the psalmist, with Jesus, asking why God has 'forsaken' us (verse 4; and see Psalm 22). And now out of the silence of exile, as in the uncertainty of the Bethlehem night, as in the stink of the tomb, God speaks. God is not silent! God has not rested and forgotten the world (verse 1)! Although imperial powers conspire otherwise, God's unlikely means of peace has shone forth like a torch, for all the nations to see (verse 2). Glory to God in highest heaven, and on earth peace among those whom God favours (Luke 2:14)!

We will no longer be called 'Forsaken', or 'Desolate'. Our name now is 'My Delight Is in Her' (verse 4). God is not simply a keeper of justice or a managerial saviour, but one who delights, perhaps like one who fusses over a baby. God is as giddy as a bride or groom (verse 5). Tatenda! Rumbidzai! Thank you! Praise the Lord!

Counsellor, Advocate, Delightful One: call me by new names this Christmas Day. Use my tongue and my breath to call the world by a new name.

Ready to be sought

Isaiah 65:1-7

Isaiah 65 is polemical. It opens a tiny window on to the public crisis as Jerusalem was rebuilt. More than one way out of crisis is on offer: the Judeans engaged in the practices named in verses 3-5 would certainly characterise their spirituality differently from Isaiah. But Isaiah's sharp words are a reminder that a prophet is always partisan, always for the moment, always 'getting up people's noses'. In her own way, Mary was this kind of a prophet. She knew that saying yes to a living, passionate God turns the world upside down. To be 'like God', as to be like Mary or Isaiah, is to be full of committed emotion in the event, not calmly above it all.

The key point in these verses is that God is not pleased with all worship or spiritual practice offered by his people, particularly where their practice ignores people in need (as in Isaiah 1:15-17). Isaiah's yardstick is helpful. God is close by, even to those who don't seek him (verse 1), but God is not readily available to self-indulgent, privatistic religious practice that ignores those in need. No profound prayer book or slick worship team or fancy spiritual practice can insulate us from the demands God makes of those who seek to walk in his way.

God of Mary, open my eyes to where you are, my ears to where you call, and my heart to others in need; and give me courage to speak your word of truth.

Blessings and curses

Isaiah 65:8-16

We are tempted to move swiftly on to the wonderful vision coming in verse 17! Indeed, the new heavens and earth emerge here in negative (verses 13-15): there will be eating, drinking, rejoicing, singing, gladness of heart. Yet here we also can't avoid the uncomfortable premise that there will be some in the coming rule who will not want to take part.

Many contemporary readers will squirm at these verses, particularly at the threat of divine violence (verse 12). They reflect a bitter disagreement in Jerusalem into which an angry God interjects. But there is no 'good cop, bad cop' God here. On balance, the God of Isaiah 65 is one who is desperate for the life of all creation, eager to welcome us and despairing at those who are lost in their own agendas. God does not delight in this exclusion as God delights in the new creation. Instead these verses remind us starkly of what is needed to overcome the interests hostile to the coming community of peace. Victims of injustices, like those killed by Herod (Matthew 2:16-18), know that those interests are not to be underestimated. God, for his part, was (and is) ready to be sought, readily available to all (65:1).

As in Deuteronomy 30, we have before us a way of life or death, blessings or curses. The two ways are not symmetrical, as we will see; but the prophet reminds us that human intransigence is real and will be finally overcome by God.

God, I want to be found among your humble servants.
Break my heart with yours for those who do not.

Newness, delight, surprise

Isaiah 65:17-20

Savour these verses today. Be astonished! They are no less incredible for us than they were 2500 years ago. The new creation takes in the heavens as well as the earth. Dare to imagine its very materialism: a full health-care programme and a just economic system are sketched here and in verses 21-25. There will be no infant mortality. There will be proper care for the elderly, so that they live full and healthy lives. This is no utopia, to be built in the clouds; this is Jerusalem herself : her walls, her peoples, her temple. Jerusalem will be a joy and its people a delight. Children and the elderly, two groups often pushed to the margins of society, are front and centre in this re-created, re-energised city. There is no cost to the life enjoyed by this city, no price paid by the environment or by an invisible low-wage labour pool. God will delight in this city and we are likewise commanded to 'be glad and rejoice forever' in what God is creating (verse 18).

My wife serves as Anglican vicar on one of the larger and more impoverished housing estates in Norwich. God's delight, or anyone's, for that matter, is sometimes hard to see. But it's there. At an afternoon service at one of her churches, I once welcomed in a young lad who was peering through the windows. 'Damien, Damien,' he shouted to his brother around the corner, 'we can go in!' Be glad and rejoice for ever in what I am creating, says the Lord. Be glad.

God, let your delight dance on me. Teach me to rejoice in the world you cherish. Share with me your life that is greater than exile and the cross.

Isaiah 56 – 66

5 They shall not labour in vain

Notes based on the New Revised Standard Version by

Nathan Eddy

For Nathan's biography, see p.360.

Isaiah 65:21-25

A real and coming vision

Isaiah's vision has a very concrete reality. We can build homes confidently knowing they won't be taken from us by risky finance deals (verse 21). We can invest time and money in growing crops, knowing our investment is not at risk (verse 22). There will be an equal sharing rather than unfettered competition; the powerful and the vulnerable, the wolves and the lambs, will feed together (verse 25). The words 'they shall not labour in vain' (verse 23) are not empty spiritual promises: our earnings, our savings, will not be taken from us. This is a new heaven and a new earth with healthy public institutions: with health care that works, with housing providers who are transparent, and a justice system that protects the vulnerable.

This vision isn't a communist or socialist or capitalist platform, but God's platform. God will answer even before we call, will hear even while we are speaking (verse 24). There are no intermediaries. Food, health care: these things are essential, but there is more to fullness of life. 'One does not live by bread alone', as Jesus told the tempter, 'but by every word that comes from the mouth of God' (Matthew 4:4).

God, many in our world don't have a roof over their heads. Give me gratitude for what I have. Give me compassion for what others lack.

Rejoice!

Isaiah 66:1-2, 10-11

Again there is the command to rejoice. The city will satisfy, nourish and care for her people (verse 11). We have seen the very practical programme for this nourishment and care in the preceding chapter. That care is not charity but the very foundation of the new city itself; the whole city's institutions are what nourishes. A city that does not care for its people in this holistic, foundational, way is not the city of peace envisioned by God.

My train journey to Lowestoft from Norwich runs across the Norfolk Broads beyond a road. Every morning I see herons and swans, partridge running to hide in the undergrowth, hares frozen upright. Often the sun is sparkling on the water and the wet grass. Praise wells up in me as these scenes flash by. But God asks me to rejoice in God's town, as well, a town that God hopes will live in harmony with this landscape; a town that God hopes will nourish its people at a consoling breast; a town where God dreams that one day, for those who wish, there will be jobs and housing and health care and delight for all.

Read 65:17-25 and 66:1-2, 10-11 slowly. Dwell on a word or two that resonate. 'Delight' … 'rejoice' … 'I am creating' … 'rejoice and be glad'. Imagine the people's faces, old and young alike. Imagine God delighting in this scene. Where do you see yourself in this vision? Go deeper rather than broader with a word or an image.

Prosperity like a river

Isaiah 66:12-14

We have had many vivid images of God in these readings from Isaiah: God as potter, delight-er, namer, seeker. We can now add 'mother' to that list (verse 13). Isaiah chooses this mother imagery not because he is politically correct, but because only a cascade of vibrant images can capture the dynamism and beauty of God. Notice Isaiah's pairs: potter–clay; father/mother–child; delight-er–object of delight. As we are drawn into God we discover ourselves afresh, as clay in strong hands, as daughter or son comforted, as an object of beauty held high in God's hand, as someone renamed. We have all kinds of reasons to resist seeing ourselves in this way, many of which church has encouraged. But God will find a way to show us that we are loved and beautiful if we let God, so that our bodies themselves will flourish (verse 14), just like the prosperous body-politic of our towns and cities.

The last verse, verse 14, recalls God's indignation against enemies, the same anger we have noted in chapter 65 and which closes the whole book (66:24). Our world is not any closer to perfection than Isaiah's, and God is no less at ease with it. Nor should we be. But as we recall God's dis-ease we must not forget the in-breaking of God's delight, God's comfort and God's newness. Isaiah wouldn't have it any other way. Let your heart rejoice as a new year dawns!

Mothering God, I give you my life that your new world may be born. Make me a part of it, each day of the coming year.

Nathan Eddy - new IBRA editor

Peter Fishpool, chief executive of Christian Education, asked our new editor some questions about himself.

When I look at your photo my initial impression is a studious young man. When you open your mouth I immediately recognise an American accent. If we got really talking, what one thing would you wish my lasting impression of you to be about?

Joyful. Up for an adventure. Imaginative. Three things! Hopefully you wouldn't get me going on about mountain bikes. Then I'd be boring.

What sparked you into reading the Bible on a regular basis?

I've always read the Bible, but my Bible was fairly narrow until my early 30s, really. I wasn't ready to let scripture disrupt my view of myself and of the world. One day I realised there was more to life than the way I saw things. God accepted parts of me that I hadn't. I liked God's version of me and God's version of the world. I read the Bible more as it dawned on me that the world revealed there, and the forgiving and accepting person I saw I could be, was not a fantasy but was real. There's a lot in the Bible I don't understand, but I'm OK with that. I see an overarching story that is good news.

You have worked with students at the universities in Manchester for some years – is studying the Bible really a head thing for educated people?

Reading the Bible is always a head thing for everyone! Understanding ourselves and our emotions involves hard thinking. Asking questions of scripture is important – but God also wants us to be open to the questions scripture asks of us. This involves thinking with the heart as well as the head. Can we imagine the world that is opened in scripture? Can we imagine that we have a role in it?

You worked for a time as a journalist, getting the important news out into the world. What persuaded you to take this different path as an ordained minister and teacher?

I always felt called to a religious life of some kind. I enjoyed journalism, but I didn't want to spend my life observing life. I wanted in. I wanted to put it all on the line.

You were born in one country but now choose to live a long way away in England – does a personal sense of exile attune you to the stories of the Jewish people – and to those of many others in this war-torn world?

My family is from England many generations ago, and I choose to live here, so it's not quite the same. But I do miss family and friends and I dream about downhill skiing. There's a reason East Anglia isn't known for its skiing!

You have two infant daughters, what are you doing to introduce them to the Bible?

Our daughters are six and three. We pray at night before bed. We talk about Bible stories over dinner. My wife Clare is a full-time vicar and I work half-time as minister. Between our four churches hopefully something rubs off on the kids.

You have studied the Bible intensively for a Masters degree at Yale University – is it possible to digest all that learning into a couple of hundred words of a daily Bible reading note?

No, but the challenge is unavoidable. The Bible is worth studying, and there are no shortcuts. Ancient Israel is very different from 21st century Britain. But digesting biblical history and context is the easy part. What's harder is being attentive to your deepest fears in the passage, the part of yourself you turn away from God. In a sense you let yourself be 'digested' by scripture rather than the other way around. That involves understanding the history and context of scripture, too. And it's not always pleasant.

What is your advice about the appropriate balance between listening for God in our prayer life and learning about God as revealed in the scriptures?

I wouldn't privilege one over the other. You need both. It's like tightening the wheel on your car, if you've changed a tyre – you tighten a bolt here a bit, then another bolt opposite a bit, then another bolt a bit, around the wheel in a star pattern. You don't force one bolt and then leave it. One balances and tempers the other. What is God growing in your life? Where is the spirit moving? Or where aren't things growing and moving? The important thing is to be honest with God about where things aren't working, and saying thank you for where they are.

One of the exciting aspects of IBRA is the contributions from Christians around the world, with their own particular dilemmas of faith. How have these very different personal stories affected you?

They affect me deeply. I learn so much from the words people find for their lives. And working as a journalist and as chaplain in a big university has meant I've been blessed with stories. Christ's teaching works sideways between people as much as up and down from God. God speaks in the Bible from listening communities to our listening communities. And the church needs to be listening if we want to be listened to.

IBRA scheme of readings 2014

Voices

Readings in Matthew 1–4
The birth of Jesus, the Messiah
Then Jesus came from Galilee

Foolishness
The wise and the foolish: an Old Testament view
Old Testament personalities – wise, foolish or both?
Human foolishness and the foolishness of God

Readings in Matthew 5–7
'Blessed are you . . .'
'But I say to you . . .'
'Strive first for the kingdom of God . . .'
He taught as one with authority

God's hands and ours
Hands in the Old Testament 1
Hands in the Old Testament 2
Hands in the New Testament: Jesus in his ministry
Hands in the New Testament: God so loved the world
Hands in the New Testament: in the life of young churches

Readings in Matthew 26–27
The last week
The last hours

Easter appearances

Readings in Joshua
Preparations for invasion
Into the promised land
Getting organised

The greening Spirit
The Spirit at work in the whole creation
The Spirit as the source of life and fruitfulness
The Spirit restores life to decaying creation

2 Corinthians

Journeys
Journeying out
Journeying towards
Journeying in and out

Ecclesiastes
Is all vanity?
What is wisdom and who is wise?

War and peace
Making war, longing for peace
Peace begins with God

Nearer God's heart in a garden?

Readings in Matthew 8–16
Jesus went about in all cities . . .
. . . proclaiming the good news of the kingdom

Faithful and fruitful
Vocation of faith
Fruitful living
On bearing good fruits

Amos and Habbakuk
'The Lord roars from Zion'
'I hear, I tremble within'

Saints and holy people
All called to be saints
Inspirational saints
Saints in the early church

Children in the Bible
Children in the Old Testament
Children in the New Testament

Readings in Matthew 13–16
Conversations with Jesus
Teaching and learning

God in translation
Rainbows, visitors and wrestling matches
Sounds and silence
The Holy One and a withering plant
The ultimate translation
What we have heard and seen, looked at and touched

Fresh from the Word

ORDER FORM

You can order using this form or through your local IBRA rep, or online at http://shop.christianeducation.org.uk, or by email to sales@christianeducation.org.uk or by phone on 0121 472 4242

Please return this form to IBRA, 1020 Bristol Road, Selly Oak, Birmingham B29 6LB

Name: ______________________________

Address: ______________________________

____

____

Postcode: ______________ **Tel:** ______________

Email: ______________________________

Postage is free. Your order will be dispatched when all books are available.
Payments in pounds sterling, please.

UK customers	Quantity	Price	Total
AA130301 Fresh from the Word		£8.75	
I am an IBRA Rep (10% discount) I am ordering 6+ books and would like to become an IBRA Rep (10% discount)			
Western European customer			
AA130301 Fresh from the Word		£13.00	
Rest of the world customers			
AA130301 Fresh from the Word		£15.00	
Donation to the IBRA International Fund			

Ebook versions are available from http://bit.ly/IBRAbooks

☐ **I enclose a cheque (made payable to IBRA)**

☐ **Please charge my MASTERCARD/VISA/SWITCH**

Card Number: ☐☐☐☐☐☐☐☐☐☐☐☐☐☐☐☐ **Issue Number:** ☐☐

Start Date: ☐☐ ☐☐ **Expiry Date:** ☐☐ ☐☐

Security number (last three digits on back): ☐☐☐

Signature: ______________________________

The INTERNATIONAL BIBLE READING ASSOCIATION is a Registered Charity

International Bible Reading Association Partners

A worldwide service of Christian Education at work in five continents

HEADQUARTERS
1020 Bristol Road
Selly Oak
Birmingham
B29 6LB
United Kingdom

www.christianeducation.org.uk
ibra@christianeducation.org.uk

and the following agencies:

NEW ZEALAND AND AUSTRALIA
Epworth Bookshop
157B Karori Road
Marsden Village
Karori
Wellington 6012

Mailing address:
PO Box 17255
Karori
Wellington 6147

sales@epworthbooks.org.nz

SAMOA
Congregational Christian Church
Central Office
Level 5, John Williams Building
Tamaligi
Apia

isalavao@cccs.org.ws

AMERICAN SAMOA
Congregational Christian Church in American Samoa
PO Box 1537
1 Kananafou Street
Pago Pago
96799

cccasgs@efkas.org

FIJI
Methodist Bookstore
PO Box 354
Suva
Fiji

mbookstorefiji@yahoo.com

GHANA
IBRA Secretary
Asempa Publishers
Box GP 919
Accra

asempa@iburstgh.com

NIGERIA
David Hinderer House
The Cathedral Church of St David
Kudeti
PMB 5298 Dugbe
Ibadan
Oyo State

SOUTH AND CENTRAL AFRICA
IBRA South Africa
6 Roosmaryn Street
Durbanville 7550

biblereading@evmot.com

DEMOCRATIC REPUBLIC OF THE CONGO
Communauté Baptiste du Fleuve Congo
Avenue Kalemie no 8
Kinshasa
BP 205 & 397
Kinshasa 1

ecc_cbfc@yahoo.fr

CAMEROON
Redemptive Baptist Church
PO Box 65
Limbe
Fako Division
South West Region

evande777@yahoo.com

INDIA
All India Sunday School Association
Plot No 8,
Threemurthy Colony
6th Cross, Mahendra Hills
PB no 2099
Secunderabad – 500 026
Andhra Pradesh

sundayschoolindia@yahoo.co.in

Fellowship of Professional Workers
Samanvay
Deepthi Chambers
Vijayapuri
Hyderabad – 500 017
Andhra Pradesh

fellowship2w@gmail.com